KARAOKE NO MORE

Karaoke No More

The Real Story of the Beginnings of Westlife

PÁDRAIG MEEHAN

A Brandon Original Paperback

First published in 2004 by
Brandon
an imprint of
Mount Eagle Publications
Dingle, Co. Kerry, Ireland

Copyright © Pádraig Meehan 2004

The author has asserted his moral rights.

ISBN 0 86322 321 4

2 4 6 8 10 9 7 5 3 1

Cover design: Anú Design [www.anu-design.ie]
Typesetting: Red Barn Publishing, Skeagh, Skibbereen
Printed in the UK

CONTENTS

LIST OF ILLUSTRATIONS

ACKNOWLEDGEMENTS AND DEDICATION

Thanks to those friends who read early drafts and offered suggestions. To Steve MacDonogh, who saw that what I was trying to do. To those who know who they are.

Dedicated to my dad, Darby Meehan.
And Tom Glancy and Mick Ronson.

INTRODUCTION

This book is the story of IOYOU, mostly as I remember it. Some details have been filled in by other witnesses and by research from material in the public domain. I missed out on being there at the beginning and also at the end, the part when the band line-up had taken on the shape of the future Westlife. The time when they secured their deal. I wish to thank the various people who talked to me, and shared their memories and feelings. As I sat down to write this story in the late summer of 2002, Westlife were off to have another crack at America; they were on the verge of releasing a Greatest Hits album. Already at least four books on the subject of the band had been published. But a big part of the story, it seemed to me, still remained untold. The nitty-gritty of the beginnings, the various characters who had come and gone, the sheer fairytale quality of the story (for those who had happy endings). And finally the place where all this began. Sligo plays like a leading character in the story of Westlife's beginnings.

Some of the story was hard to disentangle. Some of the happenings are remembered differently by different observers. I suppose we tend to remember selectively and colour things with

11

our own bias, and I know I bring to my account prejudices of my own. All I can say is I have done my best to be fair and to give balance to my story. I did not ask any of the people I talked to to go on the record. Some were very helpful, others didn't want to talk to me at all.

Certain of the events are painful for people to remember, and I hope that for them my decision to tell (or retell) the story will be a part of healing, or at least not just a reopening of old wounds. It is difficult for the guys who were dropped: go quietly and you are forgotten, you become invisible; talk about your feelings and your experience and you may be accused of being bitter, or begrudging.

Willie C., my old friend, has often talked about the clownishness of showbiz, particularly the clownishness of rock music. Rock and roll.

I mean, I used to stand in front of the mirror and imagine myself playing in a rock and roll band. I used to listen under the bedclothes to Radio Caroline, anchored somewhere in the North Sea. They played songs by Lou Reed and David Bowie and Marc Bolan and Roger Chapman (Family) and I was entranced. I felt I lived in a secret world that only a few very cool people knew of. The glamour, the sexiness, the wildness, the danger of it all was irresistible. David Bowie looked so cool, sang about things that I thought I was the only one in the world to care about (and some things I didn't understand at all, which fascinated me even more).

I pored over his lyrics. I sought meaning in them. It was terribly important stuff. Super-real business. Bowie was androgynous and mysterious and powerful. He held an almost religious authority.

But that glamour—while no one can deny the power and value of the art, of all the wonder of human endeavour in that area—the glamour does wear thin. Willie used to admire Mick Jagger, want to be like him. (That was when he didn't want to be a racing car driver.) We tried to figure out what Keith Richards was doing on 'Get Off My Cloud'. I said, 'There's two guitars going.' Willie said, 'You haven't got it right yet.' Willie could do Mick's accent. We formed a band. Think of the girls! Think of the fame. Think of being on stage, being that star, hearing those crowds.

So we did. It was called Willie and the Parasites. Willie liked that his name was in the band name, and I had no problem with that.

We decided to write songs. So we did. But we fought a lot, too. We knew that there was a lot we didn't know. A lot of connections we didn't have. But our souls were so full of excitement—at what we imagined for ourselves. An extraordinary life. A life of adventure. Then Willie left and went to England. I joined another band. Kept the dream going, and tried to learn, hunger in my heart.

When Willie came back, we went walking, near my home place in Croghan, up a great hill to the Clump, Cox's Clump, the landmark of my childhood, a clump of trees that can be seen from nearly as far away as Carrick-on-Shannon. We walked by farmers working in the fields. We both knew by then about *The Clownishness of Rock and Roll*. How unimportant and boyish and indulgent The Rolling Stones—Willie's heroes—really were. Sure, they could be admired. For their craft at writing songs. Or their musicianship. Or their good looks. For their business acumen. For being lucky. Their music could be enjoyed and imitated and borrowed from. But it was court jester stuff. *What they were saying wasn't as important as the way they made it sound.* We didn't quite get around to dissecting the glamour of the likes of Bowie and Lou Reed. That seemed too much like sacrilege. But deep down we knew.

Our fathers were both farmers, practical men, men who took themselves seriously. Far too seriously. Life was no longer as predictable or cleanly moral, or as understandable as theirs seemed to have been. But the first flush, the first thrill of discovery of the world beyond my peasant existence was being tempered. Willie reported back on the ups and downs of Irish working life in London. He had witnessed degradation, had come across emigrants who were lost, people who were disappointed. He had sought out havens of silence in the great city, a city full of jarring sights and sounds. He had leafed through papers and glossy magazines in shops.

The ads for musicians would be in the back pages of *Sounds* and *NME*.

• Vocalist wanted. No time wasters.

All new bands were influenced by The Velvet Underground.

He stopped to watch a telly in a shop window. Others lingered there, too. Looking at what? Glamour. Escape. Into a fantasy world, manufactured by big business, by the entertainment industry. It was like the American Dream. Let them dream of a better life. That holiday can by yours. That house. That make-up. That dream. Let them pay to dream. People colluded in it; everyone knew it wasn't real. But it seemed they couldn't do without it. (This was a period of figuring out about politics. Should we be left-wingers or right-wing? You could end up arguing either case.)

There was no argument about what the entertainment industry was servicing. The dream. Soaps. Footballers. Hollywood. Mick Jagger. Even David Bowie. I had just read a letter to the *New Musical Express* that a guy wrote, addressing David Bowie (my hero). He said thank you, David, for helping me to grow up. For fooling me and telling me the truth and expressing my doubts, for being my role model, for changing as I changed. For being Ziggy. For being so damn cool. But goodbye, David. I'm off to join the real world. Or something to that effect. I knew what that guy was talking about.

But, all the same, I stuck at it. I loved my dad. He showed me the stars. He was thoughtful, patient and generous to a fault. But one time when I was small—maybe in a thoughtless moment—my father said to me, 'You'd never be able to write a song.' That really angered me. I thought, I'll show him. And I did; I wrote some great songs. Rock music was something I could do. Could give myself to. So I tried that road, didn't allow it was any bit less real than farming, or milkmanning, or accounting, or being the head of a driving school. I was making choices based on what I knew about. Keyword here: Information.

I was very nervous the first time I played in front of an audience. Anthony Noone and Patsy Mac and myself did a gig in the Four Provinces in Rathallen, probably in 1973 or so. My sister and her friends endured and applauded. Patsy was a fine trad accordionist, but between us Anthony and I knew only a handful of chords. But we had a few brand new original songs.

Anyway, over time, I came to play a tiny part in the great big music industry. I practised the guitar, met more musicians, joined bands, did gigs. I got to make records and played all over Ireland. Went to London. Our band (and our representatives) talked to record companies, important ones that are called 'majors'. I walked into the very office in Soho Square where CBS executives were discussing marketing strategy for Mick Jagger's next single. I saw Brian Eno's right leg and the back of his coat as he dashed through a door. That was 1986. That year, I played to big audiences, in the Blue Lagoon, Sligo, and the Baggot Inn, Dublin. The RDS, the SFX, the Stadium. The Self Aid show, in which we played a small part, went out live to millions on TV. I was cool about it all. Not even nervous. Though the band was called Those Nervous Animals.

I sought out new role models, secret heroes, sources of inspiration. David Byrne of Talking Heads. What would *he* have done now? Someone said, we need two new fast songs. I found I had grown enough in confidence to look inside myself for answers. Build a style. Find a voice. I wrote or co-wrote most of the songs. I was learning the craft. The skills of entertainment.

To be professional. To tune that guitar. To look up. To look happy. To dance. To take on that mantle of power, of almost religious authority. To hold it, as a Zen master might. Or a dancer. Or a priest. After the shows the buzz was amazing. Unwinding was the problem. Couldn't go to bed, couldn't sleep, had to party. . .

But the buzz wore off in a few days. I used to love going home and walking on the farm, going up to the Clump. I had a great time in the rock music business. I could have made a career out of it with a bit more wisdom, and luck. I don't regret a thing. I grew immeasurably as a person. I sorted out a lot of things in my head and soul. I learned to be proud of myself. I hope I learnt a bit of humility, too. Some time, if you like, I can tell the story of getting out of the band, of the ending. Of us not becoming stars. But it's not important. It won't be a sentimental tale. It was an education.

When I came back to Sligo from the moon, my first task was to rediscover myself. It took a while to get back. I noticed that when I spoke to people I spoke slightly differently, with a different tone, more cityish, more reserved. Looked on the world just a tad differently. Even though I knew it was just a job, a role in a fakey world. I felt like an actor, like Bowie used to say, but maybe I had begun to live the role. You could get used to putting on a face for interviews. To having a guitar roadie, who wrote down your favourite amp settings, recorded any changes you made, and restored them faithfully for the gig. He would not even let me plug in the guitar myself onstage. (We had this rock star treatment for one tour only.) Sometimes I wondered. Would I have been beautiful or ugly as a man with money? With fame? What would I have changed into if I had really 'made it'?

Funny, but I think—I *think*—I know the answer. I would have come back, but by a longer route. Or just a different route. I would have been OK.

POSTSCRIPT

Deciding on the spelling of the name for the band formerly known as Six As One was a tricky issue. We never really cleared it up. A few different spellings have been used, and maybe the most popular one is IOU. I have also seen dots included, both I.O.U. and I.O.YOU. A lot of the early publicity material used the formulation I O YOU. I never liked that one. When it came to working with the graphic designer who did the *Together Girl* CD it became IOYou. Averyl liked IOYou or IO You, I seem to remember. IOYOU is my preferred spelling, and I have used it throughout this book.

PART 1: SHINY NEW WORLD

TOGETHER FOREVER

We'll be together girl forever
The way that it should be
Together girl forever, If only you could see
I know now how I'm feeling, girl
My feelings are so true
Together girl, forever, me and you

(Filan/Feehily/Meehan/Connolly)

The day of the recording, the entire band assembles at Michael Garrett's house. Michael and Shane wrestle. They are messing. They are always messing. They have been best friends for the longest time. Derek is quiet, as ever. He sits cross-legged on the couch, trying not to take up too much space. The rest are loud, jibing and joking to cover their nervousness. They do their best to keep the roughhouse stuff under control because being at Michael's house is a new thing. Michael's house is posh. It is spacious and comfortable, with tasteful furnishing. The decor is confidently understated. The Garretts are doing OK.

Dad Garrett is at work; Mrs Garrett makes tea and sandwiches. Derek thanks her politely as he takes his cup; he sips from it and makes a bit of small talk. The Garrett parents are supportive of the boys recording their new song. They are excited, too. They are proud of their son (Michael is fourth in a family of six), if slightly bemused by all this boyband lark. Solid middle-class folks, they know the Leaving Certificate (final exams in secondary school) is coming up next year, and they are concerned that Michael keep his feet firmly on the ground.

Michael's younger sisters are in school, this being a Monday. They would have loved to be here for when the band came visiting. Michael's sisters are the biggest fans of IOYOU, and are *soooo* proud of Michael.

The year is 1997. A mild, cloudy day in late September. Being in IOYOU gives the boys a certain swagger around the town. *They don't sing karaoke any more.* But none of the six band members have seen the inside of a recording studio.

Situated in a nice part of Sligo, on a quiet tree-lined road, only three minutes walk from Michael's house, James Blennerhasset's 'Doghaus' studio is small. Part of his family home has been taken over to provide the space for it. But it has all the latest in digital recording gear. James likes toys. James is bald, dapper and bespectacled and cool as hell. He has seen it all before. He has played bass with everybody: The Chieftains, Van Morrison and the Blacks, Mary and Frances. A photo—autographed by Mick and Keith—of James and The Rolling Stones hangs on the studio wall from a session the Blen did with The Glimmer Twins. He has been up early, asking his Apple Mac and his digital machines to *please talk to one another*. Behave yourselves, machines. We have a session today.

• Knock, Knock.

James and Pádraig Meehan don't need introductions to each other. They have worked on projects before, demos with bands, instrumental pieces, soundtracks, etc. Pádraig is the producer of today's session.

• Mister P. Meehan. Come in, come in! How's the goin', boss?

19

James calls everyone boss. He is doing Pádraig and his boyband co-managers in Streetwise a favour by charging minimal rates for the studio. He is curious about the boyband project. 'Have ye signed a contract with them?' Meehan's response to this query is vague. He rubs his chin. 'Yeah, yeah. That's all organised.'

Meehan has a lazy eye, and when he is tired, the left one wanders off on its own, sending conflicting and unofficial messages to his brain. Like James, he is not tall, five seven and a bit. He wears floppy casual clothes, chunky shoes. He has a paunch, and at forty-one his curly hair has receded alarmingly. Determinedly, he wears it longish at the back. His nose is flattish, his lips full above a small upturned chin. He offers a bright smile when he is not sure what to say.

The Blen multi-tasks. He talks to the computer and on the phone and to whoever is in the room, all at once. He is a perfectionist. A devoted Apple Mac-ist. His system is set up to record to computer hard disk and (audio) to videotape.

But first you have to have breakfast. James makes good coffee. The two take the mugs into the studio. Down a step and close the door on James's home. This is the second day of the session. Yesterday James and Pádraig went through the familiar ritual, starting from the very beginning. Getting a click going, setting a tempo. Pádraig played the song on guitar, singing in a silly falsetto. They decided on the ideal pace. The song, 'Together Girl Forever', is a slow ballad.

Rough backing tracks for three songs have been assembled. 'Everlasting Love' and 'Pinball Wizard' (a dance version of the old The Who song, from the rock opera *Tommy*) will complement 'Together Girl Forever'.

While the band are entertained down the road by Mrs Garrett, James Blen logs into his Internet account. Daragh Connolly's instrumental sequences for the songs have arrived by email. James sets about assembling the jigsaw, a tedious and frustrating exercise. James curses Daragh, the arranger, for his habit of inserting event changes in every instrument. Eventually they are ready to go for a guide vocal track. Pádraig gets on the phone.

• Shane and Mark, come over to the studio. Yes. Off the Strandhill Road. No. The others can come later. Yeah, we'll record their parts then.

James welcomes the two lads politely. Shane and Mark shake hands with James and introduce themselves. Shane Filan, Mark Feehily. Pleased to meet you. They are perfect gentlemen.

- Wow, this place looks cool.
- Lots of expensive stuff here.

James hits the button and plays back the rough backing tracks. The drums are Roland 808 sounds. The coolest vintage drum machine in the world. These are just samples, of course, not a real 808.

- If only we knew how famous it would become when they were cheap in 1985.

The older guys do it by habit now, they go into studiospeak. They forget the far-off days when they had wondered at people calling headphones 'cans' and bass drums 'kicks'.

The boys stand in the control room and sing along with the chords of their song.

- Well, guys. Do you want to go in and sing a bit?

The studio floor is tiny. James's cellos and basses hang on the walls.

- Put on the cans.

Mark and Shane fumble awkwardly with their headphones. With their cans. James sets levels.

- Is the track loud enough in the cans?
- Yeah.
- Can you hear yourselves?

'Can you turn me down a bit, please, it's a little bit loud,' says Mark. 'It's blowing the head off me,' says Shane.

'Let's go for it. We will take one.' Pádraig has a philosophy of recording everything, even the singing during the level setting. You don't want to miss the definitive performance. Oftentimes the best singing is done when the singers don't know they are being recorded. Especially if they are given to nerves. But these boys don't seem at all nervous. Just intense. Standing by the microphone, they sing together.

James presses talkback. He says, 'Great! Sounding good. We will do the real one later.'

- Did you record that?
- Come out, come out, boys, and have a listen.

Shane's face shines with wonder as he listens. He has a wide smile, dark brown hair, a high forehead and, below dark eyebrows, twinkling hazel eyes. He puts his weight on the back of James's engineer's swivel chair and soaks in the music. His mouth doesn't move much, but his words occur suddenly beside you.

• Not bad, is it, Mark? It's allright . . .

'We will be doing it again, though?' asks Mark. 'Oh, yes,' says James. 'That was just a guide.' The boys take a break while the musicians lay down more tracks. Acoustic guitar. Shane and Mark phone the others back at Garrett's house.

• We did a guide vocal. It's just a guide. This place is cool.

The other boys are tired of waiting.

• When are we coming down?

• Is it just ye going to be singing?

• No. We will send for ye later.

'OK, fellas,' says James. 'Ready to go for lead vocals? And after that, maybe some harmonies? Who wants to go first? Mark?'

Shane goes first. A little side turn of the head from James. James has a trained impassive expression, a kind of half-smile behind his glasses as he listens, which gives away nothing in the way of judgement. But that little nod means Wow. Pádraig knows Shane is impressive. He has a measured way of singing, almost too restrained, but it is obvious that he understands phrasing and tone instinctively. Shane has a touch of Gary Barlow about him, the smoothie out of Take That. Mr Entertainer. This young guy thinks about every note, about his approach. That is why he is so good at helping the others. Shane thinks band. He has a way of raising his hands to conduct, to measure the delivery. Shane is about control. Two or three takes and Shane has nailed his verses of the song. Every time he sings it, he sings it the same.

It is Mark's turn. Mark is a different proposition to Shane. He is imaginative but introspective. A soft boy, with baby red cheeks, Mark has a slight tendency to put on weight, especially on his legs. He is the youngest band member, only seventeen. He has pretty eyes; his eyelashes always look long. An ample pout. Mark has an innocence to him and a diffident way of talking out of the side of his mouth. He looks up at you and laughs shyly. Then he comes out with a wisecrack and you glimpse a different side of his personality. The cheeky, impish side.

Shane kneels on a chair in the control room and watches through the small glass panels as Mark gives his vocal everything. Mark has his cans on. They look at each other. Shane mimes the singing word for word with Mark in sympathy; he wills him through the notes. Mark never takes his eyes off Shane. The boys are helping each other.

James and Pádraig follow the cursor as it traces over the passing wave samples on the computer screen. As Mark sings, the machine paints his voice in these shapes, freezes his performance into a landscape of sound. Mountain ranges slip by, and their reflection in still water. Silence is a flat line. When Mark lets fly, big peaks butterfly out to the top and bottom of the page. James looks on these valleys and hills as his raw material. Later he will farm them, using onscreen tools to scrub the gaps flat of bumps and clicks. The main thing is not to get hypnotised. You have to remember to listen as well as watch.

Seated at the sound desk, James and Pádraig exchange comments with their eyes as Mark's singing voice belts out of the monitors. Pádraig is well used to hearing the boys sing. He has worked with them for months now. He has huge faith in their ability, but he knows that today's session represents an important hurdle for any musician; the recording process will put their performance under a new level of microscopic inspection.

Mark is a challenge to record.

His natural instinct is to explore; he travels the full dynamic range of his voice, from a timid falsetto to a fortissimo bellow. James will use a compressor to try and capture the performance without killing the life in it. There is a part of Mark's voice that under the scrutiny of the control room, up loud and solo, sounds hoarse, a little raw. The tone is narrower and less silky smooth than Shane's. There's a throaty frequency somewhere in there that we don't want to hear too much of. James goes hunting for it and compresses that register back a bit. Better. James tries a different mic. Much better.

Mark is full of passion, and he is a man in a hurry. Consequently he is slightly undisciplined at the microphone. You can almost feel in him the sense of escape, escape from the loneliness of dreaming of being a singer through all those boring classes in school, the ordinariness of life. Eleven o'clock break, lunch, last class, home. Mark has spent literally years jotting down lines that sounded good, trying to write songs while his classmates played football. He has been dreaming on his bicycle, sending soaring notes over the hedgerows by the rainy roads home. And can he soar! He takes a melody and plays it over in his imagination. He makes it rich with feeling.

Mark hears the roar of the crowd. He reads the glowing reviews—Mark Feehily, singing star! What a range. What falsetto! The headlines. *Mark Feehily, R&B star!*

He bends the notes blue and tails off words with little scales, like Stevie Wonder, or Michael Jackson, or Mariah Carey. Mariah Carey is his hero. So don't ask Mark to sing the same part over and over in rehearsal. He gets bored easily. But give him a soul or R&B tune and he is determined to bring an imaginary crowd to their feet. So once you get a good sound off the microphone for Mark, the rest is sheer excitement. What will he do next?

Lots of takes are recorded of Mark. He ad libs little soul bits on top of the choruses at the end. The final vocal will probably be a composite, a jigsaw puzzle assembled from the best bits of the day's work.

Graham rings James's doorbell. He is here to do his rap on the song 'Everlasting Love'. He wrote the rap himself.

Graham Keighron is angular and skinny. When you chat to him he is relaxed, warm. Graham comes from an estate in Maugheraboy on the western outskirts of Sligo town. He has a young face, though at twenty-one he is the oldest of the boys. The rest of them call him 'the Daddy of the Band'. Graham is also called 'the A.J. of the band'. That is, A.J. as in Alexander James McLean, a.k.a. Bone. Out of The Backstreet Boys. Graham Keighron is the Sligo version of the Palm Beach, Florida, choreographer, singer, rapper and fashion model. Like A.J., Graham is *his* band's best dancer. He comes up with choreography ideas, too.

Green-eyed, with light brown hair and sharp facial features, there is something black and white about Graham's looks, like he could be a character in a classic 1940s movie. He always looks great in his gig suit. On this day, for the studio, he wears tracksuit casuals, a baseball hat. He looks you in the eye. This young man is full of hunger for success. Graham is an honest worker, very fit, and he can sing reasonably well, too. He is well capable of holding a

24

harmony or a melody line and takes the lead in a number of songs in the band's set. He is conscious that he is not quite as good vocally as Shane and Mark, so he has carved out a niche for himself as the band's rapper.

There are still lead vocals to be put on the other two songs. 'Pinball Wizard' proves a challenge for all but the unflappable Shane. But James and Pádraig think he sounds a bit too smooth. Graham gives it a go. He is pretty good. He does some of the answers.

How do you think he does it?
I don't know.
What makes him so good?
(Pete Townsend)

Mark decides he will have another crack at it. As Mark improvises somewhere in the rafters, the man next door to James's decides that this is a perfect time to mow his lawn. James and Pádraig carry on recording, pressed for time.

It is time to get all the boys singing on the choruses. At last, in the late afternoon, the call comes to Garretts'. Three happy young men hurry down Strandhill Road. They sing all the way down to the studio. 'Barbie Girl'—it's a stupid song, but you can't get it out of your head. The blonde one is Kian Egan. The tall, dark one with the dimples and sallow skin is Derek Lacey. And the pale one who takes long steps that swing outward, the one who looks into the world from behind wayward locks of dark hair, is Michael ('Miggles') Garrett.

The three lads crowd in the studio booth and sing the chorus of 'Together Girl' for all they are worth. They have a few goes at it. It's a bit out of tune in places. It's a bit wild. Take four. OK. That will do. It will be in the background, anyway. Another track is recorded of all six band members singing at once. Better.

There is a sheet of paper divided into eight or sixteen boxes, whatever. The track sheet. It is a map of the song, a way to navigate around and get back the next day to as-you-were. The engineer scribbles in something, a code name to remind him of the contents of each track as it is filled. 'Mark Vox 1'. 'Shane and Mark Harmony 3'. 'Pádraig Acoustic 2'. 'Busy Bass GTR'.

The track, jokingly labelled 'The Herd', is the one track that does not bear too many listens. It's a bit scary. But the first time James and Pádraig listen to it solo and up loud another horror is revealed. There are only a couple of takes where the performance sounds usable. But then James's sharp ears pick up some unwanted interference on the best take. Audible—at very low level—in the background, is the unmistakeable two-stroke splutter of the Lawnmower Man. Pádraig says, 'Will it be noticeable when everything is in?' James says, 'You couldn't have that. No way.' What to do?

The band have gone home. Shane is back to college down in Limerick tomorrow. And time is running short. James has another session queued up for the studio.

That evening Daragh and James put on their youngest voices, and after checking that the Lawnmower Man is not at work, they sing the choruses. Pádraig does sound engineer. Pádraig looks up at one stage and sees two serious faces beyond the glass, eyes on the lyric sheet, two faces screwed up in effort and concentration. He giggles. The two well-travelled pros are totally engrossed in their parts.

Ahh. Look at those open faces, the faces of angels. The bastards are actually enjoying it! Then they spot Pádraig grinning. Caught! Once James and Daragh start laughing they can't stop. Pádraig thinks his sides will break. The would-be teenyboppers sway from side to side as they sing, each holding up an imaginary cigarette lighter, stadium-rock style. Eventually they settle and get back to getting a unison backing vocal on the chorus. Nailed. They bind each other to secrecy on their heroic act.

As evening turns into night, James puts down his final bass guitar tracks. He does some acoustic, too. James's rhythm style suits the song. He plays a lovely steady strum which sits in nicely behind the vocals. He is fast and accurate. The songs are beginning to sound good. On day three the tracks are mixed. Daragh comes in and tweaks his string parts.

It is a marathon session, James doing edits and cutting and pasting in Digital Performer. He skilfully cleans up the individual lead vocal tracks, pulls a word from here to fix a phrase there. He cuts out a foot stomp here, tunes a dodgy note bend there. He nudges a whole line a tad to the left, so that the singer comes in spot on, on the grid line that marks the top of the bar. But he has lots of good stuff to work with, usable stuff. The boys have done well. Mark Feehily and Shane Filan still sound good. Seems you can't say the word 'me' and be in a boyband. It's Meh. Kind of black.

- I need someboddayheee to hold *Meh!*

For Graham's rap, James uses a mad plug-in effect to model his sound and give Graham a huge black voice. That's good fun. Roger Brennan, a local DJ, comes in and makes suggestions for the bass drum parts and other mixes in a dance context.

In the end, the backing vocals on 'Together Girl' are a mix of all the boys singing, a double of Shane and Mark doing the chorus *and* a touch of James's and Daragh's vocals. So everyone got to be on the recording. Probably if you listen to it up loud enough you hear the Lawnmower Man in there, too.

Pádraig brings a recording of the first 'monitor mixes' of the songs to Mary McDonagh's house. Mary McDonagh and Averyl Dooher, co-managers of IOYOU with Pádraig, are there. The band is there. There are friends and neighbours, too, and other people who are working on the IOYOU project. Everyone huddles around a ghetto blaster. It has to sound good on this if it is to sound good on the radio.

It's not bad at all. It's boyband. The boys compare it to various boyband records they know. There is a self-congratulatory mood. Everyone feels the sense of embarking on a journey, of setting out on an adventure. For the six boys it is their first recording, with songs on there that they wrote themselves. The six are setting out on a quest for fame and fortune, and the managers are right behind them. They can't wait to see their first CD on the shelves, for sale in a shop.

A week or so passes. Streetwise—as Mary, Averyl and Pádraig call their management partnership—have been meeting Aidan Mannion and Kevin Flannery of Sound Records in Sligo. The local record shop owners have agreed to part with some money for the final masters of the recording session. This will help pay recording and mastering costs. James Blen, aware that Streetwise have a policy of keeping business local, has suggested Robyn Robins's Mid-Atlantic Digital Studio (MAD) in Enniskillen for the mastering session. This is where the mixed tape will start its transformation into a CD.

In late October, James and Pádraig travel up to Enniskillen, just across the border in Northern Ireland. James drives. They spend the day listening to the track on the impressive speakers of MAD.

Robyn Robins is a real laid-back American guy. He wears his hair long. His rock and roll credentials are impeccable. Robyn was Bob Seger's keyboard player in The Silver Bullet Band; they sold a lot of records stateside in the eighties. Robyn clearly enjoys the job of mastering engineer. He is on top of the mouse, like a video game child assassin. He paces himself. When it's time to take your eyes away from the screen of the Mac and give your ears a break, Robyn swivels to you and explains stuff, using snowball-throwing finger gestures. The modelling possibilities of his software are impressive. So many possibilities, it spins your head. 'We can get this sounding good,' says Robyn. 'We can widen this, lift that out.' James and Pádraig worry that they might have overdone the reverb on the original mix.

Robyn would have liked more scope. The idea of mastering was to work all the frequencies, get max volume, then compress hell out of it. But James and Pádraig had done a lot of this work in Sligo, in their mixes. Eventually Pádraig, James and Robyn settle on a final version of 'Together Girl' and 'Everlasting Love'.

The first single will—according to the management/record company joint strategy—be released only in the north-west of Ireland. Pádraig comes back from Enniskillen with two master copies of the recordings on writeable CD. One for the record company (they will send it to Trend Studios in Dublin, where a thousand copies will be manufactured for the marketplace) and one for video cameraman, Ciaran Carty, who will shoot lip-synch footage for a prospective video for the band, to go with the single.

James and Pádraig talk on the drive back from Enniskillen. Pádraig remembered Mary McDonagh telling him about her boyband idea, not twelve months before, in November '96.

• I have a boyband. Not the panto boyband. A real boyband. Mark Feehily is in it. I must be mad. Will you come and have a look at them?

• Course I'll have a look at them. Mary, you are gas!

PANTOZONE

Ransboro School is fifteen minutes from Sligo town. Out on the peninsula, a place of shifting colour, shifting contrasts. Cuil Irra, the Remote Corner. Warm light, cold light, soft light, hard light. The light on the peninsula is always changing.

If you wanted to kill time, you could spend an hour going the long way. A 7km loop out from Sligo via the north road takes you to the village of Strandhill at land's end. If it's low tide, you travel overlooking a vastness of rippling sand, broken only by the line of concrete pillars marking the causeway to Coney Island. Strandhill village is set on a descent; the land falls all the way to the beach. The tide is a surfer's dream, but Strandhill Beach is treacherous for swimmers, even paddlers. A relic of forgotten wars, an ancient cannon, points out to sea. It tilts towards the crisp horizon line of the blue-green Atlantic.

To complete the circuit, return towards town via the winding road to the south, by Cullenamore Strand and the Sandy Field. As you pass between ivy-draped walls, the weathered face of Knocknarea Mountain revolves to your left. The road cuts inland after 4km or 5km. At the crossroads before the riding centre you will pass Ransboro Church. The school stands beside the church.

The place has always had a terrific community spirit, and produced more than its fair share of quirky and funny and eccentric 'characters'. A pantomime all year round. They have a community ethos and jealously guard their amateur status, but Cooleara Players[†] boast a talented core of experienced performers. Old heads that can keep the ship steady as the young ones graduate from gnomes and fairies to wicked sisters and fairy godmothers. The company doesn't just do panto. They also tackle serious plays; they tour and regularly win prizes. They usually put something on in the New Year. The funds raised by the panto help make these more ambitious projects possible.

The Cooleara panto is an institution in Sligo. Nineteen ninety-six is its eighteenth season. The pantomime will be packed out for the run of sixteen or seventeen shows before Christmas. The actors and production team—all locals—have put in weeks and weeks of rehearsals in Ransboro School and in the back room of Michael Woods's place, Cooleara House. In 1996, as usual, Mary McDonagh is choreographing the panto. It is a tough job, organising a cast of—it seems—thousands, some of whom have never danced before. And there are one or two seasoned principals with two seasoned left feet. Magnificent size twelves. Grace may not be a word in their vocabulary, but mischief is. They love to challenge Mary to put some kind of shape on their comedy numbers. The look on her face is—always—priceless. But year after year she comes up with hilarious routines, and manages to hypnotise the lads and lassies into learning them.

The schoolroom is cold. When you sing you see your breath. The small group retreats to the kitchen area. These nights Mary is staying back late after rehearsals to get a 'panto boyband' together. It will be a brilliant lift to the second half of the show. Panto dame Brian Devaney, never short of a quip, has christened them 'Pantozone'. Barry Cawley is in it, and Cormac Carroll. And a guy with an American accent called Roger Clarke. One of the fellows in it, out

---

† Cooleara (cool-air-a) is a townland on the peninsula that still bears this derivation of the ancient name.

of Mary McDonagh's dance school, is quite a good singer. She kind of parachuted him in. His name is Mark Feehily. Pádraig Meehan, who is musical director for the panto this year, has arranged harmonies for the songs. He rehearsed the vocal parts with the panto boyband first. They have to have the singing off pretty good before they start to learn the steps. Otherwise the concentration demanded while dancing will mean they forget to sing. And Mary will have to remind them.

• Learn the song, *please*, boys.

Mark is a good singer, but he doesn't seem to have a great memory for movement or harmonies. His attention appears to wander; he is off somewhere else. But he does persist with the harmony line that Pádraig gives him. Pádraig likes Mark right away. He is a modest, personable fellow. Mark is mad into music, all kinds of music. He is interested in Pádraig's guitar.

• Where did you buy it? You are deadly on it.

Pádraig explains he is not a session musician. There are many far better guitar players around. 'But this'—pointing to his acoustic Takamine—'this is my shovel for digging out tunes, new ideas.' Mark says, 'You write songs? Cool.' One day Mark arrives and gives Pádraig a cassette tape with his ideas for his own songs on it. He says he always has song ideas in his head. Pádraig compliments Mark on his singing. Mark seems almost embarrassed. Pádraig says, 'I love the little scat things you do—you know, sliding down through all those blue notes. Do you like Stevie Wonder?' Mark says, 'I never heard anything of him.'

• Where did you hear that style then?
• Michael Jackson, I suppose, replies Mark.

MARY

Pizza in Mary McDonagh's house is a regular ceremony in the last months of 1997. The Streetwises have wine, the boys have soft drinks and pizza. Mary is *Bean a' Tí*. The woman of the house. She pays for the food. She has sold the yard at the side of her house in High Street and is spending the money on IOYOU. Mary has a sharp eye and a clean determined line of chin.

The McDonaghs had theatre in their blood. Mary, as a young girl, danced in all the Feiseanna Ceoil. This was a countywide competition centred on Irish music and dancing. There were competitions for light jigs, heavy jigs, slip jigs, reels. Mary loved the big musicals, too; her home was endowed with a selection of opera classics. She dreamt of becoming a ballet dancer. She started ballet classes with Sybil Higgins when she was four. Sybil was an impressive lady. She had an accent, a touch posh English. 'Theatah.'

Sybil did freelance teaching in various centres around Sligo. She taught swimming and dancing. Her Summerhill College swimming students won competitions regularly. An atmosphere of respect—

awe, almost—surrounded her. She had her favourites. But she understood the basics of movement.

Mary McDonagh loved to move and quickly grew into one of Sybil's best pupils. But a rural west of Ireland town like Sligo had no classical tradition of dancing, no school like the ones in Moscow where children's bodies were sculpted from infancy into works of art, physiological wonders destined only for flight, shaped only to dance the ballet. Nevertheless, Mary McDonagh had fire in her heart. When she was only fourteen, after spending two years as a boarder in the Ursuline Convent school, Mary set off on the journey by train and boat to audition for Nesta Brooking's School of Ballet and Dramatic Art in London. Her dad was a great support to her in the pursuit of her dreams. Mary was over the moon when they told her she was accepted. She had passed the audition.

Mary McDonagh walked the echoing halls of the Nesta Brooking School of Ballet and Dramatic Art. Mary looked wide-eyed at the serious people there. She took in the hurrying, scurrying, busy world of the ballet school. It was not quite like she had imagined it, but it was great. The world of professional ballet training was a whole lot more competitive and demanding than school in rural Ireland. As different as London city was from Sligo.

It was tough, she was lonely at times, and the physical work the dancers had to endure was close to torture, but Mary's fighting spirit brought her through. She graduated and eventually made it to the small screen as a dancer. She danced on various TV shows. Her journey as a performer took her in shows to every major theatre in Ireland. In 1997, a beautiful black and white photograph of Mary hung in her kitchen, a publicity shot from those times.

Mary learned from every experience, from every dancer and teacher she came across. Her studies and travels gave her a grounding, a feel for a wide scope of disciplines. Ballet, tap, modern dance. She was interested in dance from various exotic ethnic sources. And Irish dance, too, of course.

After retiring from dancing it was a natural transition for Mary to make a career in professional choreography. She worked for years in RTÉ, the Irish national broadcaster, doing shows like 'The Live Mike', 'The Late Late Show', 'Lifelines' and many others. In Bunratty Castle, near Limerick, where US tourists encountered the Ireland of their dreams through the magic of theatre, Mary used to have a regular gig choreographing the annual summer season. She wasn't snobbish about it. She would go from pro ballet dancers to Bunratty to the lads in the Cooleara panto, and keep her sense of humour.

Mary was great for having ideas. Her friends were used to her just blurting out a whole new plan, straight out of the blue.

- Do you know what we should do, lads?

It was Mary's idea to launch The Fun Company in 1982 to promote shows in Sligo. Having just arrived back to live in Sligo, Mary saw a gap and filled it. There was a lot of young talent showing in different schools in the area—why not start a company and bring them together, develop and showcase this nascent talent. This brought her into the role of producer. The first show The Fun Company did was *The Witness*, an original show in a bizarre sci-fi setting from the pen of Irish songwriter Shay Healy. *Jesus Christ Superstar* followed and *The Wiz.*

Over the years, Mary got used to juggling plenty of hats. One day she might don her choreographer hat to marshal the dancers of the *Rhythm of the Dance* for the National Dance Company of Ireland. A few days later, back from touring the world, Mary would be directing a kid's show. Back in 1996, when she had her boyband idea, she had just finished a run of *The Children Of Lir* in Cork Opera House. As producer.

It is a good bet that Mary McDonagh's most lasting legacy to Sligo will be her work as a teacher. Shortly after she moved back to Sligo, she started the Mary McDonagh School of (Movement and) Dance. At the early stages she did not have a premises to work from; she booked whatever studio was available and got an assistant to help her keep tabs on the train of students of all ages who attended the regular classes. Sometimes the people who were in The Fun Company shows got extra classes during the week. They didn't have to pay, except for their normal Friday evening classes.

Thus it happened that maybe half the population of Sligo of a certain age passed through Mary's hands. Some came to prepare for the Feiseanna Ceoil; some were daughters sent by mothers to Mary to learn carriage and deportment and elocution.

Middle-class kids, posh kids, working-class kids, happy kids, troubled kids. They have made their first dance steps in her 'babies' classes, and trust-fell backwards into her hands. And a sub-set of the female population has the Mary way off to a T—a way of carrying themselves, a slightly chilly self-respect. Mary holds herself with the iron discipline of a ballet dancer. She rarely raises her voice, but you don't see too much messing in her classes.

There is a let-your-hair-down Mary, too. A girlish, playful side. Mary has many sides. And a warm heart. Her house is an open house; over the years all sorts have come along and been nurtured and then moved on. There have been protégés, apprentices, stragglers and lost puppies. There is usually an entourage around Mary's—dancers, wannabe dancers, helpers, an old lady from next door. Mary's family, her actor dad, Walter,† and her sons, are used to it. People coming and going. Her dog Mighty yaps loudly to welcome each newcomer or current lodger. These days it's the boyband, IOYOU.

---

†   Walter also directed shows. He was one of the old guard, respected by his community for his knowledge and wisdom. Walter McDonagh's generation, in the post-war years, picked up where a previous one left off, continuing Sligo's long and unbroken love affair with the theatre.

GARRISON TOWN

The farther west you go, the wilder the sky. In contrast to the eastern shore, the western coastline of Ireland is ragged, chewed on for millennia by the hungry Atlantic ocean. Seen from the air, the Cuil Irra peninsula has the shape of a bull. Framed from above, he is frozen on the last stride of his charge into the tide. Ballisodare is scattered at his left flank, Sligo town to his right, and his arse is in Lough Gill. Two blonde horns of beach swing out to north and south, towards Coney Island and Culleenamore. The whole area is especially rich in ancient sites: passage tombs, court tombs, earthen barrows. On the back of the bull's head, close to the western tip of the peninsula, stands Knocknarea, a small cake-shaped limestone mountain with a 50,000-tonne pile of rocks set on its summit. The profile of the cairn echoes the outline of the hill. The mound is Miosgán Maeve, the Grave of the Queen.

Is the legend true? Is Maeve herself *really* inside the rock pile, standing tall even in death, her iron spear still in the grip of fleshless fingers? The cairn was built (and more than likely closed) in the passage tomb era, 2,000, maybe 3,000 years before metal weapons were known in these parts. But Queen Maeve's extravagant exploits have been passed down word-of-mouth by the hearth for generations. Monks wrote them down, when writing came in, so we could recite them today. Plans were laid a few times to open up the tomb and finish the argument once and for all, but somehow all fell through. American tourists carry a pebble for good luck up the winding path on the eastern slope and place it on the heap to help hold Maeve safely where she is.

In the late autumn and in the wintertime, the town of Sligo smokes and smoulders in the shadow of Knocknarea.[†] The Ballygawley and Ox Mountains lie to the south-west, a purple wall closing behind the peninsula. They catch the light like crystal after a fall of rain. These hills are so old that half a million years in the embrace of the great mantle of ice was just a fleeting encounter in their recent past. The last time the glaciers left was not more than maybe15,000 years ago.

Further to the south of the County Sligo, the Bricklieves stand above Lough Arrow, in a place known as Carrowkeel. The Unshin River rises close by and flows 17km north, threading between the Ox and Ballygawley hills to enter the Atlantic in Ballisodare Bay. From Carrowkeel you can watch the sun set over Cuil Irra and Knocknarea. And look down on townlands big and small. Townlands named for quarters—Carrow-this, Carrow-that. The Rough Quarter; the Narrow Quarter. In the same style as Knocknarea, the main peaks on the Ballygawley hills and the Bricklieves carry nipple-cairns, with passage tombs inside. The mark of the early farmers.

Farming carries on still. It still has a place. Knots of farmhouses and outhouses and cattle feeding places punctuate the hedge-drawn pattern of small farms. And slightly bigger farms. If you are doing

---

†   The first roundabout in Sligo town was—and still is—a passage tomb. The townland of Abbeyquarter North, on the banks of the Garavogue, has a stone circle and a few remnants of the dolmen that once stood at its centre. The place became Garavogue Villas when a housing estate was built there in the 1940s. They left the monument standing and built the road around it. In the Marian Year of 1954, a Crucifix and Blessed Virgin statue were added, standing in the circle where solemn ceremonies passed 6,000 years ago.

well, you need to climb astronaut-like up a set of steps to reach the cab of your shiny new tractor. The small grey Fergusson Twenty that served farmers so well since the fifties is becoming a rarity now. But men wearing cloth caps can still be found conversing across fences, looking not in the eye, talking to machinery and tools and pools of water. They advise each other about the qualities of a good donkey.

• You don't want him wake in the legs. I had a great ass one time, a mare ass.

There are places yet that remain untamed. High places of waterfalls and canyons and undiscovered caves. Up where the lines of fences finally peter out on vertical rock faces, the sheep are wild, or half-wild anyway. They wander up there, dodging foxes and birds of prey till the men and dogs come to reclaim them and bring them down to the lowlands to dose them or wash them or sell the fat lambs.

The first people to come to this place were not farmers. They lived here for 5,000 years before that revolution overtook them. They ate fish and hazelnuts and blackberries. They hunted. They walked. They carried the bones of the ancestors with them, half-burned but bearing knowledge of everything.

The beginning of the end of the first people's dreamtime came on a day with fair weather. When a cluster of dugout boats appeared on the horizon, a little fleet with animals in tow, unfamiliar, tame animals, animals heard of only in rumour and legend, wild-eyed cows. The cows had been borne in some kind of tackle over the narrow stretch of water to the east. Change was in the air for the people in *The Island That Would One Day Be Known as Ireland* when the first strange alien cow staggered ashore, prodded by sticks, weak after her journey across the sea.

It seems the aboriginal Sligo community started building small stone monuments a while before this time, maybe when the breaking news of the new way of life, a smell of the future, came to them from beyond the sea. The cow brought with her new ideas, new words—ploughs and longhouses and woven clothes. Royalty and their demands for taxes. Tastes ran to the milk and blood of cows. Alcohol, too, most likely. It was time to settle. Seasonal migration would eventually die out. Baked bread was in.

Of the original population not killed off by cow and chicken diseases, most took on the new way of life, or at least adapted the parts of it that suited them. There's a Sligeach in Scotland.[†] There are shell middens there, too. Another shelly place. In rural Sligo, Maugherow, Ballymote, Ballinafad, the pronunciation of the word bears a tinge of the Gaelic original. Shly-Goh. In the town they say Sligo (Sly-Go).

Sligo town is a funny old town. Sligo hides its face. It keeps hidden its passionate heart. It has a population of maybe twenty thousand and a post-colonial air.

Sligo is a place where the violet flicker of TV screens lights the faces of dark-eyed, dark-haired, Spanish-jawed men crowding the floors of bookies' shops. Volumes are exchanged here in the flash of a sharp eye. Sligo is a place where, of a summer morning, urban gridlock chokes narrow streets not a stone's throw from a different way of life. From the clusters of estates outside town, commuters make their way, joining queues of cars stacked deep behind traffic lights. Some hurry from modern bungalows and journey over a maze of country backroads. Passing shadowy, serene places where spiders spin webs and small birds startle and scatter from their morning slumber on a patch of dry tar road.

Sligo is a place where meticulous punctuality may carry less weight than the firmness of a handshake. A place where the voices of granny, mum and daughter, power suit and tracksuit, a mix of many voices, all rise. They chew over the talk of the town in hairdressers, in waiting rooms, in the fruit and veg. Whether the hairdresser is a fellow with a marine haircut in T-shirt and jeans or a hipster blonde showing lots of tanned belly below a skimpy top, they will have ways to keep stirring the pot. Juggling two or three lines of chat while, apparently independently, expert hands busy themselves parting, clipping, gelling and blowdrying.

Like Boyle down the road, Sligo was a garrison town. It stood on a place that had strategic importance for the armies of the past. Sligo wound up being the main town in this north-western corner of Ireland, straddling the route north. That experience left its mark. There was and is a big difference in the feel of towns like Sligo and of those that never hosted the British military.

† Cnoc Sligeach, a midden on Oronsay, in the western isles.

Some people did well out of the armies of occupation that came and went. Many citizens were proud to be loyal to the Crown. Sligo used to elect a Unionist member of parliament to Westminster. There were those who cared not a fig who ruled them; others harboured rebellion in their breasts. Sligo folks of all persuasions learned in those days the profit of keeping your mouth shut. Or at least immobile. Of those who could not stay their mouths, those with the best prospects had mastered the technique of the ventriloquist.

In a garrison town, the street you came from said everything about you. There were the ghettoes where the homes of the poor Catholics and the poor Protestants stood. There were the good parts of town. New money wanted to move there; old money didn't see much room for them.

The citizenry were resourceful. They fine-tuned their sense of humour. A dark Sligo humour, deeply ironic, with a twist of the absurd added in. Fatalistic and often self-deprecating. They learned to love Association Football. A ball killed in flight, trapped on the instep, rolled into the path of the inrunning striker. Or the last-ditch tackle, the ball nicked off the striker's boot an instant before he shoots. Or maybe they developed an appreciation of rugger. The raking kick to find touch under pressure. The hand-off as you body-swerved for the line.

A rigid set of social tiers existed in a garrison town like Sligo. People were supposed to know their place. And a stark divide grew between the dwellers of the county town and those of the countryside around it. You'd expect the country lads to be able to field a high ball, Gaelic football style. To fly-kick on the run, and split the posts from forty yards.

A hundred years ago, iron-clad shoes and wheels clattered over cobbled streets. Horse manure tended to accumulate; a young lad might get a small consideration for sweeping the pavement outside public houses or some of the business premises.

The merchants of Sligo were careful men. They dressed well. They wore good hats. They had long names. Most—not all—were of Protestant stock. They convened in smoky rooms to decide what was good for the town. They went to the club later. Poker, snooker, snuff. The lawmakers, the professionals, the property owners were there, too, undisturbed by the presence of women or peasants or members of the worker class.

The prudent shopkeeper would know most of his customers on first name terms. And if not, would regard it part of his vocational skills to read a face and clothes and an accent in an instant. And if it turned out you were from a good town family, or a farmer with money, you would be welcomed with open arms. But bad clothes plus bad accent equalled bad credit. The colonial era shopkeepers of Sligo could tell that this type of customer was:

(A) not deserving of attention and, potentially, a threat, or

(B) malingering, and unlikely to be able to afford such fine goods.

But all that is behind us. We are in the late nineties now. Nearing the end of the twentieth century, things are changing in Sligo. The development of the riverside is underway, opening up the north bank of the Garavogue River. Shopkeepers of today only want to know how they can help you. But they are becoming an endangered species—the supermarket is king now. The big stores buy in bulk and can afford to cut prices. The Irish economy is starting to throttle up, with a growl that has people talking Celtic Tiger. People are demanding choices. Still, you have to go to the local shop an odd time. You don't get all the gossip at the checkout from the harried looking young wans in polyester uniforms.

Sligo hides its face, and there is still a lingering reticence in the townspeople. Visitors fall in love with the landscape first and are puzzled by the town dwellers. It takes a while to get to know them, but once you do, you realise that the Sligonians are very special. In lots of ways the curious cultural mix of the town has enriched the place, made it wise. And sport and commerce and outside influences are weakening the barriers.

Association Football is no longer the sole preserve of working people from town. Pockets of soccer fans argue the workings of the offside rule in country towns like Tubbercurry and Gurteen.[†] In the Sligo scene it is common enough to find players competing in both codes of football, Gaelic and soccer. Gaelic football is a great

---

[†]   The definitive book on the experience of the country soccer crowd is Eamonn Sweeney's account of supporting Sligo Rovers from Gurteen, *There's Only One Red Army.*

theatre of ancient passions: going to a match, walking to the field carrying the colours, feels like participating in a great tribal movement. But the Sligo Gaelic team have lingered long in the doldrums. Every so often comes a flowering of hope. Sligo wins a few matches, and a minor bandwagon starts. Like the time in the seventies when town folks bumped into neighbours queuing outside Markievicz Park bearing the black and white flag of the county instead of the red of the Rovers. And shouted, 'Good man, Mickey, on your bike,' in acceptable Gaelicese as Mickey Kearins took on Roscommon, all on his own.

It is common now to see the same faces—wearing different hats and utilising subtly different expressions—at Gaelic matches and at cup or league ties in the Showgrounds.

There's a great tradition in Sligo of 'going up the river'. Town dwellers can draw on a rich store of local knowledge, put names on obscure hills and country crossroads. Names whose meaning is buried deep in language. The Garavogue is Ireland's shortest river, but it leads to the bright lake, Lough Gill. A dangerous lake, but a great place to fish, if you know what you are at.

Sligo has its own story, its own history, a history that people outside the town might not know. Sligo people, whether they speak in the short cadences of the town or the broad country *blás*, they have long memories. Michael Coleman was among the first of the great Irish fiddlers ever recorded, out in America. Back at the dawn of recording, he spawned a thousand imitators.

Coleman was a real young dandy around south Sligo at all the sessions one time. A narrow man, wearing tight trousers that didn't cover the socks; good leather shoes on his dancing feet. Outside Killavil chapel, within sight of the cairns of Kesh and Carrowkeel, Coleman told his pals all about the dizzy heights of New York City, on the far side of that ocean that broke at Strandhill. He was talking of places of which he had little experience. But in 1914, Coleman took the boat. He toured America for a couple of years with a vaudeville show. In New York, in the recording studio, he wasn't fazed by all the technology. He had to cramp his bowing style to get close enough to the big white acoustic horn that served as both speaker and microphone in the 1920s. There was a guy there with the job of nudging the musicians up closer to the horn.[†] Someone else had to wind the handle to turn the recording machine.

Coleman ignored the physical restrictions and played sweet and steady, throwing in plenty of fancy left hand ornamentation. It brought the Sligo style of fiddling to public attention. It made that way of playing cool. Seamus Tansey, historian and modern-day giant of the flute, calls Coleman the Elvis Presley of Irish traditional music. They say Coleman had a brother who was a sweeter fiddler. But he never recorded. Jim Coleman stopped in Sligo.

New York in the twenties was another world. Chinatown. Brownstone houses. Traffic jams. Shining skyscrapers of glass and steel. Michael Coleman played on the radio. Live. What a wonder as the musician's sound was transported electronically into living rooms. The farming of the invisible electromagnetic world of the ether was beginning. Coleman was one of the first, but many would follow. Like James Morrison and Paddy Killoran. They left south Sligo and went to America, too. They became legends to those who stayed at home.

At home, life went on, at a sensible pace. The ramblers would sit around the kitchen fire. Men and women who never mastered an instrument were well able to lilt the tunes. In the sixties, change may have been in the air, but country folk turned on their radio of a Saturday for Ciarán Mac Mathúna and 'Céilí House'. As the years passed, different names, different styles became familiar. And turned sepia, turned into history.

The McLynn family of Old Market Street were famous names in Sligo and beyond in the era of the folk revival. Jargon played in the Trades Club, where you had to order your drink with sign language. Talking over a song was sacrilege in a folk club. That was the time of the Ballisodare Festival and legendary nights in the Venue. Strandhill was a great centre for music in the seventies. The Baymount was still in vogue. People would head out there *en masse*,

---

[†] Trying to get level on the instrument to get above the noise was the problem in those days. They made a special fiddle for recording with an ugly horn out of it; it was a horrible yoke to play. People knew everything about you just by glancing through your cylinder collection. Recording to disk was just coming in. Production values have come on a long way since those sessions.

in buses and cars, hitching and on foot. The place was going strong up until the mid-eighties. There were no taxis in Sligo then, just a couple of hackney cars.

There was a big festival called Sounds '71 held in Sligo. Tom Paxton played the Gaiety.[†] The main open air gig was in the Showgrounds. It was £1 to get in. Gigs were organised at various venues over the June bank holiday weekend. Hearing the strains of Irish music within the boundaries of the county town was still something of a novelty. But The Chieftains would be playing, and Seamus Tansey, too. And Horslips, doing rocked-up, comic-strip trad. Dr Strangely Strange were on the bill and Fairport Convention, with Sandy Denny. A lot of strange-looking young people appeared in the town. When they felt inclined, they rested by sitting on the pavement and generally displayed a shockingly carefree attitude.

The main act in the Showgrounds was Tír na nÓg, Leo Kelly and Sonny Condell's group. A crowd built up outside the gate. Not all could afford the admission fee, so compère Shay Healy organised a whip-round to pay for their tickets, collecting £128. It was just two years after Woodstock.

Louis Stewart played Sounds '71, too. Duffy's Music Shop put a few guitars in the windows in the months after that, and there was a great run on them for a while. Cavendish's Music Shop sold a couple of guitars, too, on HP. The Jazz Workshop started around then. The jazz *aficionados* in the town went to check them out. The Jazz Lads played a New Orleans style for thirty years. They used to be The Mellowtones. Mickey Neilsen has kept the jazz tradition vigorous for a new generation. There were plenty of country bands. Sandy Kelly packed in rock and pop and took to singing country. She had a great career in front of her.

If you were into teen idols, you might have followed the Duggan brothers' answer to The Osmonds, Brotherly Love. Girls screamed when they burst onstage, in sky-blue suits with massive bell-bottoms. They were good musicians and singers, and had a sequence of chart hits in the mid-seventies. Their manager was Dublin-based, a guy called Louis Walsh.

Because the town was small there was always a curious cross-

---

†   One of Sligo's two cinemas at the time.

fertilisation thing going on. You might have a fella playing bass with the Jazz Lads one night and in a pop band the next. Séamus O'Dowd was as comfortable with a Rory Gallagher or Thin Lizzy tune on the Fender Strat as following the fingertips of his eminent dad, Joe O'Dowd, on the trad fiddle. The young guys playing heavy metal would inevitably hear older ones playing funk or blues, and join in the session. Francie or Terry or John Lenihan could take on J.J. Cale tunes or Irish ballads with equal ease. Although there were still a few musical cliques that liked to keep themselves to themselves, mixing and matching was an exciting and enriching aspect of the Sligo music scene.

Artists from abroad found inspiration in Sligo. Thom Moore came from across the Atlantic to live there and write inspired songs, write of 'The Cedars of Lebanon' and 'The Train to Sligo'. He formed a couple of great bands, Pumpkinhead—with his wife Kathy and fellow Californians Rick and Sandi Epping—and Midnight Well. Janie Cribbs joined him with her angelic-earthy voice. They should have been huge. Songwriter Dick Gaughan, too, became a regular visitor from Scotland to the Cuil Irra peninsula.

Followers of Sligo rock music could recite a long list of bands that started in Sligo in the eighties. There was a pub called Hennigan's where they used to play. Great epic events happened there, bands formed, bands broke up. Songs were written, there were tears and drama and laughter. Not one of those sessions was recorded. There was a guy who used to run the pub at one stage called Terry Browne. He was sandy, with quick blue eyes. Terry used to play practical jokes on people. He was great for a loan if you were stuck. He used to do a nervous thing with his finger, sticking his knuckle into his cheek to help him think. Terry was a soul man, he was good *craic*, and he encouraged all the young ones to come in and play.

Hennigan's on Wine Street was owned originally by Mary Hennigan. Then it fell to her son, Hal, and his wife Bernie. Brendan Rossiter ran the pub in a later era, then a few others, till Terry Browne came on the scene, originally in partnership with Kevin O'Boyle. They drew a mixed crowd. Bikers felt at home there. No-nonsense town lads would stop in for a couple on route from home matches in the Showgrounds. A woman could go into the bar alone

45

and not draw hostile stares. Gay people saw Hennigan's as a haven of liberal attitudes, and it was, most of the time. *An Phoblacht*[†] got bought there. Students drank there. Travellers—but not in big groups—were welcome. Foreigners—in a time when non-nationals were a bit of a novelty—would be in. Jews and Palestinians. Plenty of Germans with Irish accents.

When Terry Browne took over, he brought in a bit of marketing. He kept the Hennigan's name and put in sand-blasted glass logos in the windows and a new sign over the door. He got T-shirts made up and a portrait done and hung on the wall of all the characters who made the place their local. Terry's era was a time of solidarity.

Terry knew that dance was one of the ways to Sligo's heart. They always went wild when the Arts Festival brought African or Caribbean bands. The Hennigan's Blooze Band were good for dancing to. The Picture Show and Those Nervous Animals liked to get funky. Galway down the road was into cajun. Sligo liked white blues (Terry asked you every week, 'Did you see *The Blues Brothers*?') and funk. Ralph Winkler had a couple of reggae bands. It was a gas when the whole back room—a tiny space, stuffed to the gills—was bopping to some wicked groove. No musician got rich from playing Hennigan's back room. The bucket went round at the end of the night.

Terry looked after the musicians and they looked out for him. One time he was in a bit of bother, and all the musicians in the town got together and did a big gig in the Southern Hotel to help out. The musicians in Sligo were great for that. If one of their own needed a hand, they'd pull together and do a gig. The sound guys did the PA free. If a guitar player broke a finger or someone got sick, everyone would club together. They mightn't collect all that much, but it helped.

The jacks in Hennigan's, it has to be said, were never the best. You took your life in your hands. You picked your way gingerly over slippery tiles, convened with Armitage Shanks and got back to the bar as quick as you could. No one ever made a claim. Graffiti, usually rhyming, decorated the backs of unlockable doors. The pub was without functional ventilation: it was like being inside a lung, a

---

[†]   The Republican newspaper.

poisoned lung. Fifth-year schoolgirls dared each other to try and venture into the dim interior.

At different times of the day the vibe would turn. The place had its phases. Vivienne, Terry's sister, held court in the afternoon. She pulled a decent pint. She took no prisoners in the slagging stakes. She was witty and mischievous and never left a tooth in it. Terry would come in around teatime, when the pint-after-work crowd took up their shift. Conversation was conducted at this time of day at nearly-shouting volume, competing with blues music pumping from overburdened speakers. It was singles time in the late evening. Innocent-looking Yankee tourist babe chats up a couple of the local Romeos at the wobbly bar. There was a roadie and a watercolour painter, Hennigan's Department of Foreign Affairs.

You didn't have to be twenty to have a place at the bar. A good few older ones liked coming in. Vivienne had the order down before they needed to ask.

- The usual, Fred? The tourist pint?

A tourist pint is a whiskey glass full of Guinness. There was a man used to come in in the daytime. He must have been getting on for eighty, but possibility was still lighting in his eye. Fred lived in Wolfe Tone Street. He was a man for a story. He enjoyed the company of women.

It was easy to warm to Fred. The young ones took time to listen to what he had to say. They would be delighted to walk him back to his house at eight o'clock, his going-home time. He had a dog that used to do tricks, and Fred took pride in showing him off.

Fred was a happy man. He seemed to feel the lightness of his life. His funeral even had some of that quality. A good many of the Hennigan's crowd were among those who followed Fred's hearse up Pearse Road. It was a warm day, maybe a day in early winter. Passing traffic drove by slowly; people blessing themselves like they always do passing a funeral. Fossett's Circus happened to be coming from the other direction, coming down the hill. They halted the trucks a minute in respect, the wagons yellow and blue and red against the purple hills.

The live music crowd usually left it late coming in. To the annoyance of Terry, they would stick their heads in to see the band finishing after spending their money somewhere else.

Some people stayed in there far too long. It was interesting to watch the place filling and emptying, the different groups coming and going. Hennigan's was a refuge during the day for people without work. You didn't have to have money on you. Another blackcurrant in water. A few sat around the fire at the back and stared into the coals. Dark moods sometimes descended on the place. Then someone would start the *craic*. Spontaneous Mexican waves were known to travel along the five people sipping coffee on a Monday afternoon.

Fuck's sakes, Terry would say, and start telling you stories. Sligo was a busy port town way back. The famine ships sailed west to America from here in big numbers, dropping anchor at Rosses Point to take on more passengers. The channel in Sligo Harbour was prone to silting up, but they used to dredge it with tugboats. Ships sailed in and out by the markers in the bay, carrying coal and timber, Guinness and livestock. Up until the seventies there was a living to be made as a docker. Sixty or seventy years earlier the port was booming; trading enough to support a whorehouse keeper.

•   That place with the curved plate glass window in Castle Street, you know it; I'm tellin' ya: that was where they had the whorehouse in Sligo.

In Terry's day, in the eighties, a few merchant boats would still be seen tied up at the quays, among them Polish coal boats. They were exotic and communist and weather-beaten and sometimes bore contraband cargo of beers with difficult-to-pronounce names. Most of these beverages would taste better than piss, but . . . not what you'd call an awful lot better. But some of it was all right. And they had good vodka always. Certain denizens of Hennigan's used to slink darkly past the customs office and go aboard to sample the drink and strike bargains with the Polish captains.

Terry Browne was always thinking up schemes, leading the gang off on missions to other towns. Hennigan's went on tour a couple of times, to Liverpool and London and Carrick-on-Shannon. They made parachute jumps.

There were legendary debates in that house, and verbal jousts. Writers Dermot Healy or Martin Healy (no relation) or Sydney Bernard Smyth or whoever occupied a corner while they carefully dissected existential truths. Deeper in the night the tone could become less genteel over in that corner. Martin's raw passion, his angst, would pour. Venomous words. But it was nothing personal really. It was just his rage against the world and how little we know of it. In Hennigan's insults often flew, but patrons rarely came to blows. In another corner, out the front, drummers compared paradiddles, tapping out patterns on the table or on their legs. The arty crowd provided a bit of colour, but the bulk of the exchanges turned on more down-to-earth topics. Work and weather, relationships and kids. Slagging and bitching and praising.

- Where did you get that watch? I'll give you a tenner for it.

New people showed up, joined the chat for a while, then left and were never seen again. Some others hung round till they merged into the threadbare furniture. Dole spies could party there on Saturday nights incognito. Or at least they thought they were incognito. A couple of talkers spun themselves dramatic backgrounds, but everyone knew they had just wandered up from the mental hospital. None of those who knew Hennigan's could ever think of another place quite like it.

Many music people started off in Hennigan's, particularly in the early to mid-eighties. A young guy called Ciaran Gorman from Pearse Road used to come and watch the bands, then go home and write lyrics.[†] The Hennigan's Blooze Band started off out the back. There were others, many, many others. There were different town gigs that time, too, but Hennigan's was the mecca.

Terry Browne managed one band for a while called The Last Picture Show. They played Grace Jones and Steely Dan songs. Susan Rowland was the singer. Terry used to go up the country to gigs with them, just for the *craic*, the odd time. He used to perform himself in some of Mary McDonagh's shows in the Hawk's Well, too. He had been Jesus in *Superstar*. And Kenickie in *Grease*. He wore the leather jacket well, singing 'Greased Lightning', a crazed robot Elvis. Then Terry was tragically killed—hit by a car as he crossed the road. The pub closed.

Even in 1997, on the surface, Sligo still can wear its old-time, forgotten, neglected air. A stranger to town walks it on a Sunday

---

[†]   Ciaran changed his name in the mid-nineties to Perry Blake and struck for fame.

morning. A few scraps of paper turn on the wind. Where is everyone? The town sleeps dreamless and uneasy, like a man who will awake hungover. The grey oppressiveness of the large seventies estates around the town marks a stark contrast with the beauty of the surrounding landscape. There are social problems, unemployment, an underlying sense of seething anger. What is a working-class boy to do?

There are a few pubs that have music. They might do a bit of karaoke. There are three or four dance clubs; the DJs play charts and techno. There's a growing DJ scene in the more hip clubs, like the Clarence Hotel. Guest DJs bring a frisson of excitement and a promise of the exotic. The DJs specialise in a myriad of sub-genres. House and techno and jungle and trance. Ambient. The nightclubs' licences allow them to stay open for a couple of hours past the half-eleven deadline. Some of the pubs have DJs, too. They are cheaper than bands, and they play what people want to hear.

There are few live music venues any more. Most of those that existed in the eighties have disappeared. But there are hints of a revival in the live scene.

Martin Carr has started putting in a few bands in his newly done-up pub opposite the railway station. Mickey Kane, vocalist and guitarist, is just back from a long sojourn in foreign parts with an astonishing new vocabulary.

- Don't smoke my speakers, maan.

Mickey's new band is called The Bubblemen. Yvonne Cunningham sings. Jonathan Goodwin has a place going called the Weir, on the Mall. A couple of young bands get to play in the back room there, Fiction and China Red. A band called Redrum. Jonathan books the odd out of town act. Kian Egan's brother Tom plays with Fiction.

There is a Sligo Arts Festival: they have been going thirteen years or so and they've brought in some good music acts. They might give a local band a gig.

And there are two theatres in this small town. The Hawk's Well is where Mary McDonagh's students get to show their steps, when she puts on shows. It is compact, and well equipped; seats 350, and the bar serves a good pint. They have just reopened after being done up in August 1996. The Factory Theatre down the road concentrates on new works, experimental theatre; they have an influential director and writer at the helm. The Hawk's Well mixes the art with a dash of popular entertainment. They take touring pro shows, local stuff, the pantomime at Christmas, and occasional music gigs and comedy. A lot of Sligo people know the inside of the Hawk's Well.

Mary's shows are always popular. As well as producing musicals and plays, she does variety shows, comedy shows, kiddies' shows. Mary especially loves working with the little ones. It is amazing what the wee tots can do. They are totally natural, totally honest.

MICHAEL AND SHANE

The Carlton Café is not Sligo's most glamorous eatery. Its faded plastic exterior leads to a dark narrow room smelling of chips, with bucket seats, the modernity of another era. It has not changed an awful lot since the early seventies.[†] Those were the boom years. Three tonnes of spuds a week had been turned into chips and had passed across the counter. Chips with curry, chips with vinegar, chips with fish. Salt on your chips? Chips from real potatoes, mind you. Served with a smile. Peter Filan, the chirpy man who runs the Carlton, has an unusual claim to fame: he was the man who sold the very first burger in Connacht.

Peter and his wife Mae live above the restaurant. They have a family of seven: four boys and three girls. The youngest is a boy called Shane, born in July 1979. His green-brown eyes and willing smile made him popular in school. His first school was Scoil Fatima. After four years there he moved to a different primary school in Sligo town, St John's. Shane was always a good pupil, his favourite

---

†   Since 1997 the Carlton has been dismantled, and the Filan family have installed a glamorous clothes shop, Morgan De Toi, on the site.

subjects were maths and English. He did not grow fast; he was the smallest fella in most of his classes and got nicknamed 'Shorty' for a while. But he was strong and mobile.

Shane could have probably have made it as a rugby player. He played under-twelves out in the Strandhill Rugby Club. (He won a medal for under-twelves soccer, too.) Shane was an out-half. He was left footed, kicking right. He was always the captain, the natural leader. Shane had the ability to make decisions. He had great vision and a good pair of hands.

In 1997 Sligo Rugby Club were sending a couple of useful young lads along for a trial with the provincial team, Connacht. Shane Filan had impressed his rugby coach so much that he was virtually an automatic candidate. He acquitted himself capably in representing his province, and the opportunity soon presented itself of a trial for Ireland. His coach was terribly disappointed when Shane rang him to say he would not be attending the trial to play for his country. He had a bit of a knock to his knee. But anyway, Shane had taken a decision. He had a gig coming up, in the Hawk's Well. He was going to concentrate on music and forget about the oval ball.

Shane could also have been a jockey. The Filans had always been horsey people. Shane had been riding ponies since he was a toddler. He loved the outdoors, the space of the countryside. And the animals. He won loads of show-jumping competitions; his mum kept all the cups in a cupboard in the sitting room. Shane was one of those guys who seemed to be good at everything he did.

Shane met Michael Garrett in St John's National School, when they were both eleven. There was about a month between them in age. But Michael was a lot taller. Michael carried a bit of weight at that time, and he was surprisingly strong. Shane showed off a few kick-boxing poses—he had just started classes. They might have wrestled a bit, though they didn't fight. Maybe Shane decided it was better to be friends with this big geezer.

Michael was a new boy in St John's. His family had just moved to Sligo from Cork. It was a second move for the young Michael. He was born in Galway, and when he was seven or eight they moved to Cork. Michael was a live wire. He had straight dark-brown hair. They were both good mimics; they could 'do' any teacher you cared to name. Michael's favourite subjects were maths and geography. He was useful on the football pitch, too. The boys discovered that they both adored Michael Jackson.

Michael Garrett lived on Strandhill Road. And Shane was from town. Michael's dad drove a nicer car. Peter Filan was a low-key but astute businessman. The boys had more in common than they realised. Both Michael and Shane's rural roots were only a generation away. Both their fathers would be able to size up a bullock at a cattle mart. Shane didn't bother much about bullocks. He dreamed of faraway places. He dreamed of fame. He practised his autograph when he should have been studying. Sometimes you could talk to him and he would be somewhere else. You would yell his name. No one home. Then he would say, 'What?' It was one of his maddening traits.

Shane always loved singing. He revelled in an audience from the time he learned to toddle. Everyone was used to him singing along to records at home with a mock-up microphone. 'Uptown Girl' by Billy Joel was his favourite party piece. But it was back in 1987, when he was eight, that Shane's whole world was set on fire. That was the year Michael Jackson brought out the *Bad* album.

Michael, the youngest of the Motown Jackson family, had grown up in public. His solo career really took wings after he teamed with producer Quincy Jones and made some of the funkiest, danciest pop music. Ever. *Thriller* (1982) was a record-breaker, selling forty-two million copies. Each single release from the album went with a visually stunning and groundbreaking pop video. The *Thriller* video featured a *'Living Dead'*-style schlock horror setting and flocks of tightly choreographed dancers. It was directed by filmmaker John Landis.

Through his videos and TV appearances, Michael Jackson introduced a whole new way of moving—a brand new dance. OK, so he borrowed a lot from street culture, breakdancing and B-Boying. Locking and popping and freezes and power spins would all have been familiar moves to breaking crews like the Nigger Twins, Clark Kent, and the Zulu Kings in Brooklyn in the mid-seventies.

Breaking crews were gangs of black urban youths. They were not just competetive. Dance was for them an alternative to actual battle.

Battery-powered portable stereos, 'ghettoblasters', had just come out. The blaster lived on your shoulder till it was time to get on down for the break. They were not interested in the verses and chorus of the song. They weren't into the singing. It was the instrumental or percussion break they waited for. Some adventurous DJs might lift and drop the stylus back to repeat the break. Some even rhymed over the beat, long before rap was named. For the breaking crews, the stage was the street. The competing crews danced on cardboard boxes spread out on the pavement. Each dancer had an individual style. They borrowed ideas wholesale for their routines—from gymnastics, from disco dancing and from martial arts moves out of Bruce Lee films.

Michael Jackson went into the studio around 1985 to record his follow up to *Thriller*. He was arguably at the peak of his career. The eccentricity and disturbing allegations that marred his later years had not yet become evident. Quincy Jones produced again. Quincy and Michael took their time over the project, mixing and remixing until it was just right. Michael had written a new song, a song called 'Bad'.

> *Your butt is mine*
> *Gonna tell you right*
> *Just show your face*
> *In broad daylight*
> *I'm telling you—how I feel*
> *Gonna hurt your mind*
> *Don't shoot to kill . . .*

For the *Bad* video Jackson and his team wanted something outstanding to surpass their past glories. They brought in big-name movie director Martin Scorsese, maker of so many classics. De Niro was in a lot of them. *Taxi Driver. Raging Bull. Cape Fear. The King of Comedy.* Scorsese had prior experience of working with musicians. His name was on the greatest band documentary ever, *The Last Waltz,* about The Band. Now the movie director had six minutes to work with. He made the most of it. Jackson's image had up to now been nicey-nice guy, the baby of the Jackson family. Martin Scorsese placed Jackson in a gritty New York subway, in leather and chains, leading a chorus of angry street-fighters. Scorsese's lens tracked the feet of the dancers; he brought the viewer into the hot centre of a gravity-defying, parading (Jackson grabbed his crotch a lot), breakdance battle.

Shane Filan loved it when Michael Jackson did the drop. Suddenly stricken, the dancer hit the floor, like a puppet whose strings have been cut. Of course, the knee-crunching move known as the drop had been coined by the King of Soul, Mr James Brown, in the sixties. But Jackson brought all these moves—and a few new moves of his own—to a whole new audience. Put together with Jackson's great songs and singing, Quincy Jones's grooves and Scorsese's craft, *Bad* was dynamite!

Michael Jackson was born on 29 August 1958. Shane Filan on 5 July 1979. The boy/man that Shane was watching on the screen was, at twenty-nine, twenty-one years older than he was. But it made no odds. If Shane saw an age gap, he did not care.[†] You don't quibble. A hero is a hero.

Michael Garrett saw *Bad*, too, in his sitting room at home in Cork. He watched Michael Jackson moonwalk across the screen of his telly, wearing his fedora hat and one white glove. The figure on the screen tilted his hips, and froze on the downbeat. A wave ran along the dancer's outstretched arms. A little flick-lift through fingertip; wrist; elbow; shoulder; head/neck; shoulder; elbow; wrist; fingertip. A wave like a wind through corn. A force possessed the dancer, causing the neck to present the head in different frames, like two cobras striking out of the same basket. *Bad* blew Michael Garrett's mind, just like it did with Shane Filan up in Sligo.

So Michael Jackson was a major topic of conversation for the two new friends in the schoolyard of St John's. Both wanted to be Michael Jackson. Getting presents to keep Shane or Michael happy for hours was a cinch. Michael Jackson videos. Shane watched and tried to copy the moves Jackson made. He pushed the chairs in his living room back and did the moonwalk. When he had it off fairly good, he did it for his friend Michael in school. 'Jesus, Shane,' said Michael. 'That's feckin' brilliant.' Then Michael did his version of it. 'Not bad, Michael,' said Shane.

[†]   In the same way that the kids who bought 'Rock Around the Clock' in 1955 didn't care what age Bill Haley was. The father of rock and roll was thirty when he shot to superstardom.

One day, much later, when they were sixteen and both students of Summerhill College, Michael and Shane sat on a park bench in the Bishop's Garden, the Peace Park, a little walled haven of green at the heart of Sligo town. Between the Cathedral and the Hawk's Well Theatre. It was a dry, crisp kind of day. They sat in silence. They were able to sit in silence now. Their friendship had deepened. Shane was miles away, as usual, when Miggles remembered a good joke he'd heard lately.

• Shane? Did you hear the one about the guide dog? Listen, Shane.

• What? Oh, hey . . . Michael?

• What?

• I'd love to be in a band. You could be in it, too. I'm thinking of a name for it like SC4, if there's four in it, like the Summerhill College Four. Wouldn't it be great to be famous?

• Yeah. That'd be deadly. Let's form a band.

ONE DAY IN THE SHOWGROUNDS

One day Mark Feehily and Ciaran Carty were at a Sligo Rovers game. They came separately and bumped into each other beside the stand, the place called the Shed. Mark was with his dad. The Rovers were doing OK that year, after a recent crisis that saw half the team depart. It was early 1996. Ciaran was with his cousins. Mark said, 'Could you do some backing tracks? I want some music stuff to sing along to. I know you can do that technical stuff. I can do karaoke on it. I want to practise singing in front of a crowd. I am thinking I might even get a band together.'

- You want me to make up some karaoke tracks?
- Yeah.
- No problem.

Ciaran always said no problem, even if it was a problem. He always tried to please people. Ciaran was an only boy. He was a hardy little guy. He smiled a lot. Ciaran loved sport and was good at it. He played Gaelic and soccer. He won under-twelve All Ireland soccer and Gaelic medals. He was mad into music, too. But Ciaran Carty loved film more than anything. He was a Spielberg fan. He had all the videos and watched them over and over. His favourite was *ET*.

Ciaran first met Shane Filan in the Rugby Club in Strandhill. Ciaran didn't play rugby, though he lived beside the pitch. But they ended up playing under-twelves Gaelic football together. They got on well. Shane was the only one of the future band Ciaran knew before he went to Summerhill. Shane made the move to second level from St John's a year before Ciaran.

Summerhill College was a fine old edifice standing close by the Bishop's Palace. The entrance to the college grounds—flanked by stone pillars—was across the road from Sligo Cathedral. The school buildings stood at the end of a curving leafy avenue. The grounds were extensive; there were football fields and handball alleys. Summerhill had a good name as a school; it was a respectable, disciplined place. The Catholic kids went there. Boys only. Summerhill boys always succeeded above average in sports competitions.

Summerhill had mostly lay teachers, but it still was a place where the Roman collar generated the tremor of real authority. Where God was in heaven and decent people all knew the goodies from the baddies. In 1992 the Irish Catholic Church still had its self-confidence. Bishops were comfortable telling their people how to vote in referendums. Divorce was still not legal in Ireland.

When you knelt inside the college chapel and faced the altar, time stood still. Jesus looked down from his cross, eternal, inescapable, all pervading. This was how it was, how it always will be, he seemed to say. The old way. The hard way, but it's for your own good. The school would give the boys a solid grounding in traditional values and orthodox religious teaching.

Ciaran made friends with Mark Feehily on the first day in his new school.

- This class will be called *One-F-One.*
- Yes, teacher.
- You don't call me teacher, you call me sir.
- Yes, sir.

Tall windows. You go from being the big boy in national school to the very small boy in secondary school. It is good to have an ally. Mark Feehily was a nice lad, quiet, with a country accent. He had a low fringe topping a roundish, friendly face. Ciaran and Mark clicked from the start. Ciaran was a gatherer, a jackdaw. Ciaran collected CDs. But Mark spent his time robbing Ciaran's Mariah Carey CDs.

When he was fourteen and a half, Ciaran's dad bought him a camera. It was an 8mm video. Ciaran was in heaven. He used to get a bunch of kids together and go down to the quarry in Strandhill and make movies. Ciaran was the producer, the director and the cameraman. Some of the kids made up prop guns. The girls sometimes got shot at the beginning and had to lie still for ages.

- • I can see you breathing.

Sometimes dead people came back to life. The baddies got sick of *always* being baddies. Sometimes there were fights. Ciaran didn't like aggro or conflict. He would coax his team back on track, and there was always a great laugh when they watched the finished masterpiece in Ciaran's sitting room later. When Ciaran was fifteen, his dad died of a massive heart attack. It was an awful shock and a terrible loss, a sad time for Ciaran and his mum.

Young Ciaran had a business head. On Sunday mornings, he would head off to film matches and sell the players his VHS copies for twenty or thirty pounds. He even did a couple of weddings. He saved up and bought a better camera. It was the bee's knees at the time, a hi-8. He learned some good tricks on that camera. He got more work. Again he saved every penny. He wanted an even better camera.

Ciaran got to know lots of people in Summerhill pretty quick. He was always fixing or working an angle. He saw everything. Knew nearly everyone. Michael Garrett was a big strong guy, a year older than Ciaran. He was in the same year, but in a different class; One-F-Two. Michael sometimes ended up in the same technical drawing class as Ciaran. Michael fancied himself. No one could beat him up. Ciaran, being small, needed more negotiating skills than Michael Garrett.

Kian Egan came into the picture in the third year. He was in English class. He was a real tough guy. At that stage, bands didn't appeal to Kian at all. He certainly had no interest in boybands. He was hanging around with a crowd who would probably beat up a boyband if they met them.

Kian Egan and Mark Feehily first crossed paths in Mr McGann's English class. Mark was drumming under the desk. Drumming under the desk could be annoying. Kian showed him pretty quick who was boss. These roundy-faced country fellows were good for a bit of mockery; you could push them around and get a laugh. Mark knew a lot of guys who got a laugh out of calling him names and roughing him up. But he was an irrepressibly cheerful chap. He accepted mistreatment as stoically as a juggler accepts a wayward ball. As a cow accepts flies. He just dusted himself off and got on with it.

After a while things changed. Kian started to listen to Mark. He wasn't sure how that got going. Mark Feehily was a 'Boeuff' (Not From the Town). He was fat (fat in schoolboy terms may mean just a teeny bit more rounded). He was pretty low down on the ladder of people you needed to listen to, but he talked. He was always talking. He was mad into sports, into tennis. Nothing special about that. But Mark was kind of different. He liked to sing. He was a shy guy who wanted people to hear his voice. And Mark knew an awful lot about music.

Kian had begun to think lately that music could be kind of cool. Not that performing was anything new to him. Two of his brothers were musicians. When Kian was younger he loved the stage; he used to win poetry competitions in the Feis Cheoil. He had acted in plays in St John's primary school and danced in the chorus in children's shows under Mary McDonagh's guidance. But he had been through a phase where stuff like that got filed under the headings of: childish, embarrassing and best-forgotten.

There was a guy in Summerhill from the town called 'Boeuff' who played the drums. His father might have been from Leitrim. A few other guys were good on the guitar. There was a crowd who knew the names of a lot of metal bands, real heavy stuff. Grunge was in in America. Nirvana and all that. It was wild and dangerous and good for your image.

Kian decided he liked Mark. Mark gave Kian ideas.

- Anyone can write a song.

Kian and Mark sat together for a spell after that. It was a boost for Mark's credibility in certain quarters. He got no more hassle from a red-haired boy who had been picking on him. Indeed Mark and

Kian talked so much, Mr McGann had to split them up. They still sat together in art classes though. Kian picked up a guitar casually one day and strummed it, and everyone admitted he sounded *not bad at all*. Kian Egan had secretly learned to play the chord D on the guitar.

SUMMERHILL

There was plenty of theatrical and musical talent among the Summerhill teaching staff. Joan Fitzpatrick gave classes in speech and drama. And music. Kenny Donagher, a fine trad box player himself, taught music and computers. He had imaginative ideas.

In 1992, the year that Ciaran Carty and Mark Feehily and Michael Garrett started in Summerhill, a new teacher, giving Irish and music, came to the school. David McEvoy was not from Sligo, but from Portlaoise, down south. He turned up full of energy and enthusiasm. The school musical had lapsed for a few years, and David McEvoy dived in at the deep end right away, proposing a revival. He volunteered for the job of musical director.

Nineteen ninety-two was a big year for the college: its hundredth anniversary. In August David McEvoy and a core of staff colleagues picked the fifties musical *Annie Get Your Gun*. It had a good storyline and the songs of Irving Berlin.

The nearby girls school in Finisklin, the Ursuline Convent, was invited to come on board. Joan Fitzpatrick would produce. They could be talking about a cast fifty strong. Time started looking tight to get the show on before the end of the year, what with other demands on the hall and other centenary stuff. Eventually the show was postponed to the following March.

In the first days of the New Year, Mary McDonagh staged *Grease* in the Hawk's Well, her second production of the musical for a Sligo audience. She wanted a raunchy, rocky *Grease*. Terry Browne from Hennigan's was Kenickie. Local vocalist Joe Hunt had the leading role of Danny. Ann Marie Byrne played opposite him. Ann Marie had sparkle.

Mary came up with a bright idea to showcase the next generation of talent coming through. She wrote a part specially for two young ones, Shane Filan and Olwen Morgan, to do a duet. Shane had to say, 'You dropped your books.' Olwen had to say, 'I don't have any books.' Then they did a song and dance routine. The song was 'We Go Together'. Both kids were a sensation at the start of the second half of the show. Olwen wore a long dress and she sang and moved beautifully.

Mary McDonagh first spotted Shane Filan's emerging flair for the stage when he had just turned twelve. She would have been doing the Community Games (another voluntary gig she used to do). It was mostly a community sports competition, but there was always a part where the children did a bit of singing or acting. Mary knew Mae and Peter Filan, Shane's parents. It was a short walk from the Carlton Café around the corner and up the hill to her house.

There was a story that Shane missed a few rehearsals. He was doing great in his song. But he had so many irons in the fire—Gaelic football, rugby, riding. Things to do for his mum. A few places to check out that, with him not being thirteen, his mum might not appreciate.

Missing rehearsals—even for Community Games—was not guaranteed to impress Mary McDonagh. She told him off when it happened first, and when he reoffended, Mary said, 'Do that again, Shane Filan, and you are out of the show.' Shane went home and told his mum that he might be out of the show. He didn't say much about the missing rehearsals bit. Mae Filan said, 'Who does Mary McDonagh think she is?' One day Mae marched up the hill to Mary's and gave Mary a piece of her mind. Shane was standing behind his mum, signalling to Mary to cover for him, to say he had

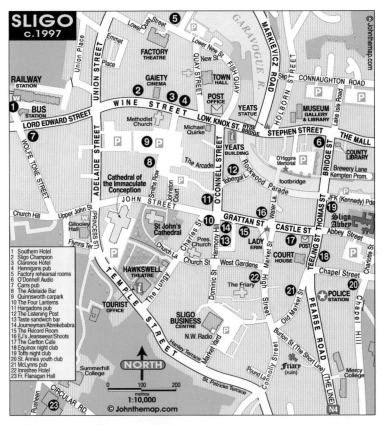

SLIGO
c.1997

1 Southern Hotel
2 Sligo Champion
3 Clarence Hotel
4 Hennigans pub
5 Factory rehearsal rooms
6 O'Donnell Audio
7 Carrs pub
8 The Adelaide Bar
9 Quinnsworth carpark
10 The Four Lanterns
11 Hargadons pub
12 The Listening Post
13 Taste sandwich bar
14 Journeyman/Abrekebabra
15 The Record Room
16 E.J's Jeanswear/Shoots
17 The Carlton Cafe
18 Equinox night club
19 Tofts night club
20 St. Annes youth club
21 McLynns pub
22 Innistree Hotel
23 Fr. Flanagan Hall

▲ Sligo map, ca. 1997 *(John the Map)*

▲ Six As One poster: Derek, Kian, Michael, Shane, Mark, Graham.

▲ IOYOU as a five-piece, in May 1998, prior to Sligo Arts Festival gig:
Michael, Kian, Mark, Shane, Graham. *(James Connolly, Picsell8)*

▲ Sligo smoulders at the foot of Knocknarea. *(Mark Keane)*

▲ The cast for Mary McDonagh's production of *Grease* in September 1996. Shane, Kian, Michael, Mark and Graham are in the picture. *(Jimmy Eccles, Sligo Champion)*

▲ The 'Mammy Shot' taken by James Connolly at the end of Mike Bunn's photo session with IOYOU, 9 November 1997: Shane, Michael, Derek, Mark, Graham, Kian, with Mary McDonagh. *(James Connolly, Picsell8)*

been at the rehearsals. Mary felt the force of Mae's tongue. And so did Shane, all the way to the bottom of High Street. Shane stayed in the show. He came to rehearsals religiously after that.

Mark Feehily's parents took him to the Hawk's Well Theatre to see *Grease*. He loved the show, didn't stop talking about it for ages. One of the best bits was when they brought the car on stage, a real vintage car![†] Danny and the gang driving it, hanging out of it, doing the big number in it. He was particularly star-struck by the contribution of Shane Filan. He didn't know Shane at the time. Mark was a first year; in a school of thousands of boys, second years lived in a foreign country. He didn't know anyone who could sing and act like that—except for himself and Michael Jackson! It sent him dreaming again.

Mark had young, cool parents. He had a great extended family, grannies and aunties. All adored Mark. Everyone knew Mark had faraway eyes. Eyes full of dreams. His mum and dad knew—they and his two younger brothers were his captive audience.

• I want to practise singing in front of a crowd.

Sitting in the theatre that night, it seemed to Mark that this boy Shane, in his white T-shirt and dark pants, under the lights, looked very grown up. Even though at thirteen he was a good four inches smaller than the girl he was dancing with. It didn't seem to matter.

Mark decided to go for a part in the *Annie Get Your Gun* musical in school. After auditions the leading parts were cast. Phyllis Wilkinson and Niamh Crowley—Niamh was making a name for herself as a prodigious young classical violinist—would play gun-totin', rough-talkin' Annie every second night.

Mark Feehily was thrilled when his singing voice won him a place in the chorus. He joined a bunch of other lads in his year, including Kian Egan.

Shane Filan and a few of his friends from second year got to be in that show, too. David McEvoy saw Shane's 'We Go Together' cameo in Mary McDonagh's *Grease* in the Hawk's Well and thought he did well. Shane ended up getting offered the part of a girl, Jesse. Shane wasn't heard to complain; at least he would be onstage, singing.

---

† A Ford Anglia.

The venue for *Grease* was the Father Flanagan Hall, in the college. The room doubled as a gymnasium. It had no permanent stage; everything had to be built there from scratch: the sets, the cyclorama. Maribeth Milne, an art teacher from the Ursuline, designed and painted the sets.

Annie Get Your Gun ran for five nights and attracted full houses every night to the Father Flanagan Hall.[†] A different Annie was occupying people's minds the following week. Gay Byrne never normally let the identity of his guests on 'The Late Late Show' be known in advance, but RTÉ made sure the whole country knew that Ms Annie Murphy, ex-lover of Bishop Eamonn Casey, would be there on Friday night to tell her story of bearing a son to the bishop. The whole country sat in front of their TVs and the story made headlines in all the papers.

In December of that year, David McEvoy and his Summerhill team put on a second school show. This time Mary McDonagh— whose sons were attending the college—came in voluntarily to choreograph the dancing. The show selected was *Oliver.* Another co-production with the Ursuline Convent.

Mark Barr and Conor McSharry played Oliver. Both Mary and Dave agreed early on that Shane Filan was a dead ringer for the Artful Dodger. He didn't disappoint in rehearsals. Kenny Donagher was Fagin.

Mark Feehily didn't get a part in *Oliver.* But he went to see it. There was Shane Filan again, in a cloth cap, singing, cracking jokes, getting loads of laughs.

Both Mary McDonagh and Dave McEvoy enjoyed working together on that school show. David did Trojan work with the singers. What Mary got out of the group of young boys and girls in a short few weeks was nothing short of sensational.

In 1994 Summerhill didn't do a musical, but they held a talent competition. David McEvoy announced the deadlines and the rules. There was a solo/duo section. It turned up some gas monologues

---

†   The school hall/gym was named after the campaigning priest from Ballymoe, County Roscommon, who founded Boys Town, a shelter for homeless children in Omaha, USA. Father Flanagan was made famous by Spencer Tracy in the 1938 movie *Boys Town.*

and duologues. Mark Feehily went up and sang a Garth Brooks song, strongly and well in tune.

The most exciting bit was the battle of the bands. Most of the band entrants were seriously heavy; Judas Priest, Metallica, Guns 'n' Roses, even Deep Purple material was preferred.

The sound of distorted guitar stirred memories for some of the longer-serving staff. Rock music was nothing new to Summerhill. The Generation Gap used to gig in the Bottom Hall in the college in the early seventies. Frankie Langan, Billy Kelly, and Seamus McLoughlin were in the band. Kevin Sweeney sometimes, too, on vocals and guitar. Frankie was the Mick Jagger of the band. '(I Can't Get No) Satisfaction' was his big song.

Back in the early seventies Thin Lizzy were just setting out on the road to becoming an Irish rock legend. They played more than once in the Father Flanagan. Those gigs were fund-raisers for the school soccer team who travelled far and wide to matches, even to Spain and France. The gigs funded it all.[†]

Phil Lynott and Eric Bell tried out a new song in Summerhill one evening. A rock arrangement of the traditional ballad 'Whiskey in the Jar'. A few months later it would give Lizzy their first British number one hit and provide the intro that every learner rock guitarist for thirty years would torment their fingers with. Thin Lizzy looked fierce cool in their big hair and wide flares. Phil Lynott was black and proud, doing the work of two people, a powerhouse bass player and a masterful lead singer. A live wire beanpole in painted-on trousers. Boys played air guitar down the front, riffing along with Eric Bell on virtual Stratocasters.

Twenty-two years later, for the battle of the bands, the students were the stars. They posed with real guitars, twiddled real amps. The crowds in Father Flanagan Hall were just massive, the guys down the front yelling support for their favourites. Local musicians Dave Moriarty and Rhona Grimes were persuaded to come in as judges. They made their calls in a feverish atmosphere and made a quick exit.

Ciaran Carty brought his video camera to school and added to

†   Summerhill foreign ventures and fundraisers straddled the reign of two priests: Fr Michael 'Ricky' Devine and Fr Cyril Haran.

the excitement by filming proceedings. A band called SCROD almost won. They blasted their way through a couple of death metal versions, including The Troggs' 'Wild Thing'. They came second and were presented with a silvery trophy with an inscription. They split their £150 or so winnings between them. The teachers didn't know—only the band and a few friends—that the name SCROD was an acronym; each letter represented a word, the first of which was Smelly; it was an x-rated expression about the hygiene problems of older ladies. The guitarist in the band with shoulder-length brown hair, decked out all in leather, was Kian Egan.

The Factory Theatre used to be an abattoir. By January 1995 cattle were no longer butchered there: pigeons and bats lived in the rafters. The auditorium was a bare-walled box with a high roof of corrugated iron. A raw but functional and somehow perfect space to spin illusion. A great workhouse. The new theatre space had its problems, but it was a challenge that Mary McDonagh relished. She had a good team working backstage. Make-up worked almost like a production line, all those boys lining up. The principals were going over those few lines that never seem to stick in memory. Michael Kilcoyne as Fagin. Ursula Smullen as Mrs Sowerberry. Nicola Morrison as Mrs Corney. Young Rowan Rossiter as Oliver.

Shane Filan got the Artful Dodger again, his first major role outside of school. But he had to share it on alternate nights with Damien Ginty. Damien could do a great London accent and had a feel for the timing that makes good comedy.

• Considah yesself pa' of th' furni-chah!

Shane Filan had the edge in the singing and dancing department.

Mary brought in David McEvoy, the young music teacher from Summerhill College, as musical director. David's band included Sligo's legend of the skins, drummer Fluky Gorman. Everyone in the biz in Sligo town has a Fluky story. Like When Fluky Ran Off and Joined a Circus (and hitched home with his drum kit from Dublin) or when Fluky Used Paint Brushes for Drumsticks (and got a better sound than any stick merchant in town). When Fluky Ran for Election with his All Night Party and got more votes than plenty of 'serious' politicians. Or how—if you can track down the elusive Fluky—he will still put down the grooviest back beat in town.

Mary McDonagh was reaching new heights of experimentation

with her theatre shows. The sequence of *West Side Story* (1992),[†] staged in the round, *Grease* (1993) and *Little Shop of Horrors* (1994) had set the standard. A fantastic buzz was abroad in Sligo about the latest show, and *Oliver* got repeated photo spreads in the local press. Night after night happy crowds filed out of the Factory Theatre with chorusing children's voices ringing in their ears. After the run finished, Mary wondered how she would follow that.

The Hawk's Well was still closed for renovations in those times, so Mary would have to continue to think creatively in terms of venues. The best slots for putting on shows were early in the year, just after Christmas, and maybe in the autumn, provided nothing was running against you.

Nineteen ninety-five turned out to be one of *the* great summers. Sligo baked under skies of uninterrupted blue for weeks on end. Tar rose and bubbled and burst and stuck to tyres, staining the backroads black. Everyone retired to the beach any time they got the chance.

Someone in authority had the bright idea that '95 was the 750th year in the life of Sligo town. A committee was organising various events to celebrate. In August local music promoter Robert McNabb put on a week of gigs under the banner Sligo Live '95. The Festival Arena, a large marquee, was located on the grounds of Summerhill College. He booked Boyzone, the new up-and-coming Dublin boyband. One band member, Shane Lynch, had an unfortunate accident the week before, hopping over a stream after a ball. He fell short, got wet and landed on his ankle, cracking the bone. A four-piece Boyzone appeared for Sligo Live '95, singing along to a backing tape. Lots of girls showed up. Not too many Summerhill boys. They eyed the tent from a distance, curious but publicly disdainful. It would not be a cool thing to be seen at a Boyzone gig; you would be thought a wuss or worse.

In November that year Mary McDonagh staged *A Slice of Saturday Night* in the famous Sligo rock venue, the Blue Lagoon Nightclub. With a cast of just eight. Four of her strongest guys; four of her strongest girls. It went off well. A great laugh, once they got

---

†   This was the second time Mary did the show. The first *West Side* was in 1984.

in the rhythm of the show it played tight and pacey, and *very* rock and roll.

In November 1995 leather was big in Summerhill. The scores for *Grease* arrived in a big brown parcel from Samuel French, London. Dave McEvoy gave the conductor's score a once-over. Grand, not too much of a roaster, this show was going to be great *craic*. They were going to be working again with the Ursuline.

The lead role of Danny went to a guy by the name of Adam Pierce. Cathy Burnside from the Ursuline would be Sandy. Shane Filan was delighted to be cast in a supporting role—that of Kenickie, the car-racing hardman, Danny's best buddy and mentor.

Shane Filan was partnered in the show by Ursuline student Orla McSharry. The girl acting as Frenchie, the beauty school dropout, was an old friend of Shane's, a cute blonde with frizzy hair called Gillian Walsh. Shane knew Gillian from St John's primary school, and she was a cousin of Kian Egan's. Gillian probably would not have minded Orla's part, opposite Shane. Kian, wearing his mid-brown locks shorter now (but long enough at the front for a quiff) was a T-Bird. You didn't want to be paired off with your cousin. Mark Feehily played Vince Fontain, the over-the-top DJ and competition judge. And Michael Garrett got his first big part, as T-Bird Roger.

On opening night the atmosphere was supercharged in Father Flanagan Hall. Teachers made entrances in unteacherish outfits. Parents dropped off out-of-towners. Flustered looking parents and other adults helped out backstage with costumes, props, make-up and other minor jobs on the night. By a mile the coolest person in the place was choreographer Mary McDonagh. Bombarded by a constant flow of queries, she calmly responded to each in turn and continued with her task in hand. Mary, with her coterie of attendants, was queen.

David McEvoy was king, or at least crown prince. His band tuned up their instruments as people took their seats. The rehearsals had been hectic, fraught at times. At the dress rehearsal some of the main cast showed signs of losing their voices. Anxious consultations had ensued. But now the hour of reckoning was at hand. After a studiedly worded announcement by one of the convent girls, the lights dimmed, and David nodded to bring the singers and the band in. They set the school hall rocking. David swayed as he played.

David McEvoy found a silver dress jacket in a cupboard upstairs in Mary McDonagh's ages ago. He got a terrible slagging when he wore it for his musical director gig in some show. The silver jacket had now taken on a life of its own. David gave it one more outing when he played in *Hickory Dickory Dock*, the Cooleara panto. Now Vince Fontain was wearing it, Mark Feehily literally dazzling under the lights.

The audience comprised mostly parents and other students from the girls' school and the boys' school. A great audience, they got involved, clapped along, cheered lustily in the love scenes. The two schools getting together meant lots of people getting to know each other, lots of crushes and enmities and vibes. Hormones flew. The show ended in a cauldron of emotion. Shane Filan said goodbye to Gillian Walsh, even though he would likely see her tomorrow. The stage characters were saying goodbye, all going off to college maybe never to meet again. Kenickie was going to Harvard Law School, and Frenchie was off to Hollywood to do make-up for the stars.

There was chaos in the car park, solemn speeches at the end of the show. It was an unforgettable time.

GREASE (IN THE HAWK'S WELL)

You can't go wrong with *Grease*. *Grease* equals bums on seats. The younger ones love the music and the slight raunchiness of the language, and the parents relate the era to their own youth. It's safe rebellion. Domesticated rock and roll.[†] Even though some of it might be a bit puzzling to a west of Ireland audience. Everyone calls the dot at the end of a sentence a full stop. Only a few Marvel Comics buffs could know the American term for it.

- What's with you tonight?
- I feel like a defective typewriter.
- Huh?
- I skipped a period.

When you first read your lines out loud in rehearsal, it can be a bit embarrassing. All those phrases about 'flogging your log', and 'biting the weenie'. But once you have a few shows under your belt,

---

[†] Jim Jacobs and Warren Casey, best friends of seven years standing, came up with the idea at a party: a musical about the fifties. As they wrote, the sixties were turning into the seventies.

it is all tame enough, it's *normal stuff*. In fact it's kind of cool saying those lines in front of the women (and vice versa). Easily beats all that cowboy malarkey in *Annie Get Your Gun*, and lines about workhouses and whatever.

September 1996: Mary McDonagh Productions' *Grease* in the Hawk's Well Theatre is going to plan. Booking is solid.

Mary lines up the chorus. The best movers will be in the front line of the group. They will lead the weaker performers. Front row places are coveted and jealously guarded. Mary's canon is meritocracy: the hard-working and talented people can expect to progress. Starting maybe in the back row, but working to the front of the chorus, then maybe getting noticed enough to place themselves in line for a leading part. The healthy number of talented boys available for this show particularly delights Mary. It has never been easy to get talented boys interested enough in the stage to commit, to learn their parts and rehearse. This time round she has a bunch of boys who know the show; it is only a few months since they were all involved in the Summerhill production of *Grease*.

Jacobs and Casey's story of teen behaviour is well observed; it has a universal ring of truth to it. The kids are dealing with this stuff; it's all part of their lives. Of course they relate to it. Mary McDonagh has never tired of the show.

Mary has two good actresses vying for the peach role of Sandy: Louise Parkes and Michelle Feeney. She gives the part to both of them. They will play Sandy on alternate nights.

Shane Stephen Filan—he is seventeen now—doesn't even have to contemplate sharing his part with anyone any more. He is an outstanding success as Danny. He has landed the leading role in the show at last. Some of the other young guys envy him, even look up to him. Shane can sing. He can act. He is just a natural. John Travolta, eat your heart out. Shane is 'Shorty' no more. A sudden spurt of growth has brought him past five foot seven, and he is still growing.

Mark Feehily still looks up to Shane Filan a little bit. Shane has thought a lot about ways of doing things. Mark listens. Mark has thought about a lot of the same stuff himself. Shane seems to really know what he's at.

To be fair, none of the male leads share parts, there are a lot more girls coming forward, so while the boys in the T-Birds gang play every night of the run, their opposite numbers in the Pink Ladies gang only do alternate shows. Mark Feehily actually plays two characters, that of Teen Angel and Vince Fontain. It's no bother to him; he is committed to his parts, projecting his voice strongly. The stage is by now a comfort zone for Mark.

Mark is eager to help in any way he can with the show. He designs posters and does up a show programme on his computer. Nicola Morrison helps him. Nicola is doing assistant to director for the show. She has dance ideas and is a talented actress herself. She, too, is learning her trade from Mary. The programme cover says 'Enjoy, as the *M.M.D. Production Company* presents. . .'

Michael Garrett is Roger again. Michael has lost a lot of weight; he is looking lean and mean.

The tomboy of the group, Baby Blue Eyes himself, playing Kenickie this time, is Kian Egan, who manages to generate onstage chemistry with both Rizzos.

Kenickie/Kian speaks in a hoarse-husky kind of voice. He glances out to the sides and then ahead, like a pro boxer might after arriving first at a weigh-in.

Kian has a little scar on his right cheek and has appeared recently sporting an eye-catching shock of blonde hair, parted in the middle. He has started to spell his name with a K. He has been doing a bit of training, too. Kian reckons he has a pretty decent physique. His head tilts down just a tad as he listens to Mary giving instructions in rehearsal.

Kian comes from Lyndale. His dad, Kevin, works for the ESB. Of the Egans' seven children, Kian was one of the middle ones. He was born on 29 April 1980. He displayed plenty of stage presence even back in the SCROD era, and the new blond Kian has not lost it. There is a little surge of electricity when he strides on. There is something funny and honest and innocent about Kian Egan. And something dead keen, streetwise.

He walks with his elbows held slightly out from his body, a swinging walk, his weight on the balls of his feet. Not a country walk. The Sligo town walk. He is not known for shyly avoiding conflict if it comes his way. But he is eager to learn from Mary, even prepared to endure the slagging of his macho mates. The old crowd he used to hang around with. The jibes can be vicious. 'What's with the new hair? What are you doing with that crowd of queers? Dancing? Jaysus, Egan, will you cop yerself on.'

- Dat stuff is feckin' stew-pid.

But Kian grits his teeth, puts his head down and learns his lines. With a gauche grin he makes the steps in the dances, threatening to punch anyone who slags him off.

Emily McEvoy is in *Grease*, too. She is sharing the part of Cha-Cha with Helena Heraghty. Emily is one of Mary's favourites. She has a great scene with the nerd-like Eugene, played by Damien Ginty.

Ian Fox is doing Doody. A guy by the name of Graham Keighron, from Sligo Technical School, is Sonny. Graham used to be in Summerhill, up until third year. Then he transferred to the Technical School. He was a couple of years ahead of the others. It was gas how Graham got the gig in *Grease*.

Graham arrived at Mary McDonagh's auditions for *Grease* with his pal Kian Egan. The two boys were neighbours. Graham lived in the housing estate next to Lyndale, Maugheraboy. Even though there was a gap of four years in their ages, the two had hit it off right from their first meeting—around 1994. Music was their common interest. Kian was getting into Metallica at the time. Kian considered Graham well cool. Graham spoke from his heart and his heart was in music. He knew how important image was, too, and looking after yourself. Graham was getting into rap music lately, all that black culture stuff.

Graham and Kian were in the queue when Mary McDonagh came out asking for the next lot onstage. Right off she says to Graham, 'OK, Mister, you are on, up you get.' But Graham explained he was just in with this guy here beside him, to give *him* courage, to give *him* moral support . . . Mary said, 'Yeah, but can *you* dance?' Mary and Kian encouraged Graham to have a go. Graham had always loved dancing but did not have formal training. He loved to watch guys doing breakdancing in videos and was always trying out stuff at home. Anyway, he did the audition and he got it.

In the wings, helping with the sets and props for *Grease*, is another Summerhill boy, Derek Lacey. Derek is from St Bridget's; he lives there with his mum. Derek jammed sometimes in one of the heavy metal bands in school with Kian Egan and some other guys from his class.

He is tall, a good-looking lad in a Latin kind of way, and quiet. Yet he is observant and sensitive, and attractive to a certain type of girl. Derek has brown eyes. He didn't get to be in the show, but this is the next best thing. Derek doesn't complain. He is a rock. Derek is loyal to his friends and happy for them.

Mary's touch as a director is light but nonetheless demanding. She can join in the laughter, crack everyone up with her wit. But if things get slack and discipline and energy wanes, she will call the group together for a pep talk, try and get the motivation back on track. If that doesn't bring results, Mary is capable of delivering a corrosive group ticking-off. If you get told off, it is usually fair enough. Mary has an inspired eye for casting; thus no one is being asked to do stuff that is beyond their ability.

The rehearsals move from Mary's studio into the theatre. The Hawk's Well has just opened its doors after refurbishment. They have had the formal opening, speeches, wine, and all that. The great and good all present in their finery. The development cost a million or more, it was reported. Everyone is dead curious to have a peek inside to see what all that money has bought us.

The place looks well; some thorny old issues have been sorted. Apparently the lines of sight from the balcony are better, and the dressing room space is improved. The foyer has a better layout and they put in a nice bar. But the young cast are oblivious to all this. They are in their moment, getting ready for this stage, a stage much bigger than the one in Father Flanagan Hall. The Hawk's Well stage is dark. There is a smell of building site there. There are guys hammering and painting and asking loudly about gels and Fresnel's while you are rehearsing. The 'tabs' are the curtains, but no one tells you that.

Two days to the show and the car has not arrived yet. Mark sees it in his imagination as he dances on the black-painted stage floor. It's hard to remember all the moves. Mary has changed the sequence on one number. Everything *sounds* different in the Hawk's Well. Your voice does not disappear in front of your face like it does in the energy-sapping echoes of the school hall. It's a bit scary to hear yourself this clearly.

At least the show is familiar territory. And nearly all the friends are there, the girls and fellas from the school shows; there is a little bit of history there. And musical director Rhona Grimes is good with the singers. She plays your line on the piano, she listens and gives you time to get comfortable.

You sound different again when a sound engineer straps a little box to your waist at the back and fits you up with your radio mic. Radio microphones themselves are no novelty, the leading players in the Summerhill shows wore them. But loud onstage monitor speakers *are* new. Your voice, naked and unfamiliar sounding and hard to control, has grown to grotesque proportions. It fills the empty auditorium. Barry the sound guy says you better remember during the show to knock off your receiver once you come offstage and begin to make remarks about someone or noisily go to the toilet. To emphasise the point he has a stock of horror stories; of mortal embarrassment, of friends lost; of *people who forgot.*

The dress rehearsal is ropey enough. Mary doesn't seem too happy. Her talk is a mixture of 'Go for it, lads, you know you're good' and 'Wake up, everybody, put some life into it; *people have bought tickets to see a performance'.* The show has got a write-up in the *Sligo Champion.*

Out in Lyndale, Kian Egan's mother Patricia is watching the clock.

- What time do ye have to be there at?
- Half-seven in the Hawk's Well. That's the call.

Showtime.

Mary is asking for quiet backstage. The house is open; the auditorium is filling. There is a big crowd out there. Anxious faces crowd the dock as the people in the opening number mill around waiting to be called. In front of stage in the 'pit' there is a bit of excitement, too. The drummer has done a runner. Rhona Grimes has had to have a replacement drummer drafted in at short notice.

But in the end *Grease* works. It works a treat. The first night the audience stay applauding for ages at the end. Mary hustles the cast on to take a second bow. They leave to clapping and calls for more. Tabs. Back through the narrow corridors to the dressing rooms. The stage is empty again.

The stage door is open on to the car park. Chill air from the street outside breathes into the dock, making the curtains sway. People are hurrying off, saying see ya tomorrow. Mark will follow them out in a minute or two to rendezvous with his dad at the back of the theatre.

The T-Birds car is cool. Well, if you had to be picky, it has more of the breed of a Fiat Panda than a Mustang convertible in it. Or even a Ford Anglia, like the car in the first *Grease* Mark saw.

But the show has such energy, and everyone involved is so thoroughly enjoying themselves, it doesn't matter. The car is grand. It's so cool to be involved, to be part of all this.

You can't miss the T-Birds. Ian Fox, Kian Egan, Graham Keighron, Shane Filan and Michael Garrett. The lads singing behind the scenes has been a feature of *Grease*; other cast members have been treated to their harmonies right from the day of the auditions. They sing after rehearsals, during intervals, in the dressing rooms. They sing in the corridors. They sing at the back of the stage. Backstreet Boys songs mostly, like 'Just to Be Close'. The core of this band of songsters is definitely Michael Garrett and Shane Filan. Michael is real confident and brash and outgoing. The other regulars are Kian Egan and his buddy Graham Keighron.

The public response to *Grease* is such that Mary decides to extend the run for one more night. There have been four scheduled shows, three evening ones and one matinee. Now the final night will be Wednesday, 25 September.

After the encores and the final curtain on the last night, everyone is fired up. There is that mixture of relief and pride and slight sense of loss that goes with the ending of a show. A high-spirited group from the production go out to the carpeted foyer bar and gather at tables. Averyl Dooher, who has been working in the theatre, and her friend Xavier join Mary and a larger group of friends. Everyone has words of praise for the young cast.

- We have to put on *Grease* again, in the New Year.
- No problem, says Averyl.

Everyone is a bit giddy what with the new surroundings and all. The principals in the show are at a table down the back of the bar. People's heads turn when Shane and Mark start up a song amid the post show chatter. The girls in the group laugh and clap and cheer them on. The two boys sound good; Shane takes the lead, Mark has a harmony thing going. Michael and Graham and Derek Lacey join in. And Kian Egan. A hush falls over the crowd.

I'll make love to you, like you want me to
And I'll hold you tight, Baby, all through the night
(Boyz II Men)

Mary joins in the applause. She says, 'We have to start a boyband.' Everyone laughs. But she says, 'I am serious. I will put a shape on the dancing. . . Next time we do the show, the boys can do their boyband act at half-time.'

The boys are delighted with Mary's suggestion. Deadly. Mary asks Derek to come in on the boyband with the others. Shane thinks it's a good idea. You need good-looking guys, and Derek is good-looking. He's a good singer, too. And all the lads are friends. Shane is fascinated by Mary these days. He knows she knows a lot. He spends a lot of time at her house. She's like a teacher, but also a buddy. You can tell her things. She always has good ideas. If Mary is helping us, it is bound to turn out great.

After Mary starts talking about the boyband, the core membership almost self-selects. Michael and Shane have to be in it. They are sure of it and Mary is, too. The last person chosen is Mark Feehily. Mark wasn't a T-Bird, of course, and didn't sing that much with them before. But he is a fine singer. Shane and Michael (Michael is taking it real seriously) reckon Mark will be a useful addition. Ian Fox is not chosen. He didn't show much interest when the band thing came up. It is maybe not so much his scene: he is working, doing carpentry. And Ian's not really part of the Miggles/Shane Filan clique. Who is doing the choosing? At this stage it appears to be a combination – of Mary and the boys themselves, Michael Garrett and Shane Filan in particular.

Mary suggests a fellow called Fintan Whelan who can help the *Grease* boyband with singing. Fintan comes in and works with them on vocal technique and harmonies. Fintan played in Mary's productions of *West Side Story* and *Little Shop of Horrors*. He is just back from working in Disney in France. Fintan is good at explaining stuff.

•   We will try doing that part *a capella.* Yeah, you know, singing it without the music.

Sometimes when they learn something new the boys go off and practise it by themselves. The Filans have a space above the Mayfair

Café—another property they own—on High Street. Mary rehearses them in the Factory Studio. When Mary isn't directing, Shane automatically takes over the leading role. But when she's around, he is her lieutenant, deferential, getting them to listen to her. They are a great group of lads to work with. She knows she can take all this further. She can do a lot with the boyband idea, and she will have an excellent helper. Averyl Dooher is the perfect woman to do admin and PR. Mary has known Averyl a long time.

Averyl and Mary have done a few projects together before. For the hell of it and to make a few pounds. There was the Lip-Stuck idea. *Lip-Stuck! THE PROFESSIONAL KISSERS! FOR HENS 'N' STAGS, BIRTHDAY GUYS AND DOLLS, RETIREMENTS, ENGAGEMENTS, BIRTHS, MARRIAGES AND DIVORCES!! FEE: £70!* Kian Egan has done a few stints as a kiss-o-gram.

That had been great *craic*. So Averyl and Mary chat. Averyl thinks the boyband thing is an excellent idea. She could organise gigs for them. She is definitely into it.

AVERYL AND PÁDRAIG

A veryl Dooher has blonde hair and blue eyes. She has cute dimples. She is only twenty-three. But don't be fooled. She's a sharp one. Averyl has a degree in marketing and a self-assured, can-do, go-getter attitude.

Averyl is currently employed as assistant manager of the Hawk's Well. Her job description includes doing their publicity stuff, putting together the blurbs and dealing with the media. She has made lots of contacts locally and has a good grasp of how things work in the town. Most people in the business take to her bright, bubbly personality. There is one major newspaper, the *Sligo Champion*, and Averyl knows all the lads there. Jim Gray, journalist, is her main contact. Everyone reads the *Champion* in Sligo. Advertising works in the *Champion*, and they are usually good for a photo or a few column inches, when you need to push a show. There is also a free advertising broadsheet, the *Sligo Weekender*, which has an arts page. There is the local radio station, NWR. And the national broadcaster, RTÉ, have an office in Finisklin; there is a local correspondent and a couple of stringers who give them footage and stories.

Averyl is a bit of a flirt. All the IOYOUs fancied her the minute they laid eyes on her. She always dresses well. Little tops. Labels. She's pushy and young and loud. She's touchy feely. She likes the camera, the little bit of attention.

Averyl has that grown-up kid thing going on. She knows that she has ability, and yet she lets people think she's a bit blonde, then gives them the hop of their lives. It's a good way to get taken seriously.

She is an ex-student of Mary's. Averyl could have been a star herself, the host of her own TV show, where her mix of acid wit and naiveté would have stopped the most distracted from touching that dial. After Tom Cruise came on, Averyl would bump his knee and say, 'Arrah, how are you doing, Tom, pet?'

John had a plan, he said he'd never go away again
He stayed up every night, just to get the detail right.
When you got a plan, you gotta put your best shot in,
So I heard him out, and made a commitment.
(Lyrics: Pádraig Meehan)

When Pádraig Meehan arrived to Mary's studio in November '96 to have a look at her boyband, and she asked, 'Am I mad?' he had a ready answer. He said, 'I am not the best person to be asking, Mary. You know I have been mad for years myself.' Mary knew Pádraig a while. In 1990 he had phoned her out of the blue and told her about his new sequencer. He was supervising a FÁS scheme on songwriting. 'If you need to put together music for a rehearsal, I can do it on this machine. The Ensoniq EPS. Great machine altogether.' Pádraig had great hopes for it. Maybe it was the end of the band as we knew it.

He had just used it to do 'Walk Like an Egyptian' in the Clarence Hotel's St Patrick's Day float. Unfortunately the driver had got lost and the audience and judges never heard or saw the results of his labours. The girl dancers, all students of Mary's, were devastated. They arrived back at the Clarence, drenched to the skin and in floods of tears, long after the parade had dispersed to the pubs and St Patrick was driving his tractor home at high speed out the Pearse Road.

Mary knew Pádraig from around the town in the mid-eighties.

They danced together now and again at events; in the Silver Swan or the Blue Lagoon. Pádraig was the bouncy guitar player and songwriter in the Sligo pop band Those Nervous Animals. He came from Croghan in County Roscommon, where no one ever *showed*, or *just got here*, or *turned up*. No. In Croghan all arrivals come by way of the air, or maybe from the sea. They *land*.

• She's landed.

Pádraig was born in 1956. Nutan, the Belgian photographer who was a lecturer in the art college, told Pádraig one time that his was the lost generation: the generation that was too old for rock and roll, too young for punk. At art school Pádraig had made a few videos. Those Nervous Animals' handful of releases garnered a lot of Irish airplay, especially the song 'The Business Enterprise (My Friend John)'. In 1985–86 the Animals played at Self-Aid and in the National Stadium, before Moving Hearts. They put out a mini-album called *Hyperspace*. Pádraig felt a shiver of excitement when he slipped the black vinyl record out of its sleeve when the first pressings came from Tara Records, saw the rainbows on the grooves.

For a couple of years Those Nervous Animals were the next big thing, doing 'The Late Late Show' and supporting Chris De Burgh in the RDS. They went off to London to sign with CBS. And then they disappeared off the radar. Everyone always says, 'What happened with the Animals? They should have been huge. . .'

Mary got Pádraig a gig doing a bit of sequencing for *West Side Story* a while after that phone call. And he had done bits and pieces for her since. He had nearly paid back the bank for the EPS. He has been trying to get a band going, he has some new songs, and has found a useful singer in Yvonne Cunningham. The Good Zoo. He has been ringing up some musicians he knows and trying to put together a band to do original stuff. Eddie Lee is working with him on it. They have plans for a few gigs over Christmas.

Mary has booked rehearsal space for the boyband in the Factory Studio, above a bicycle shop, close to the southern bank of the Garavogue River. Pádraig climbs a narrow wooden stair. The squeak and thump of rubber-soled shoes. There is a ghetto blaster on the floor, but no music plays. The cluster of boys facing the large mirror on the wall are walking slow-mo through a series of choreographed dance steps. Mary McDonagh is in front of the group, keeping in eye contact through a large mirror.

- You're there. You're there. Back. Then you're there.

Emily McEvoy is in attendance, giving individuals quiet words of guidance. As Pádraig gets up near the mirror, Mary, bright-eyed, glances, says hiya. Mark Feehily grins and says hiya to Pádraig. His face is flushed from exertion.

Mary takes a break to say hello. She introduces Pádraig to the five band members he has not met before. There is a small area in the corner walled off with board as a dressing room and office. Then Mary tells Emily to start the CD. 'Let's do the fast one again. Right, fellas, positions.' 'OK,' says Emily. 'Are ye ready?'

Mary's mark on the dancing moves is unmistakeable. She has a style. It's a bit more show than boyband, but it looks real slick. Always when Mary dances, she demonstrates *giving energy*—fingers extended, taut, every muscle, every cell in the dance. That's it. A bit of an audience helps get the energy up. These boys are putting themselves about. The song is 'We've Got It Going On'. They sing the song as they dance, mostly in unison. Mark has the harmonies off pretty good. Pádraig watches and listens, soaks it in.

It is something to see guys that age so *into* the boyband thing, into the dance. . . And all together. Pádraig says, 'Great. I wonder could we hear them singing without dancing?' They do their slow song.

These fellas just love singing together. Pádraig sees that right away. He is already well acquainted with the showy vocal skills of Mark Feehily. And what's the little guy's name? Shane can sing some, too.

Shane has cool poise. Graham has a cool pose. Pádraig Meehan spends some time with the band, getting them to make eye contact, to use their eyes, to confide, to play to an imaginary camera.

- The length of notes is as important as where they come in.

The lads are talkative and curious. They ask Pádraig does he know this and that band. He has heard of The Backstreet Boys. The other band names are unfamiliar. Pádraig asks the lads will each one sing a bit for him. Oh, no. They are not keen on being singled out. Everyone does a bit of the melody—solo. The lad called Michael attempts singing it in the same range as the others, but

Shane intervenes. 'Sing it down, Miggles, like you always do.' Shane gives Michael the key. 'It sounds good low when everyone is singing,' he assures Pádraig.

'There is something special about these guys,' Pádraig tells Mary. He thinks they are excellent. 'You are not at all mad. You have obviously done a lot of work already. This can be huge.'

- Averyl is helping me.

Mary is thinking of getting a show together, mixed in pace between fast and slow numbers. The boyband thing has its own rules. . .

- Great idea, Mary. An awful lot of stuff can be done now, here in Sligo.

The boys are full of nervous energy. Michael does monkey tricks, swinging upside down from the low roof stanchions. Graham tries breakdancing spins on the floor. He is good at it. Pádraig says it would be no problem to sequence up some backing tracks in the right keys to suit the lads' voices.

- You have to come and see *Grease* after Christmas.
- Yeah, definitely.
- We will talk soon, again.
- We'll talk soon, Mary. Good luck.

A White Christmas

Sligo Junior Chamber is a voluntary organisation that sees its role as promoting the interests of young people. The organisation is dedicated to a number of charitable causes, and they regularly stage events. For Christmas '96 the Junior Chamber organise a fashion show in the Southern Hotel. Mullaney's clothes shop in O'Connell Street is providing the fashion, and Eileen Magnier, the RTÉ reporter, is the presenter. Choreographer: Mary McDonagh. Also appearing, says the advertisement in the *Sligo Weekender*, is Sligo's newest boyband group, the local version of Boyzone.

The president of the Junior Chamber is a lady by the name of Christina Farrington. She approached Mary McDonagh a month or so before to provide the entertainment for the night. Mary said sure, the proceeds were going to a specific charity, either Share a Dream or Vincent de Paul. Mary would organise the kids from her school to sing and do some modelling of clothes. Christina trusted Mary's judgement and readily agreed when Mary suggested that she could add another element to the Junior Chamber's show: the unveiling of her new boyband.

The *Grease* boyband's swashbuckling debut appearance brings the Southern Hotel crowd to their feet. The six likely lads strut the catwalk with abandon, giving heart attacks to Mary and her colleague Steffen as well as to the girls in the audience. Milky clouds of dry ice or stage smoke swirl behind them. The band has no name and just two songs to sing. Shane and Mark lead the vocals on 'I'll Never Break Your Heart' and 'We've Got It Goin' On'. 'Break Your Heart', by The Backstreet Boys, is a big song for them. They have practised it a thousand times. It has been their project. The more they listened to the original, the more they heard going on. What a forest of vocals! But they have it down pretty smart. They don't do all the parts, but you'd need twenty in the band to do that. This is their *version* of it. Graham sings harmony above the lead. Michael and Derek and Kian do the playful interspersed backing vocals. They punctuate Shane and Mark's lead vocals with crisp harmony. Derek Lacey really embodies it.

Ooo. A-a-ai. Know-your're-'fraid. Feel-ings show. And a-a-ai. Un-der-stand. Girl-it's-time-to-let-go.

The karaoke CD with The Backstreet Boys backing track belts out through the sound system behind them. The spotlight bobs and follows Shane Filan as he goes on a minor walkabout. The boys are dressed in dark pants and shirts of varied colours, blues and yellows and reds.

The show is on at two in the afternoon, so the band have to miss one of the highlights of the pop year, the *Smash Hits* Magazine Poll Winners' Party on BBC TV. Mary has someone taping it, so everyone gets to watch it later in the evening. It helps to wind down from the excitement of the Southern Hotel show. Ant and Dec, the BBC comedians, do the links. And Paul O'Grady from Channel Four in his 'Lily Savage' persona, six foot six, large make-up and enormous blonde wig. Alicia Silverstone wins best female and best actress for *Clueless*.

East 17 perform. And the Spice Girls. They do their latest hits— 'Wannabee' and 'Say You'll Be There', and collect three *Smash Hits* awards. Dublin's own Boyzone collect *six*. Their clean sweep includes best haircut, Ronan Keating, and most fanciable person, Ronan Keating, as well as best album and best single. Four miles out a country road from Sligo, in Colga, Calry, on his couch before the TV screen, Mark Feehily should be collecting a *Smash Hits* award for happiest vocalist. He has fulfilled a life-long dream. He sang with a band in front of a crowd. And he has a whole bunch more gigs lined up.

Four days later Mary McDonagh watches Mark Feehily walk on stage again, this time with a different band. The Cooleara pantomime is on its first night in the Hawk's Well. Mary always goes to the first few shows, to iron out any problems. 'Pantozone', the panto boyband, are slotted in as the second last item in the show, just before the finale chorus with 'The Lambeth Walk' and 'Roll Out the Barrel', when Dick Whittington gets the girl and the evil Captain Hook is suckered and everyone lives happily ever after. The music starts in blackout. Then with flashes and whirling lighting effects, 'Could It Be Magic' by Take That sets the mood of celebration.

Panto is fun but it's hard work, too. Two shows on Sundays. After the matinee, Mark is among the youthful chorus members hanging around the theatre car park, waiting to be collected. Cars murmur past, Christmas trees sticking out of boots. The smell of sauces and roasts on the frosty air. While everyone else is having Sunday dinner, panto people must rush off to grab a bite and be back in costume and paint in two hours when the lights dim for the eight o'clock show. Mark can be back a little later; his call is only for the second half. He is always punctual.

Pantozone get a huge cheer every night. Mark's colleagues from the *Grease* boyband come out to support him. The T-Birds are impressed. Mark is great. Roger and Cormac and Barry do well, too. The kids love them. Mary gets a great kick out of it, watching from the back of the theatre. Lights, music, a couple of good-looking guys. And the roof nearly comes off. Pantozone's success strengthens Mary's confidence in her boyband idea.

Christmas '96 is a white Christmas. The roadsigns on the Curlieu Mountains wear beards of ice. The flakes come small and infrequent at first, but as the snow turns heavier towards evening, the snowflakes grow bigger, heavy enough to make a noise; every impact on single-glazed window glass an audible soft bump. On Christmas Day, two inches of snow crunch underfoot in some parts of Sligo as children explore uncharted territories. Travel is disrupted on Stephen's Day.

By New Year's Day the snow survives only in patches on the hills. A terrible flu bug is raging in Sligo. Sligo Rovers have only four players fit to train for their match with Derry. The Gaelic team, preparing for league matches, are affected, too.

Averyl engages a photographer she knows, Angela Campbell, to take photos of the band. The Hawk's Well is the meeting place. Mark Feehily arrives early. The photographer is on her way, says Averyl. When the rest of them come, they space around looking for good locations. The Bishop's Garden would make a good background. They pose. Mark positions himself right front of the group and produces a moody, lippy stare. Kian balances and tenses his body. Sucks in his cheeks. Derek looks happy at left back. Graham stands in the middle of the back row, tilting his head sweetly for the imaginary camera. Letting the slight turn accentuate his cheekbones in a way he considers looks good. He looks sharp as hell.

Nearly out of shot in the background, Michael Garrett is agitated, climbing the ivy walls, maybe hoping to be frozen in a decisive moment, a perfect moment of pure drama. He will get with the programme in a minute.

Afternoon park strollers pass by with uninterested looks; they see a crowd of young fellas messing around. Playing at being pop stars. It would be easy to miss how much in earnest these gentlemen are.

Shane Filan steps out of the group and frames the picture with thumbs and fingers at right angles, a neat rectangle frame. Turns it over, landscape, portrait. 'Right, lads.' Shane already has formed his own picture of how things should fit together. He seems to have dreamt these passages, peeked into the last pages of the book and has a good idea of the plot. He has somehow absorbed the code, has sussed out certain principles of the music publicity world. And he wants to explain.

• What's happening today? It is just a woman taking a photograph. It will last just a minute. Just a second. *But you have to put your best image into it.* Concentrate. You have to give the photographer something. *This is how we will be seen.*

Like recording. It is forever. It is important.

He instructs each individual: Kian face this way, Mark that way. He looks at how the light strikes each of their faces. He has an opinion about the pose that best suits each one. Shane is grooming them. Conducting them. 'Don't be messing.' They go along. When Shane speaks, the others believe him.

He almost forgets himself. He steps into the picture and turns on a showband, punter-friendly smile. When Angela Campbell arrives they go inside. They use the stage of the Hawk's Well for the shoot.

Grease is advertised in the local media: six performances in the Hawk's Well, from the first of January to the fifth, with an afternoon matinee on the Sunday. The holiday season still has life in it, and *Grease* draws full houses. Every night at the interval there's a hectic costume change. Six of the lads from the cast step out of the eternal summer of '59 and become teen idols of '96. Dark pants, loose white shirts. Marcus Counihan, the stage manager, puts on his American DJ voice and roars close into the open backstage microphone.

• *Ladeeees and gentlemen! Would you please welcome— live on stage—Sligo's newest boys band! Six—As—One!!*

The girls scream obligingly. They go wild. The lads stroll onstage, grinning and waving to people they know. They appear full of confidence. Their first tune is 'I'll Never Break Your Heart'. It's their slow one, so first position is a line-up downstage, six backs to the audience as the opening bars play. Heads bowed. Each boy turns smoothly to face the audience on cue for his entry line. Kian is first to sing. Shane is next. Until Six As One are all facing out, shoulder to shoulder, making expansive hand gestures as they sing. One of the nights, there's a problem with Kian's microphone, but he soldiers on bravely through a whine of feedback.

They up the pace for the second song. Twelve arms slice the air in unison. Six sets of hips swing. Mary's steps are adding excitement to the snappy funk groove of 'We've Got It Goin' On', another Backstreet Boys tune. At one stage, Miggles does a brief bit of a moonwalk, just like Michael Jackson. He leaves one foot in place and drags the other back, lifting up the heel. Then he does it with the other foot . . . It gives a sliding effect, of moving on Vaseline or talcum powder, the ground treadmilling past while the dancer stays on the spot.

Before the show Mark did up a new show poster with a bit about the band. It included the new boyband in one of Angela Campbell's group photos. *Grease* '97, starring Six As One. He even has a logo done, with a magic marker, using the same 's' in 'as' and 'six', a big snaking 's' weaving like a mountain boreen, like a country road.

That name, the band don't love it, it's just you have to have a name, and no one could think of a good one. Shane had said one of the days, 'Listen, lads. Look—for now—we will just call it . . . anything . . . Six of Us, Six . . . Six As One. OK? OK? It's shite, but we're bound to think of a better one after the show.'

'*Six As One?* I'll go with that,' says Miggles. 'Six As One, that'll do,' says Mary.

On the final night of the show, as Six As One finish their first song, doing the *a capella* ending, the boys take a breath before the last dramatic resolving note. In the gap, before they sing 'Heart', a female voice rich with that Sligo twang pipes up '*Ye beauud-Ts!*' The final big harmony *Hearrrrrrt* is nearly lost in the laughter of the audience, which soon turns to applause.

Funny how the lads all still remember the story of that evening long ago when Shane's mother made her surprise visit to Mary's house. It is always good for a tired laugh. Shane laughs uncomfortably.

- Remember Shane, the day . . .
- My mum! That's my mum!
- She was in such a hurry, she nearly fell in the door!
- Ha, ha.

It gains weight with the telling. Everyone thinks it is hilarious. Shane's mum. Up in Mary's. Shane's mum is a bit of a legend. Shane grins, his wide grin. 'Ah, yeah. That's my mum!'

Shane adores his mum. He is a bit of a mother's pet, really. Mae Filan has always been an authority figure in the house, rarely challenged. She is used to having the last word. But his mother thinks the world of Shane.

Now Shane feels a bit torn. A bit pulled two ways. He kind of wishes his mother had not gone up the hill to tell Mary what for. How is it that other people's parents always seem cooler than your own? Other people have young, glamorous, hip mums. Mums who would be far too cool to go to someone's house to try and stand up for you. Mums who could let their hair down and have a laugh with Mary and her acolytes, the in crowd in the Hawk's Well.

Mrs Filan and Mary have not had occasion to talk to each other that much. They felt no need to. When they meet in the foyer of the Hawk's Well, Mrs Filan and Mary are nice to each other. In a kind of formal way. Young Shane's excellent performance is reflecting well on both of them.

A couple of months pass. March sees the return of the snow. There's a week of white weather. On the eighth, the Sligo Grammar School hold their transition year fashion show. Graham Keighron's old school. The show is not in the school; it's at the top of town, up in the Sligo Park Hotel. Steffen Jorgensen and Mary McDonagh are working on the Passion for Fashion show, doing the choreography and movement for the models. The transition years are the models. Some great outfits are on display; all the rag trade businesses in the town have contributed. And some highly original hats, too, by Mudita Proctor. Carbury National School take part, showing the children's wear. The commentary is bilingual, in Irish and English. This was a gig Mary considered pursuing for the new boyband. But then she said no. She had bigger plans for them.

Mary is in rehearsals at this time for a production of *Annie*.[†] It's opening on 11 March. Graham Keighron has a principal role in it. He is enjoying the acting. Graham is Rooster and Gillian Walsh is Lily; they are the gangster couple. Liam Winters is in it. Kian Egan and Mark Feehily get parts in the chorus. Ursula Smullen is the horrible Miss Hannigan. Maggie Villarining and Louise Burns play Annie on alternate nights. Both girls were in the MMD Production last year of *Oliver*. There is a big, very cute brown dog in the show called Andy, playing a dog called Sandy.

[†]   *Annie*, the story of the orphan, is not to be confused with *Annie Get Your Gun*.

THE NAME

The rain stops. The sun comes out on the shiny new world. The next bunch of showers is queued up on the north-western horizon, out beyond Ben Bulben. But for now there is bright sunshine and an expanse of blue sky, interrupted only by a few windblown jet trails. The blue sky blues everything. Dark blue hilltops, green-blue bare pastures. April is cold. The blue sky reflects off the wet surface of a narrow country lane and off a battered purple Toyota Corolla van hissing through the puddles. Pádraig is low in diesel.

He is doing some research in the college library. On the way in, he bumps into Mary McDonagh. She greets him with that wry smile.

- Did you get in to see *Annie?*
- No . . .
- Tsk tsk, well, you missed a great show. You are a terrible man. You missed *Grease* as well.
- know, yeah, I meant to . . . I was doing a few gigs, I was away . . .
- What are you up to these days?

- I have a few songs done. I did a video with Barry. And I got a gig from the Arts Festival for The Good Zoo. Yeah. You know, like we were saying last year, I would love to do an original musical.
- That would be deadly. Sure, give me a listen if you have some stuff on tape . . .
- How is the boyband going?
- Yeah, the boyband, the boyband went off great. They did another gig last month. That's something we must chat about.
- Yeah. It would be no problem to sequence up a few tracks.

A few weeks on, Mary McDonagh meets with Averyl and Pádraig in her house in High Street. To talk about the boyband project.

Mary and Averyl already have in place what appears to be a loose verbal agreement. The two women even have a name chosen, Streetwise. Their idea—originally—was to have a production company. A production company to do more than just put on theatre shows. Maybe get into management and promotion and development of talent. Provide rehearsal space, market new ideas. There are so many talented young people. They often approach Mary looking for advice, and sometimes bring tapes. An outlet is needed.

But now Averyl and Mary have a particular focus. They want to develop the *Grease* boyband. To record and do gigs. They need some help on the music side. Pádraig says he is willing to help. He can't resist a project. Averyl Dooher, Pádraig Meehan and Mary discuss working together under the banner of Streetwise Promotions on the boyband project. Yes, say the women, they have talked to the boys.

Between the three at Mary's living room table, they reckon they have a lot of the skills needed to manage and promote a boyband successfully. 'And those we don't have—we know how to get them,' says Mary. 'Let's make it a Sligo thing as much as possible,' says Pádraig. They all agree. Averyl and Pádraig do not have much money, and Mary says she will spend her money on the project. She has a bit of money from the sale of the yard at the side of her house.

Averyl says when we make money from managing the band, Mary will be paid back. They do not write this down. They simply agree on it. The next day Pádraig writes a note in his word processor, listing the areas of responsibility each of the three partners have agreed on.

Mary has her promotion skills and, of course, her movement and choreography. She has authority with the boys; they listen to Mary. Averyl has marketing expertise. She has the theory and the engine. She is a dab hand at the word processor. She will sell the product, book the gigs. Talk to people. Averyl is a worker. Mary suggests things, and Averyl always follows them up. She never complains.

Pádraig would look after the technical side and the music and singing. He had dealt with record companies before and done tours.

• But what do we call the band? We need a good boyband name.

Six As One go to see Remix, the new Limerick boyband, in the Gilhooley Hall in early May. There are five in Remix, a couple of really great dancers. Pat Egan is managing them. They are more a dance act than a singing one, the Sligo guys reckon. Some of them look real hard. You would call that guy a 'shank' if he was from Sligo. The acoustics were tough for them. Ah still, they have deadly dance moves, Graham has to admit.

'OK,' says Averyl, next time everyone meets. 'Let's all put our minds to it. Let's try and think of a good idea.' Do the boys have any ideas for a name? They are thinking about it. You would have loads of ideas when you didn't need them. Pádraig says it will come. They give themselves a deadline of two weeks. It passes. It's not that there are no ideas. Just nothing everyone loves.

Pádraig tries to think laterally. A boyband name? Pádraig has been doing a few gigs with his pals for a bit of *craic* in a pub. Barry Brennan, the lead singer, was the original frontman in Those Nervous Animals. The pub band didn't have a name either. But Barry and Pádraig were known to down instruments in mid-song and race outside M.J. Carr's pub, pointing to the heavens. There, a pale elongated wisp hung in the evening sky. The Comet Hale-Bopp.

It had been at its brightest in April. Pádraig found it strangely moving to gaze on the long-tailed visitor in the sky. The ancients would have seen it as an omen, a harbinger of change. When it was away from the earth, out in the cold depths of space, it didn't wear its spectacular tail. It only wore it when it came to visit. The tail was out-jetting, caused by the heat of the sun and the stresses of gravity and the solar wind in these parts. Pádraig read somewhere it would be back in 2,380 years. Does that mean it swings around the Earth and sun at regular intervals? It seemed a reasonable assumption. Pádraig was enthusiastic about it. If his theory was right, the last time Hale-Bopp stood in the Sligo sky, we were in the Iron Age.

Times were tough. Queen Maeve was doing her thing, comparing bulls with the neighbours and putting her name on the heap of stones on the breast-shaped mountain. Warlords roamed the trackways and trails, seeking heads.

The time before that was a happier time. The crowd around here were mostly farmers, ruled by a few chiefs and a warrior class who liked to dress up in colourful gear and dance in boulder circles. The cairn was on top of the mountain that time, too. The hereditary priests of the sun were not as powerful as they used to be, but they still burned great fires up there and predicted the future for the local chief. The old chief wanted a cairn to be built for *him* on a suitable hill, maybe the hill above the lake, so people would remember *his* reign forever. But the locals just didn't seem to be in the mood.

If Hale-Bopp passed this way in 5140 BC, some people were occupied building passage tombs out in Carrowmore, in the sacred place near the foot of the mountain. Shattered from days and nights of dancing, of drumming, from walking with the sun god, from talking to the ancestors. The witch-doctor led the chant as patterns were sketched out on the burnt ground. Then the dolmens were raised, lightness and space sketched out in 12-tonne rocks.

Forests covered the land, dark and deep. Bears lived there. Hunting and fishing and moving around with the seasons was the way of life; everyone had to do it, even the tribal elders. It was a golden age. Hunting was good, the weather was warm, and sea levels were at their lowest. The language spoken would be utterly unrecognisable to anyone in the Ireland of 1997. The people in The-Place-That-Would-be-Called-Sligo had yet to see a cow.

Maybe they had a word *like* Sligo though, a word like *Sligeach*, for the Place of Shells. The fruits of the sea kept the people strong. The oysters were big and plentiful. The divers went out in dug-out boats and lifted them out of the deep water. Salmon ran freely in the two rivers, one on either side of the peninsula. In those times, there was no cairn on top of the mountain.

7520 BC was the first time Ireland was occupied during Pádraig's imaginary circuit of Hale-Bopp. A few brothers were resting from a boar hunt in a forest clearance a couple of miles from the coast. A band of womenfolk were gathering berries for a meal. Did one of them look at the brush-stroke in the sky and wonder on it? Did they have a name for it?

Every time it passes, it gets a new name. When it swings around 2,380 years from now, chances are, we won't be calling it Hale-Bopp.[†]

The boys behind the bar in Martin Carr's instantly hit on a name for Barry and Pádraig's band. The Space Fanatics. That's Sligo humour for ya.

Early June. The Arts Festival has come and gone. Pádraig's big moment was his gig with The Good Zoo in the Southern Hotel, supporting English band Edward the Second. The new songs sounded good. Election week, a week of blistering heat, has come and gone. So has the coalition government of John Bruton. We will be having Bertie Ahern in charge for the next five years. There is tension in the North, flashpoint, Drumcree. The NASA Pathfinder spacecraft, a low-budget explorer, lands on Mars and starts to photograph the surface. A little robot car does a runaround. It stops and scratches a rock, which American boffins have christened 'Big Joe'.

Averyl has run clean out of patience. She stands on the floor of Mary's living room, hands on hips. She says, 'Come on; this indecision has gone on too long. We need to pick a name, *any name!*'

Averyl arrives the following week with a sheet of paper on which she has printed a list of band names. Her friend Fintan Whelan—the guy who helped with the singing for *Grease*—has been brainstorming. Fintan runs a sandwich bar, called The Amazing Sandwich Taste Experience. He has come up with a bunch of names.

There's one about an elephant. Trunk or Tusk or something.

- *Trunk?* Hmm.

---

†   Hale and Bopp were the two astronomers who discovered the comet independently in 1995.

Averyl suggests L-O-V-E. 'What about L-U-R-V,' says Pádraig. 'What about C-U-R-V-E,' says someone else. 'Supply, Demand and Curve were in the sixties.' 'What about KISS?' says Averyl. 'No. There was a band of that name in America in the seventies.'

The band straggle into Mary's dining room later that evening and everyone hotly discusses the name. The band doesn't love the name favoured by Averyl and Mary and Pádraig. *IOU*. Neither does anyone else, it seems.

'We could spell it *IOYOU*,' says Averyl, drawing big on an A4 sheet. 'Or I-O You.'

- Io is a moon of Jupiter, actually. It's got volcanoes.
- I Owe You. Mm. OK. Sounds like YO YO. Or YO, Bro!
- I-L-You would be better, like I-Love-You . . .
- No, that's shite!

But no one can think of a better name than IOYOU that a majority can agree on. The meeting moves to the sitting room. It is a week later. Shane is standing with his back to the fireplace. His usual spot. The person in this spot has the floor. Shane has been listening to other bands and has some new discoveries. 'Listen, lads. Backing vocals have to be smooth. Not like the lead vocal. You have to go "aaaaa . . ." '

'OK, then.' Mary cuts in. Mary asks the band, 'Did you check with your parents? Has anyone any questions? Are we all agreed to do this?' The boys say, '*Yeah*, Mary,' in a tone of, 'Like, have we not been saying this for weeks, have we *not* just picked a band name, how could someone *not* know this?' Pádraig explains a record deal, about sending off promo stuff and demos, and doing showcase gigs, and getting signed up to do an album. 'Is that what we are looking for?' '*That's exactly what we are looking for*,' say the boys.

On this summer evening, all agree that they will have a go at fame and fortune under the name IOU. Or I-O-You. Mary and Averyl and Pádraig will be the managers. The band all agree, they say their parents have given the go-ahead. There are whoops of glee from the boys. Averyl and Mary are cracking jokes. A ritual pizza is eaten. Everyone leaves in high spirits. The boys head down the hill. They are evolving a walk, *a springing walk*, a hand movement that evokes Harlem. Especially Michael and Graham. That's not a Sligo town walk. That straight-arm thing, a cupped hand swivelling, arms out, arms back, arms tangled up all over the place. Shifting weight from foot to foot. It's a black, rappin', cussin', dissin' b-boy walk. Mary goes to bed, wondering what she has got herself into. What next? Managing a feckin' boyband, she laughs ironically to herself.

But when Shane goes home and tells his mum about the new name she is raging. 'What was wrong with Six As One? Who came up with this new name?'

- Oh, Mum!
- Ye were always Six As One. That was the name you made up yourselves.

LEAPS AND SONGS, HAIR AND MOZZARELLA

Of course, Mary got herself into this a long time ago. Only now Mary, Averyl and Pádraig have a new band name and a verbal agreement to 'go for it' as a band and management team. They are happy enough. They feel they are on to a good thing. All the boys are nice guys. They trust Mary, and they all adore Averyl. There is consensus among the six band members that Averyl's arse is a magnificent feature. And Mary has been like a mother to them. They have spent a lot of time at her house. She has been keeping manners on them, feeding them and giving them dance classes.

By and large everyone in the band pulls fairly well together; now and again there have been minor bust-ups: Averyl has a big part in keeping order. She is a big sister who could read your thoughts.

• Never come in here again with drink on you!

How can they win? Mary is on the other flank.

• And as for the lover boys, you know what happens if you make anyone pregnant.

Averyl and Mary agree that keeping manners on the boys is a full-time job. OK, there are the quiet ones. Derek or Graham rarely cause any hassle. But a couple of the others have been guilty of breaches of house rules. Issues have come up around time keeping or rivalry between different boys. Occasional tantrums have been thrown. Mary has had her shoulder cried on. With the band, she doesn't play favourites. She is fair. She will give out, but the clouds never last long. Sometimes individuals sulk for a while. The lads all have different ways of coming back. Kian's style is to return with a breezy grin as if nothing has happened.

Six sets of dancing feet have made the floor of the Factory Studio quake, twelve large and not totally clean runners making heavy contact beside the small shoes of younger dancers. The six IOYOU fellas have watched Mary leap balletically, and almost caused an earthquake trying to copy her.

Now Mary introduces Steffen Jorgensen to the rehearsals. The boys watch Steffen fly gracefully through the air. He lands fluidly, into the next move. They all want to try this stunt. Steffen looks on, wearing an expression of mock horror while flailing bodies hurtle across the studio floor as if they had just been shot from a circus gun.

Steffen was born in Denmark. He is bright as a button; he has strength and lightness like a willow. When he was only a baby his family moved to Sligo. He started with all the other kids in Mary McDonagh's classes. Steffen shone, and Mary supported him when the time came for him to journey across the water to London. Just as his teacher had done, he did the audition and got it. Except Steffen's destination was the Central School of Ballet. His career as a professional dancer took him to Europe with the Wiener Ballet Theatre. He danced *Swan Lake* and *Nutcracker*. He performed with the Pact Ballet in South Africa. Steffen starts to take IOYOU for regular rehearsals.

Steffen has a camp air and a dramatic flourish to his personality. At first, some of the lads seem a bit doubtful. So Steffen gives them a few frights. They find out that Gaelic football is a doddle compared to ballet. The strength, the discipline needed. The physical pain barrier you have to go through. After trying a few of the moves, the IOYOUs are glad to go back to a few boyband type

105

routines. Steffen has a few cool ideas for these, too. His authority is established.

Being in a boyband takes up a lot of time. Averyl sends them from the studio to the hairdressers. Mary and Averyl know Erich Conlon from Peter Marks hairdressers. After an approach by Averyl, Peter Marks come on board as sponsors. Erich will be doing the boys' hair.

• Hi, lookit, Egan. He hasta have the boxers showing so people can see the label. Calvin Kleins?

Everyone watches a video of Boyzone in Mary's sitting room. An Irish boyband, and they are huge internationally. IOYOU laugh scornfully. The production is sloppy.

• They are not dancing at all!

The boys say 'and they expect people to pay money for this rubbish?' Mary says, 'Well, people do. It's the baby audience. It's marketing. It's all image. It's *Louis Walsh.'*

• Yeah, Louis Walsh.

A debate begins about whether Boyzone are singing live in the show on the video. When you look at boyband/girlband shows it is usually possible to know whether or not they are singing live. Miming is a difficult skill, as thirty years of 'Top of the Pops' has shown. If the vocals are all coming off tape, there will be bits where the singers mouth words that are not sounded, or bits where they are away from the mic or shut-mouthed when you hear them sing. And if it was pre-recorded, there will be no pops or mic-blasting 'B's. It will all sound too perfect . . .

• No way are they singing!

Pádraig says, 'Ya gotta be at the gig to know for sure. You can't trust TV or videos. Nowadays there are all kinds of in-between stages. It's down to money. Remixes can be done. Post-production lip-synchs, even.'

It always comes back to The Backstreet Boys. The funky, hard-edged, original sound of The Backstreet Boys. The way they move. They *definitely* sing live. They have a *backing band.* That's what IOYOU would love. Cooler boy/girl groups have backing bands for their shows. Others have to make do with tapes or sequences. Sure, that is just hi-tech karaoke—that is, if they are *actually singing at all.* Bands that mime to tapes are crap. Graham says we need to be doing more breakdancing moves. Street dance. He is trying to figure out how A.J. does it on a particular Backstreet's video. He will bring it up to show Mary the next day. Mary says, 'Ye have to get the basics right first. I don't want injuries.' The lads all say, 'What a lot more work we have to do.'

Mary asks the boys, how is the study going? 'Aw, not too bad,' say Shane and Michael. Graham is glad he has his Leaving over and done with last year. Shane is now in the same year as Derek and Miggles and Kian and Mark. He is repeating. Michael says his studies are going OK. But these days the subject foremost in Michael's mind is bands and music.

The boys have various tastes in music nowadays. Kian still likes his rock heavy; he has been having a go at drumming. The others listen to a lot of varied stuff, from REM to Bryan Adams. Shane and Mark both model themselves on The Backstreet Boys. Graham, too. It's not just that he tends to like what Shane and Mark like. Bone is his main man. Has been forever. And Bone has led Graham into other cool areas; he always watches good rap stuff now if it comes on telly. The dancing is the thing. Graham is interested in martial arts as well as dance. Anyone that can move the way that A.J. can is OK by him.

Michael Garrett still likes Michael Jackson.

Pádraig Meehan has been listening to lots of music he would not normally listen to. The charts, 2FM, Boyzone. He is feeling old, all these new bands he never heard of. But he knows how important bands are for growing up to.

It must have been 1972 that Pádraig saw David Bowie do 'Starman' full face to camera on 'Top of the Pops'. He was in Cahill's pub in Croghan, where he used to go on summer evenings to view the black and white TV positioned high on a shelf above the end of the counter. Other kids would be there, too—consuming crisps and minerals, playing draughts. Patrick Cahill, the bald-headed publican and undertaker, would sit beside the stove with his feet up and pass judgement on what came on the television. Patrick thought this Bowie fella was awful funny and mad as a hatter. Pádraig just stared at the screen. It was awesome. It was like a space alien had just made secret contact.

•   Don't tell your fath-ah or he'll get us locked up in fri-ght.

In 1973 a carnival was held in Croghan. Pádraig and his sister heard heavy rock guitar riffs floating across the fields. They went to the village and inside the canvas marquee and met the band after their soundcheck and got all their autographs. The band was called Time Machine. One of the band guys chatted away and let Pádraig have a go on his guitar. They talked about the bands they were into. The Time Machine guy showed off his hammer-ons. He liked Steve Mayall and all those blues guys, but he had a cassette of *The Rise and Fall of Ziggy Stardust and the Spiders from Mars*. Bowie. Pádraig had that one, too.

Even though the Meehans didn't own a record player, after seeing that monumental piece on 'Top of the Pops', Pádraig had sent away for all Bowie's albums to England. He cycled down to Tom Glancy's house and taped them off Tom's stereo player. The tapes got worn out from playing them on the little portable cassette player that he and his sister Bernadette had purchased by mail order for £16.

In his bands Pádraig was always the sideman, like Mick Ronson or Keith Richards. You played rhythm guitar, a bit of lead; solos were kept short. You needed a frontman, a clown prince to take centre stage. You had a hot rhythm section. Bass and drums. You needed songs. Great songs with cool chords of darkness and drugs you could only imagine.[†] The Kinks were masters of it. Songs to scare your parents.

Listening to Bowie would make you want to write songs. He would say and play things so dark and promising. Sometimes like a half-overheard conversation of terrible import. You would go home thinking of how to complete the thought. Of how to assemble some magical sentences of your own. Lines that maybe don't resolve or make any sense at all, but serve as bones, a cage for all of us to make dreams and journeys and nightmares in. Pádraig would rehearse the songs in his head on the bus to school. He kept discovering new stuff in the songs, as he learnt to sing them. There was no bottom to them.

The first band was Warsin, later known as The Parasites. Rory and

---

[†] Your experience of drugs being limited to tea, experimental beer and cigarettes. There were a few 'heads' around who might share their treasures, but the results were generally disappointing.

Willie Conlon and Anthony Noone and Brendan Mac were in it.[†]
Willie was the singer; both he and Pádraig wrote songs, and they
wrote some together, too. Willie always talked about ego. Ever since
Freud discovered him, ego had been causing trouble. But Willie
asked good questions.

• Lou Reed writes great songs with two chords. How come
your songs always have six?

Punk was happening in England. The Jam and The Clash.
Shockingly, glam rock was becoming uncool. Scaring your parents
had reached new heights.

Meehan met a few guys around Drumshanbo who wanted to be
stars. They had a manager, a fortysomething from the north of
England. Hugh Evans. The band was Ivory Coast. They did Bay City
Rollers numbers. They congregated in the manager's house. He gave
them grave advice on how to survive in this world.

• There are *shaaks* ou' theah.

Ivory Coast played Deep Purple songs, too. 'Sweet Child in
Time'. It was kind of a mixture of a heavy metal band and a
boyband. They didn't go for any of that limp-wristed stuff, or tearing
your clothes and spitting like the punks, but they tried to get their
harmonies right. They were studious about arrangements. Donagh
and Feargal Woods and the Geoghegans. Pádraig used to sleep over
in Woods's house. Mrs Woods had qualities of endurance and great
kindness. James Tivnan, the drummer, used to give Pádraig a lift
home to Croghan on his motorbike. Ivory Coast played loud, and
lots of girls liked them. Then Pádraig went to college in Sligo and
met some guys who listened to Todd Rundgren and Led Zeppelin
and Gentle Giant.

Barry Brennan was a great singer. He didn't just have a powerful
and distinctive voice. Barry had a lyrical lightness to the way he
used his voice, a musicality mixed with passion that could make
your heart leap. Up to this point Pádraig had never heard anyone as
good as Barry. And Barry had plenty of good song ideas, too. Barry
was also a Master of Miraculous Pool. He would lull his opponent
into false security with a few normal plays starting off. Then Barry

---

[†] Pat Roche and Sean O'Boyle played in The Parasites' later
incarnations.

would come to the table and produce a shot—using a high-powered technique—that involved the use of at least three cushions. The cue ball would zip around the baize, ending up simultaneously potting two of his reds and taking out all your carefully cultivated positions over the pockets. Then he'd smile at you and look entirely surprised with himself. You would be thinking, poxy hoor; what a fluke. Then BB would return to the table and repeat the feat, overturning major laws of physics with whimsy.

Barry and Pádraig got a drum machine someplace. They jammed for hours with guitars. At one stage Robbie Cribbs helped them to record some of their ideas on his reel-to-reel tape machine. They even got James Blennerhassett and Fluky and Mickey Neilsen in to play on their recording session.

Barry and Pádraig went down an alley one evening and, through the galvanised iron gates of Morgan and Bourke's coalyard, heard two guys playing bass and drums. Carl Smith and Eddie Lee. The band that Barry, Pádraig and Eddie formed became Those Nervous Animals. Eddie Lee turned Pádraig on to D-Funkt and Frank Zappa and Was Not Was. Eddie always came up with good bass lines. He had an ear for what was cool, what worked in a band sense. It was the early eighties. Pádraig and Eddie tried their hands at writing songs together. They used to play pool upstairs in the eighties version of the pub called Beezies and write choruses about video games. The Animals went close to getting a great record deal, but the ball was somehow dropped a yard from the line.

Boybands don't try to scare your parents. They try to make your parents buy you things. You still have to work on three-minute pop songs though. Only now that means a lot of syrupy love ballads. Listening to Irish daytime music radio in 1997 is a trial. A test of endurance. Meehan has to listen to a lot of Irish DJs with dodgy mid-Atlantic accents.

It appears that a boyband in Europe means something slightly different to a boyband in America. The UK is strictly pap. Seven-year-olds have to like it. To impress the US (which seems to be a slightly older market), a boyband needs a slight hint of darkness in their image. They can come over a bit rebellious, funky and rock and roll. Not rock and roll like Lou Reed. Not scary. They can't ever be imagined walking on the *real* wild side or mocking the president or using vulgarity. They have to be dreamboats, finished off with a cosmetic dusting of street cred. Just dressed and posed rock and roll. With a polished production, great tunes, cool guitar riffs. And excellent snappy dance routines. Just like The Backstreet Boys.

And—of course—to throw the dreaded sugary love ballads in there with enough regularity for a generation to grow up to.

IOYOU are going to write their own songs. 'We have been trying to write songs already but we can never finish our ideas,' say the boys. 'Will you teach us guitar?' Kian can already play E minor and A as well as D on the guitar.

• It's the changes that are tricky. Keep at it. It will be a great help writing songs.

Pádraig hauls his guitar, the Marshall 50-watt amplifier and his old trusty EPS sampler/sequencer into Mary's front room. The EPS was cutting edge—for the price—in 1990 but it's a bit out of date now. You have to boot it up with a floppy disk every time. But the boys have never seen a sampler before. They arrive in ones and twos, bringing in the air of different places. Ringing the doorbell, the startling staccato bell. Mary answers the door herself. Hiya. Some have their sweaty football stuff, muddy boots in plastic bags. They are coming from a match. 'Did ye win?' asks Michael.

Pádraig has hired an SM58 microphone from Tony O'Donnell for the evening. He gets the boys experimenting. They record voices into the sampler and do the stutter thing by jabbing the keys. '*Eye-Oh, eye-oh, eye-oh Yewwww! Co-Co-Co-Co-Cool!*' 'Let's do something constructive.' Pádraig lays down a groove—a bass drum beat, a hi-hat and a back beat on a tight funky snare. The lads like it. Michael taps in the snare pattern. This is cool, impressive stuff indeed.

They are fascinated, but plenty confident; confident enough to try out singing to the grooves. These lads have imagination. Especially Shane and Mark. Pádraig introduces the idea of song structure. All about the elements of a song, intro, verse, chorus, bridge, middle eight, etc. They lap up these terms. Within minutes they are using them like they had talked this stuff all their lives. 'Hey, what about this for a bridge,' says Michael. They are not afraid to sing out and improvise ideas. 'This is *deadly*. This is cool *craic*,' says Kian.

111

Next evening, all the boys come prepared for the session. They all have song ideas. Mark Feehily and Shane Filan have a good one, a melody and lyrics. It seems Shane wrote most of the lyrics.

- Dreams are for believing.

They even have a name, 'Together Girl Forever'. Pádraig puts chords to it and extends the harmonic structure. Soon there is an intro, middle eight, even an outro. The seven boys—the one on acoustic guitar balding and with a bigger belly than the rest—sing it over and over. They try out different harmonies. The sequencer provides a ready-made band, the drums and bass are KICKIN'. Pádraig drives away from Mary's on a high. He knows how the boys feel. After only two sessions, they have (with a small bit of prompting) written their first song.

Early June comes along. It rains a lot. Rain is no harm when you have to do exams. If it was sunny outside, it would be harder to concentrate.

THE LEAVING CERTIFICATE

Your English teacher has shrunk two inches in stature overnight. He/she smiles at you going in and wishes you good luck. You enter another realm in the exam hall. The seats are isolated from each other to make cogging difficult. You are a number. You find the desk with your number. It's kind of unreal. Two and a half hours and then it's all over. Next day is maths. Last-minute revision is an exercise in prescience, of divining the future. Was that what those years of classes were all about? The luck of the draw? Did your memory serve you well? Did calculus come up? Or did you sit there blank, in horror, as the other lowered heads scribbled in their foolscap? Shane and Michael and Kian and Mark seem to be doing OK.

But even now, they still can't keep IOYOU out of their thoughts. There is a great hooky chorus Mark has, which he can't find a verse for. It plays in the background of all his thoughts. It's well for the others. This very second, they are dossing down the town, checking out girls, having the *craic*. Derek and Kian and Graham, slagging and daydreaming out loud. Telling each other what they'd buy if they were rich, big-time pop stars. Beautiful cars, everyone goes for cars. It would be hard to choose . . . Beamers or Mercs or Rollers?

Mary has been telling the boys to keep at their schoolwork . . . The parents are all weary of repeating the mantra, 'Just concentrate on getting your exams first, have something to fall back on . . .' His career guidance teacher has tried valiantly to drum realism into Mark Feehily. But all the lads have found it hard to concentrate in school.

Thinking of doing gigs in front of loads of people and trying to keep your mind on school. It is not that easy. How do you guide someone who is not even in the room?

•   OK, it would be nice if we could follow our dreams.

'But it is no harm to ask, is this realistic?' says the teacher, in a sympathetic voice.

Mark doesn't care if it's realistic or not. He wants to be a singer in a band. He does his best; he does a pretty good essay in English. Shane feels he has done OK in most subjects. The others are not too sure. They are glad when the weeks of exams come to a close. It's an anticlimax then. School is over. Can you believe it?

When you are seventeen or eighteen and dead cool, it is not easy to avoid a complex relationship with the nightclub bouncers, or doormen as they like to be called. It is their job to seek to ensure that underage people don't get in, or inappropriately dressed people, or drunk or boisterous people. Some doormen will just look at you and not like the look of you and that's it. Nothing will change that man's mind. In Dublin especially, the guys at the door act as an exclusivity filter, making sure that just any old riff-raff don't get in. The Sligo ones seem to have been to Dublin and want that image, too.

What do bouncers do in the daytime? Maybe they don't get to boss anyone about much. Some of them certainly like their little bit of authority. They make bad jokes. They are totally indifferent to grovelling. They have heard every scam before. They are all brown belts in karate and are not to be messed with. And they have earpieces in to hear what the assistant manager upstairs is seeing on his video monitor. Or maybe they are just listening to their favourite sounds. Who knows?

Some doormen are OK. They get to know you, they forgive past sins, they are polite and open to persuasion. But the guy in charge is usually a bollox. Bollox (sometimes spelt bollocks) is not a swear word—a court in England decided that in 1978. 'Never mind the bollox', in England, means to ignore the irrelevant distractions, the banality and nonsense that might obscure the vision of a punk poet.

But if you use that same phrase in the west of Ireland, people will look around to see where the bollox is standing. OK, 'bollox' means—historically—a mediaeval monk's cassock, and in modern slang usage, a man's scrotum. But a bollox in Sligo means a person who is not good to have at your side at a moment of peril. Bolloxes are nearly always male. They would go through you for a shortcut. And doing them a good turn would be a complete waste of time.

The opposite human condition to being A Bollox is being Dead Sound. But people found to be dead sound for years can, in the heel of the hunt, turn out to be a total bollox. So there is a refined theological argument, a critical judgement call in attributing Soundness. Only those close to the individual could know the truth. But the boys are satisfied that there is no point in trying to get into a certain nightclub in Wine Street while some of them are of dodgy legal age. Yer man on the door is a complete bollox.

Two girls in white micro-miniskirts are trying to hail a taxi. There are a bunch of lads on the bridge, talking loud.

- D'ya see yer wan? A pure briar. Goodnight, girls.
- Hi, fellas!
- C'mere. One of the lads needs a light.
- I don't smoke.

Keep walking. People are spilling out of Toffs and Equinox.

You have to keep your ears open. A Honda Civic sprints from nowhere. Don't walk. Listen out for the next guy; when you see one there's probably another coming. Another 'sham' with a souped-up engine. Blasting Stuka-snarls through humungous twin exhausts. As the cars shoot by, the mechanical pulse of techno—though the speakers are inside the car, the sound gets over the engine noise—rises and falls in pitch, the upshot of the Doppler effect. Why are boy racers always small guys? Why are they so . . . private? The windows are deeply tinted. The driver's head is set so low it's almost out of sight below the window frame, the woman on the passenger's side low, too. They go riding out of town, low in their sports seats.

Wearing steel alloy wheels. Go-fast stripes. And the Mother Of All insurance premiums.

After the nightclub, the friends and band members need to 'duke' (to move unobtrusively) in someplace for some fast food on the way home. The Four Lights, Sligo people call the Four Lanterns takeaway. Burgers and fish and chips. Or Abrakebabra. Abrakebabra stays open late. It's Shane's turn to stand in the queue and listen to the voices of late-night Sligo. All sorts of people in the narrow plastic seats. Students, trios of married-looking girls with dirty laughs, black-wardrobe Goths, a few lads with skint heads and earrings, a group of country boys and girls out together, packed six to a table. A well taken out lovey-dovey couple and a loner with a jaded expression share a table. Tables are piled high with half-eaten food and packaging.

• Two doner kebabs and a shish kebab.

Kian and Graham are looking at expensive sunglasses in an optician's window.

• Now *they* are cool!!

• Nah! I want *Ray Bans!* I don't like Wires, I like Jackets! . . . Did you ever see those ones, Oakleys, I saw them in a book, jeez, *they were class*! Like, you'd pay . . .

Graham eats another chip.

• Two hundred quid *easy* . . .

• But the replica ones, you get them in Spain, anywhere, you can't tell the difference, but . . .

• I know. *Revos*, they're the best. You know like Puff Daddy wears . . . You won't get those in Sligo, you have to go to Dublin . . . I wonder what you call the ones A.J. McLean wears?

• I don't know, maaan! Don't diss me, Graham maaan! Ice— T! M.C. Hammer! Can't touch dadt!

Graham ignores Kian's OTT Graham impression. He is on a roll.

• *He* probably gets *his* for free! It's publicity for the manufacturers; he probably has shades for *life* . . . Hey, Egan! I'm goin' in tomorrow and gettin' a pair of those! I swear! They're deadleee! I'll say, 'Yo! What up! I need to try these shades . . .'

• It's not cool to say *shades* now, you call them *sunglasses* . . .

BLISTERS ON BLISTERS

Averyl has organised a gig. Three gigs, actually, over two days. She has spoken to her boss, Denis, at the Hawk's Well and struck the deal. Two evening shows, and a matinee at five p.m. for the younger audience. IOYOU's debut performances will be on 29 and 30 August 1997.

Mary is moving some of the new songs. There is real communication happening. Most of the moves are Mary's ideas, but Graham and Shane and Michael have ideas of their own. They show Mary what they think the dancer in the video is doing, and Mary shows them how to do it safely, with an economy of movement. Sometimes it works, sometimes it doesn't. If it doesn't Mary has another suggestion. They move on. Grabbing your crotch seems to be an essential move in a boyband video. Mary discourages too much of that.

The upcoming gigs have set a new mood; a mood of sober industry prevails in Mary's dance rehearsals. Now she *really* has their attention. She praises them. The boys' dancing is coming on well. 'You lads are getting a lot fitter.' She's right. They notice it themselves.

Mary is paying the Factory Studio for the rehearsal space. She has booked extra hours for the band project. In the evenings, after regular dance school lessons are finished, the band come in. Sometimes she takes them, sometimes Steffen does. Mary is upping the ante, workwise. As the regular Friday evening exodus from work to home slows to a crawl in Wine Street, IOYOU are sweating down by the Quayside. The session can go on for two hours, or over, as the lads are put through their paces relentlessly by the choreographer. No one complains. Many a night sees Michael come home limping, blisters on his feet. He has blisters on his blisters. It is just as tough for the others.

Michael is the excitable one. His heart starts to pound. He is sensitive. He feels the power, the awe of it all . . . He knows how important these days are for him and everyone around him. He feels the history, the future. Then he gets very excited. Wired. Then he is hard to control; he finds it hard to keep himself in check.

Shane is steadier. He seems to be able to keep all the balls in the air at once. Shane stayed cool in the exams. He is cool in rehearsals. He is cool with girls. He always has a girlfriend.

Derek has a girlfriend these days, too. Her name is Helena. She is pretty. And smart. He is very proud. She plays in the girlband Fusion.

This is a summer that goes by slowly for the six IOYOU boys. Time passes very slowly when you are eighteen, in a brand new band, waiting for the day of your first gig to come around.

It is a Sunday evening, in late June 1997. Mary has new flowers sown. When Pádraig calls, she shows him her garden. It is an explosion of colour. Mary is in contemplative mood. She is thinking about her life. Turning forty makes you think about stuff. Things are going well for her. Life is good. But she is working hard. She is teaching a course in the Sligo Institute of Technology. And doing regular classes in the Mary McDonagh School of Dance. Mary has a valuable assistant in Steffen. And Emily McEvoy is a great help. If all this work is not enough, Mary has shows in Cork and all over the place.

And now, of course, there is the boyband, IOYOU. Whew!

Mary has a computer now. She's thrilled with it. The monitor and tower have black casing.

- It will be good for doing boyband stuff.

Mary doesn't have a car. Pádraig has never seen her driving. She just shows up, anyplace she has to be. Her entrance to a rehearsal room (unlike his own, it seems to him) is an event.

Like all relationships, this one has ebbed and flowed. The present time is one of growing and building trust. Of figuring out where other people are at. Sometimes Pádraig has found it baffling to get his head around Mary, to know what he thought about her.

She inspires so many feelings. Her generous nature stirs affection. She can trigger . . . something you might call awe. She stands alone, an independent. Defiant, tough as boots. Yet she carries a spark in her eye, a challenge to any and all. The implicit challenge there for Pádraig was to meet her halfway in invention and improvisation.

He remembered the feeling of the first jobs he did with her. Emerald Green musical director, meet Highly Experienced Choreographer. When you were functioning in an area *Not of Her Expertise,* like driving, or maybe tying two tunes together with a turning chord, it felt odd, a rare privilege. Oddly uncomfortable it felt, and exciting in an unforgivably childlike way. You would both be somehow waiting till it was time for her to switch back on.

When he was a raw musical director and Mary was the choreographer, trying to pull their respective parts of the panto together, Mary would have identified some good tunes. Better ones than Pádraig picked and listed and argued for. This process was not exactly transparent. She didn't get bogged down in meetings with people. So certain tunes might get drafted in miraculously to rehearsals. Certain grooves, certain pieces, fired her imagination. Others clearly did not.

She'd say, 'C'mon, let's try this.' And he'd go along. It would work great and save the day. And then he'd want to bitch about her later, for being so controlling. Mary was a leader. She had her caprices.

Later it was more relaxed. Mary turned out to be great company. And a bit of experience working with her showed she was human after all. A few differences of opinion arose, but these turned out to be one-day wonders. They only served to strengthen the working relationship. It was how respect was earned. It meant both parties knew the other was passionate about the work, about excellence. There was, it seemed to him, a genuine mutual esteem and regard on both sides. Mary guided you gently sometimes, brought your attention to what *she* had done. She *explained.* It was an eye-opener. Pádraig learned a lot from Mary. She was practical, could problem solve, could size up a situation fast, could build the confidence of youthful performers. And there was a genuine warmth to Mary. He liked her a lot. He felt slightly guilty that some part of him was still wary.

What was that about? Was it that he felt things could change, could turn? Was it the clique thing, always these hangers-on? Was it that she seemed proud never to have darkened the door to the Clarence or Hennigan's? Why was that? There would always be closeness and distance between him and Mary. It was kinda good, Pádraig decided.

Anyway, he knew he lived in his own quirky, homemade, rock and roll view of the world. He had internalised a manifesto grown out of the library of eighties art school (*Suspend Judgement!! Process not Product!! Be Suspicious of Technique!! Avail of Happy Accident!! Difficult Equals Good, sometimes but not all the time*). Mary's ballet school training was knowledge from a perfectly opposite angle. The classical mindset. Practise, practise, pursue excellence. She was the earth, he was the moon.

And he was well aware that this working relationship had not been harvested for all its promise. He wanted to challenge Mary more (as well as himself) to push out the boundaries, but hadn't gotten organised yet, or maybe hadn't quite mustered the courage.

It has turned out to be a rotten summer. Rain, rain, rain. There is a week of hot weather towards the end of June. The boys have got tickets for Michael Jackson's gig in the RDS. It's part of the HIS*tory* tour.

They are full of anticipation about seeing the King of Pop. Mark and Shane visit Pádraig's cottage in Rosses Point one evening to work on some ideas. Mark has some new lyrics, written in biro on foolscap.

- Baby, what do I have to do to get your love again?

He brings along a poem by a girl they know called Mary Doran. 'Always Returning' is the name of it. Maybe it could become a song. Mary is always writing, they say; she comes up with excellent words.

Songwriting sessions occupy a series of evenings in Mary's front room. Pádraig puts emphasis on phrasing, on making words sound good together. On timing, clapping on the beat, off the beat, keeping it varied, keeping it interesting. He tries that thing with taking a phrase and emphasising different syllables each time you say it.

• The way *that* girl moves. The way that *girl* moves.

Mark and Shane are quick on the uptake: they welcome new ideas, new ways. They try to improve on them. They have ideas of their own. They like to challenge everything.

Pádraig hires mics. There are different types—condensers and dynamic mics. There's a chat about microphone technique. How you get more bass out of it the nearer you get to the microphone. You can compensate for weak parts of your voice by getting real close. 'And you can move the mic away a bit if you want to go for it a bit more.' 'Yeah, we know,' says Graham, 'you bring it out like this.' They know a lot already. They have seen people do these moves in videos.

Averyl orders pizza. By now she knows the toppings by heart. The boys have another lyric with a partly completed melody. It is Mark's idea. He wants it to be funky. 'Every now and then I get a little bit cold, and I need somebody to hold me.' It is called 'Everlasting Love'. Pádraig puts chords to it. He tries to force it to be major. It is a bit R&B. The beat is faster, a good one to dance to.

But the chorus puzzles Pádraig somewhat. Mark sings:

'Cos when you need somebody till the day that you die
And (if) the everlasting love was taken away from my—Life
I couldn't tell you what I would do
'Cos I need somebody to hold me

Or at least that's how Pádraig scanned it in the end. First time he hears it, he narrows his eyes, and asks Mark to explain the words he was singing. Makes Mark repeat it a few times. The second line sounds like:

And the everlasting love was meant to always be.
Lie if I could and tell you what I would do . . .

'Can we tighten it up? Lyrics have to mean *something*,' Pádraig asserts. 'People will read them.' 'Aw,' says Mark, 'it just *feels right*.'

121

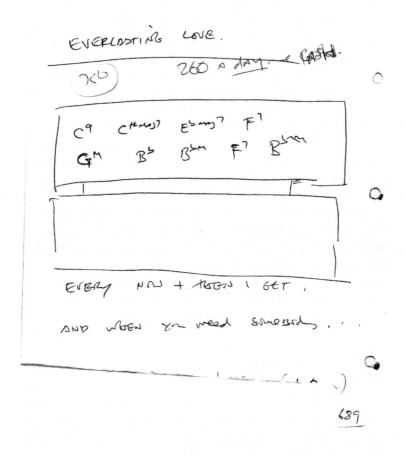

- You know you used to say it has to *feel right* . . .

Pádraig drops the subject. He is fairly happy with the finished track overall, only for wishing he had found a more definitive, a more honest, rockin' riff to hold it all together. Stronger than the dissonant funky thing he ended up doing on the guitar. (James and Pádraig treated the guitar a lot so it ended up kind of keyboardy.)

Shane alternates vocal lines with Mark. The others, at Pádraig's suggestion, do the response, as in call and response. Like in soul. Mark sings his line. The band answers. Shane sings. The band answers. It sets up a groove.

Mark and Shane are more equal in their relationship now, more equal within the band, too. They both recognise each other as IOYOU's best singers. They consult each other in almost a businesslike manner. They know they work well as a team. They complement each other. Nothing needs to be said. When you hang around with people a long time, you get an understanding. You know their next move.

Pádraig explains to the guys in the band about IMRO, the non-profit-making organisation of Irish songwriters. They protect your interests if you are a songwriter. There is a lot of money to be made if you write a hit song. And if you get your song on the radio, you are qualified to join IMRO.

Pádraig is already a member; he gives the band the handbook to take home, with all the information. 'Could we get a song played on the radio?' Pádraig asks Averyl who her contact is in the local radio station.

Averyl is going full tilt these days, too. Press releases have gone out to the *Champion* and the *Sligo Weekender*. She has Angela Campbell do another photo shoot. Brenda McArdle is designing posters and flyers and publicity material. Averyl has set up a meeting with Phillip McGarry of Equinox nightclub, and Phillip has agreed to come on board as a sponsor.

Averyl has made up a letterhead, with Streetwise on it. The letters are expanded: she goes letter, space-space-space letter. It's a spaced-out crescent, the letters grow taller in the middle of the word. Mary's phone number is below that, in smaller print.

A publicity package, including a cover letter and a press release on IOYOU, is ready to go out to business people in the area. But to

STREETWISE

PROMOTIONS COMPANY SLIGO
Telephone: 071 43025

Dear Philip,

Lowaclug

...motions Company are actively seeking a sponsor for Sligo Boys ...in effort to launch the band at a national level. ...hands material will be the vital ...and independent

Runaway

(verse 1)

If I told ya some...
listen to me
it, if u...
tell

Always Returning

Starlight, (reminding me of) your smile so bright
...me of) your love shining through
...our darkest night

By Mark Tehily

...what do I have to do, to get your love
...top

Sligo Arts Festival

I.O.U

Plus Guests • Fusion
• Baby Spice • Image
• Deep • U-16 Dancers
MERVILLE COMMUNITY
CENTRE, MAUGHERABOY
Saturday 30 May
EVENING SHOW FOR TEENAGERS
8.30PM PRICE: £4

THE SLIGO CHAMPION · Wednesday, September 10th, 1997

...ys are
...town

complete the promotion package, the band managers feel they need to give people something to listen to. 'A song on the radio? Have ye a song ready?' Averyl is enthusiastic. 'Yeah, that would be great. I'll chat to some of the lads up there.' Averyl knows a good few DJs in North West Radio. Tommy Marren says he will give her a spot, no problem.

So in early August 1997, IOYOU and their (growing) entourage crush into the small studio of the local radio station. North West Radio. NWR get a huge listenership for the local death notices. They play plenty of country and western music. DJ/proprietor Paul Claffey knows his people. He started off doing 'relief disco' to the showbands in the Casino Ballroom in Castlerea. NWR plays to the background of industry in the factories around the town of Sligo.

Tommy Marren's live interview with the boys goes out first. All over the town, sisters and friends, aunties and grannies are tuned in. Some are taping the proceedings. Averyl has prepared the questions. She and Mary watch from the room outside through the studio window. The boys are nervous but answer well.

Then, accompanied by Pádraig on acoustic guitar, they as one sing their song out proudly. 'We'll be together girl forever . . .'

PART 2: LOOK AT US NOW

THE FIRST GIG

The Hawk's Well is buzzing. Stage smoke drifting in from the wings. Piped music thumping from the public address system. The house has filled quickly. Any glimpse of the boys sets off the chorus of teenaged screamers. The screams are somehow different now, sharper and more primal, not like the 'let's scream for the lads' screams during the *Grease* interval show. There is wildness in the air. The set has a ramp. It looks mysteriously like the ramp in the last *Grease* show. Francis the carpenter has done a great job of constructing it, but when you are at the edge of the envelope doing Mary's extreme dancing routines, it can seem narrow, slippery and precarious. The rehearsals are over; the time of reckoning is near. The first gig. Backstage everyone is nervous.

Mark has his teddy and is introducing it to all and sundry.

• This is baby bear and daddy bear. And here is Mary, our manager bear.

Averyl tapes set lists on the stage monitors so the band can see them clearly. The list of songs. Pádraig and Mary—there was some consultation with the band—have plotted out the show, to make it run smoothly from song to song, and rise and fall, and finally wind up the night with a bang. Everyone came in at two thirty. For a sound check. And a technical rehearsal. The band know what encores they will do. 'Together Girl Forever' and 'Get Down'. Averyl typed them at the bottom of the set list. Averyl has sat at her word processor to script the speeches the boys are to deliver, at certain points when they have to take a breather.

She tries to calm the band guys down, even though she is excited herself. Derek does not want to do a speech. 'That's fine. Kian, can you run over your lines one more time?'

• OK. It's . . . 'Hello from all of us on stage to all of you in the audience and welcome to IOYOU's debut concert performance.'

• Shane?

• Ummm . . . I know it . . . 'We hope . . . We hope that you enjoy the show. On stage tonight we will be performing for you sixteen numbers, most of which you'll recognise as the work of other artists, but to which we have added our own IOYOU touch. We are also very excited to be bringing to you two new numbers written by ourselves later on in the show, which we very much hope you'll enjoy . . .' What's the next bit, Averyl?

• 'But right now . . .'

• 'But right now we want you to kick back and relax as Sligo boys band IOYOU slide you some grooves and moves . . .' Miggles? You are up.

• I love this. 'Awlriiiiight! How you doin', folks? I hope y'all enjoying the show. I'd like to take this opportunity to introduce you to the members of IOYOU, just in case you don't know us all. On my right is Kian, next to him is Graham, beside me we have . . .'

• OK, OK. Do the band . . .

• The band, ah, 'Hittin' the high notes and makin' life a hell of a lot easier for us tonight is Sligo's own Pádraig Meehan.' Then I do Daragh?

• Do your one. Mark? Do you know it? . . . Don't tell me you haven't learnt it?

• Course I know it. 'IOYOU have been performing for you all evening the work of other great artists; now, however, we want to present to you, for the first time ever, our own work. We will do two numbers. This first is entitled 'Together Girl Forever'. We thank

BURN BOBY BURN -- BM. (SO GOOD)

We've gotta go now (AS IS) gone

~~I'll make love to you~~ (everything)

① I'll NEVER BREAK your HEART . ___

① Just to BE CLOSE (Acapella)

TOGETHER (BOYZONE) (Seqs) → DEREK P

RELIGHT, MY FIRE + ___   IAN
                         SUONE P
                         MORE
COULD IT BE MAGIC +   GROMON

~~mmmmmmmmmmmmmm~~ (NOT TO BE done)

                         GROOM

① HERE I AM . ___

① FOREVER LOVE . ♯

① BABE . (TAKE THAT) +

① TOGETHER FOREVER . (OWN SONG)

EVERLASTING LOVE . (___)

GET DOWN . ___ (MAJOR WORLD!!)

                    KEV +
EVERYTHING CHANGES (TAKE THAT)

OPEN ARMS (MARIAH CAREY) TONE AND WAIR
                                   down

BLACKSTREET DONT (LEAVE . ✗/

you again for coming along to make this such a successful show. This . . . *the birth of a boyband!'*

- Graham?
- Well, I'm in the second half, amn't I?
- Say it anyway . . .
- 'Tonight we're gonna perform for you those numbers which helped make *Grease* the huge success it was. So get ready as we take you back to 1950s America and to the schoolyard which is . . . Ryderdale High.'
- OK, guys, you're on. Best of luck, give it *LOADS!*

The boys pad onstage and take their positions. They hold dead still, counting the bass drum beats, waiting to start their dance routine to the power chords of 'Pinball Wizard'. The vocals will be live, backed by Pádraig's guitar and the sequenced drums and samples from Daragh Connolly's machines.

'Pinball Wizard' was Pádraig's idea. He wanted to put a dynamic in the set, an explosive rock opera opening. The idea was, could we do a dance version of the *Tommy* song? He wanted it fast, at 130 beats per minute. Daragh came back saying he had done a groove for it at about 125 BPM. Any faster would be silly. Four to the floor like you wanted.

When Pádraig had first brought the tape in of The Who, the band were not at all sure about the song . . .

- It's not boyband.
- It's rock and roll.
- We don't do rock and roll.
- It will be a dance version though. The Backstreet Boys are rock and roll.
- That's different.

Kian thinks 'Pinball Wizard' is cool. Mark is not too sure. Graham doesn't like it. Derek explains patiently why sixties rock won't work for IOYOU. Even Michael is not agreeing with Pádraig. Shane has his doubts, too. Shane is listening. Then Shane says, 'Give it a chance, lads. Let's try it.'

The final version has a four to the floor techno beat, but keeps the power guitars of the original. Mary comes up with a sensational dance routine. This had to be the opening number, and Mary had a great idea—'Could we segue it straight into 'Disco Inferno', the

▲ Mark, Michael and Kian at Graduation party, 1998.

▲ Image from the front cover of the *Together Girl Forever* CD: Mark, Derek, Kian, Graham, Michael, Shane. *(Mike Bunn)*

▲ Mark Feehily at Michael Jackson's
HIStory Tour gig in the RDS, Dublin,
in Summer 1997.

▲ Shane Filan and Michael Garrett, Summer 1997.

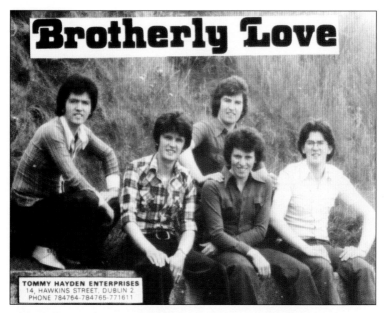

▲ Brotherly Love, from complimentary band photo, c. 1974 *(Brotherly Love)*

▲ Those Nervous Animals 1982: Cathal Hayden,
Pádraig Meehan, Eddie Lee, Barry Brennan and
Christy Behan. *(Those Nervous Animals)*

Tina Turner song?' Daragh programmes a neat segue . . .

Boom—boom—boom. The sixteenth bass drum beat sounds. The flashes go off. The teen screamers begin the clamour that will continue throughout the evening.

Ever since I was a young boy I played the silver ball . . .

Graham is enjoying being lead singer for this song, and he is making a pretty good job of it. Mark still has not learned the verse he was supposed to sing. But the gig is going brilliant. The girls in the stalls call out the names of the band. They stretch out their hands to try and touch them.

Mark blasts into 'Disco Inferno'. *Burn, baby, burn.* Shane winks, an old-time, showband wink. Where did he learn that? A girl in the front row feels he is looking at her, singing to her alone. Already something has changed in the boys. These are no longer the boys we all know from hanging around the studio. They have entered another world, dressed in their cool suits from EJ's Menswear shop. To the fans, IOYOU are stars.

Ten feet and about 1,000 miles away from the mayhem in the front row, the computer screen of Daragh Connolly's Apple Mac blinks in the corner. They have a few seats left unsold right at the front so as to make space for the music gear. Bringing his actual computer was a big deal for Daragh. He has packed his beloved Apple Mac in blankets and ferried it in the boot from his home in Offaly, all the way over the bumpy roads to Sligo. He could have simply taped the backing tracks, for the three IOYOU gigs, but he wants more control, to be able to change tempo and stop and start with the band. He rides the mouse all night.

Daragh is a grumpy old bastard but a nice guy really. He has a famous and fearsome snarl that makes no one interested in finding out what his bite is like. But he is a tireless worker and a master of knocking no-nonsense pop tunes together. He, too, has been listening to more boyband songs lately. Since Pádraig asked him to sequence the backing. He is a keyboard player and has toured with lots of bands, Johnny Logan, Dolores Keane, etc. He has plenty of stage shows behind him. Daragh has done a lot of work on sequences for this IOYOU show. Big pop snares, solid drum grooves. Mixes that suit a live gig.

There is no pit in the theatre, and the musicians have to duck to

137

keep out of sight. But they don't need to worry tonight. Daragh and Pádraig are practically invisible. The audience just hear the powerful bass and drum sounds pounding out of the PA system. All eyes are on the mesmerising movement of the boys.

Vinnie Higgins, a local sound engineer, is behind the desk. He operates the radio mics and mixes the music. At first the idea that the boys would use hand-held microphones did not entirely please Mary, who was used to choreographing dancers with two free hands.[†] At the pre-show rehearsal Vinnie had introduced another difficult problem. There are a limited number of channels available for the radio mics before they start to cause problems. 'Like *how* limited?' 'Well, five max,' says Vinnie.

- Max?
- What do we do?

There is only one thing for it; they will use one mock-up mic and five live ones.

Averyl mocks up a radio microphone with a Quix bottle and some Gaffa tape. The person with the dud mic will do a sleight of hand swap for a real one when they have to sing or speak. Miggles is unhappy. He feels he has to bear the baton of the dummy mic for too long in the set. Why does it have to be him? The managers are firm. 'Look, it's a team thing. This is the way the cookie crumbles. Just go out and do your best.' Michael is not best pleased. But in the gig he responds magnificently. Instead of sulking, he puts all his energy into his singing and dancing, dud mic or not.

Shane has a way of swaying left and right from the waist as he sings the ballads. He crouches and cradles the mic in both hands, like it's a baby bird. Any time someone takes a solo vocal they go walkabout. Mark picks up the verse from Shane. Radio mic to lips, he explores his confines like a caged tiger. Almost like a rock and roller he stalks that stage, pulling the eyes of the crowd with him. All the while, the other band members keep the smooth dance routine pumping in the background.

They drop their eyes, mock shy. What is this boyband way? It's

---

[†]   For a boyband gig, as opposed to a stage show like *Grease*, the music will be much louder, and thus you need good, close microphone contact to be heard.

men as peacocks, males as sensual objects. Standing to wait their turn to woh-oh, with wrinkled-up noses, to exchange falsetto lines with eyes raised to heaven. These lines are not about Squeezing my Lemon or Looking in Jagger's Eyes and Scoring . . . Nor peace and love, or *The Year 2525*, or any of the myriad topics tackled by pop songs of the past fifty years. These tunes have one main theme. They are about hurt and male vulnerability. They are generally addressed to the girl, pleading to her not to break this poor boy's heart, or promising never to break hers.

There are sixteen tunes in the IOYOU set. Boyzone feature, and Take That, and of course we have to do a few numbers of The Backstreet Boys. There is a killer *a capella* version of 'Just to Be Close'. 'Could It Be Magic' by Take That was listed but dropped later by Mary. So was 'I'll Make Love to You', the Boyz II Men song that started it all.

The encore is a *Grease* medley. *Grease* is not boyband; it's a bit twee now, verging on the uncool. But it's in their talk. In the words the lads use every day and take totally for granted are certain expressions; expressions they must have heard first in *Grease*. Mooning and creaming and making out. Anyway, *Grease* is home. *Grease* was at the very beginning. When Mary suggests doing a *Grease* set, everyone says, ahhh, *yeah*.

• We *have* to do it.

Mary watches Shane become Danny Zuko again for 'We Go Together'. He turns on the voice, the movement. Shane Filan as Danny Zuko as Elvis. Shane is class.

How many Dannys has Mary blocked and moved on this Hawk's Well stage? Mary's first Danny was Frank McCusker in 1986. Frank is a well-known pro actor now. Ursula Smullen—a real Fun Company stalwart—played opposite Frank in that show.

For the run in the early nineties, Joe Hunt played the male lead. Joe was a great singer. He had been a powerful lead in *West Side Story*, too. Joe was tall and dark and swarthy. He was a mean, moody Danny. Shane Filan is a cheeky, happy Danny.

We go together
Like rama lama lama
Ka dinga da ding-dong

139

Remembered forever
As shoo-bop sha wadda-wadda
Yippity boom de-boom
(Jacobs/Casey)

People linger around the foyer in the Hawk's Well after the show. There are a few little groups at the bar, chatting. The political generation.

• Were you out canvassing? Good man. You will have Dana in the Park yet . . .

The theatre crowd.

• *The Full Monty*, did ya not see it? Ahh, you *have* to . . .

The parents are at the tables. The Leaving Cert results are out a couple of weeks and the offers of college places have been arriving. There are rugby trials on. Shane Filan was invited. Pádraig says hello to the Feehilys; they greet him warmly. He shakes hands with Graham's mum. He introduces himself to Mr and Mrs Filan and joins them at their table. Mrs Filan is smiling. Peter has a Pioneer pin in, on the lapel of his suit.

• You are a Roscommon man. There's a strong Roscommon connection in this organisation.

• I am surely.

• Good country people.

• Sure, Mary's people came from Roscommon, as well . . . Tulsk.

• We are from Tulsk, you know. Well, the Filans are; Mae comes from Kiltimagh.

• That's a good one. You are only neighbours so. I'm the other side of Elphin.

• Yes, we used to live in Tulsk. Then we had a shop in Castlerea. Before we moved to Sligo. Shane was born in Sligo . . .

• There were Filans in my school in Croghan . . . I wonder are they related . . .

Shortly after the parents have finished their drink and said goodbye, the shutters come down. The bar empties fast. All the band and a few select friends are clustered round a table down the back. The lads still wearing their show suits.

It's only a short stroll from the theatre down the Lungy and over

Church Street to Mary's. A few people drive. Pizza from the Bistro Bianconi and some nice red wine is on order. Coke and other fizzy stuff for the lads. Some of the boys will be having big pints of Carlsberg later, in the nightclub. Shoulder to shoulder with the older guys.

Heavy traffic on the stairway to the loo in Mary's. Pádraig sees Michael and Shane trip past each other. The whole scene a merry tableau, so much going on all at once. In the sitting room, Derek and Graham are sharing pizza, totally unselfconscious, just lost in the moment, happy, eating, telling a story. Talking about what they'll do and say tomorrow night. Steffen the choreographer, bright-eyed, teeth flashing, is cracking up after hearing a line—a new joke? A slag? A bit of tasty gossip?—from Mary. Kian pays no heed to anyone. He is perched out on the arm of the couch, blue eyes contemplating his next mouthful of pizza.

Confucius say, you are made in a day. Getting older is not a ride on a slow escalator with well-oiled pulleys. Growing up and growing down don't happen gradually. Rather, we are taken on a series of boneshaking jumps or surges. Mushrooms, when the moon is full and dew is on the leaf and no one is watching, bloom suddenly. We mature secretly, too.

It is maybe like you are floating down a great slow flood. Things might stay the same a long time. Then all of a sudden you are sucked under by a whirlpool and find yourself surfacing in a different landscape miles and miles downstream. Or even upstream. Sometimes people get younger: they stick their heads up somewhere back up the river (you might get good news) in a different part of their life stream.

Look at your parents. One day you look at them and they are the fifties or sixties or seventies children they have always been. Then one night your father goes to bed and wakes up old. His heart is that of an old man. His movement is that of an old man. His eyes the eyes of a thousand other old men. Shane Filan will wake up tomorrow after IOYOU's Hawk's Well gig a little further downstream from the pint-sized prodigy who sang 'We Go Together' with Olwen Morgan. He will enter his day not quite a man, but definitely less of a boy.

Mary McDonagh has her chequebook out. She writes cheques for the sound system and the theatre; the various expenses that have to be paid. Averyl is collecting the suits to bring them back to the sponsors, EJ's Menswear in Castle Street. It is Averyl's negotiating skills and her persistence in writing to business people all around Sligo—and Mary's chequebook—which procured the suits and the sound system and all the trappings of stardom. 'Did we do OK on the door?' 'Yeah,' says Averyl. 'Thank God to see something coming in.'

But the boys don't notice all this unglamorous stuff behind the scenes. Manna is falling from heaven. They are on the crest of a wave. Everyone is more confident now, a bit cocky even.

SQUEAKY CLEAN

The forms from IMRO have arrived. The boys' birth certs, too. You will need those. Mary sent away for the birth certificates. Pádraig and Mary read through the agreement with the three boys. The ones who have written the songs. They could have gone the road of distributing song credits as a band, rather than as individuals. But perhaps this is the best way to do it. It will encourage those who have the initiative to write. So for the moment, Shane and Mark and Graham (who gets a credit for writing the rap on 'Everlasting Love') will join up to the Irish Music Rights Organisation.

Everyone will get to join in time. Kian and Michael and Derek also have song ideas. 'We will get around to these.' The other boys need to be reassured that they will not be left out. Pádraig encourages them. 'Just get writing. Think of words, we are going to need loads. Songs, raps, whatever. Or a tune. Even just a few notes.' Derek and Michael and Kian say OK.

When you join, you have to give details of some songs you have written and which have been performed. 'Together Girl' and 'Everlasting Love' have been played on NWR. Pádraig and Daragh will get one-twelfth credit each on both songs, for arrangements. 'Is that fair?' The guys say, 'That's OK, is that the usual?'

- That would be about right for putting shape on the song. Five twelfths each for Shane and Mark for 'Together'.
- Sound.

Pádraig says he has never had an argument with any of his co-writers in times past over authorship. Everyone knows what they have contributed. People have to trust each other.

Mark and Shane and Graham sign on the dotted line. Mary's dad, Walter, watches with a grin. He says, 'Good luck to ye, lads.' Pádraig signs the forms as a witness. Averyl and Mary and Pádraig say congratulations.

- This is a . . . another big day.
- Hopefully the first of many.
- Best of luck, boys, for a bright future.

Mary will post the forms later.

- Can *you* do it, Averyl?

Mary invites Averyl and Pádraig to stay for dinner. Afterwards, they get around to discussing the next stage in their project. They have to put out a single.

Already Averyl has put out feelers to some business people in Sligo who might help fund a promo release. She has drafted a letter to nightclub owner Phillip McGarry. She had given her draft to Pádraig and he made a few changes and gave it back to her. The estimate was that it would cost three grand to put a song out nationally. The letter listed the record companies that Streetwise would approach. Polygram. Sony. EMI. Gael Linn. BMG. Celtic Heart Beat. The sponsor, Streetwise promised, will receive brand recognition on all publicity material in relation to the band for the duration of the sponsorship deal and have their logo prominently displayed on the CD sleeve, posters for the single, posters for performances and related publicity material.

The trio brainstorm. It might be time to chat to some people in the business. People who could provide advice on how to navigate deeper into the uncharted waters of managing a boyband. They mention influential people they know. Bill Whelan? Nicky Ryan? Mary has plenty of contacts from her years in showbusiness. She might try entertainment promoter Maurice Cassidy. Averyl knows some other people, publicists who would get airplay. Some of them are more famous than the artists they plug. Mary says, 'What about Louis Walsh?' He might help. Louis is manager of Boyzone. He is the biggest pop manager in Ireland.

He must be very busy.

- It might be no harm to ring him.
- All he could say is feck off . . .
- It might be no harm.

How would he look on us, they ask. As competition or no threat? Would he help us out or . . .? 'He arranged a couple of gigs for us one time,' says Pádraig. 'I found him OK. Some people say he's a bollox. I will see can I find a number for him.'

Pádraig will start by consulting a record company who has supported Those Nervous Animals in the past; they did independent releases of music on their label, Danceline. They would know about distribution, etc.

He calls Dublin on the phone in Mary's living room. Eddie Joyce puts him on to his marketing colleague, Pete McCluskey. Otherwise known as Pete the Roz.

- Hmm . . . Interesting idea, a boyband. Not original though. How long will the craze last? It is mucking up the scene for original bands.
- Can a boyband not be original and interesting musically? Like The Backstreet Boys?
- Some are saying the boyband thing is past its peak. So you are managing them?
- Well, there are three of us.
- Something like this will not be cheap to launch. Image is vital, you know that already.
- Yeah . . . OK.
- Well, you know this has not been done yet by an indie company, because of the expense. The big companies spend a lot of money on visual shite. It is at least as important as the music. You will need a fashion photographer. A pro. There's plenty of them here. Check out the fashion houses. Not a rock and roll photographer. You will need to shoot video. Loads of video. You have to get the look of everything right, stylists, hairdressers . . .
- We have done some on that already . . .

- A video. Record the process, and you can use the footage later.
- Good graphic design . . .
- Good graphic design—you need to make the package look squeaky-clean. White is the big colour. Remember, a big section of the market for boybands are parents. Sure, get the singing and the dancing together, get the recording right, but don't forget to concentrate on the visuals.

Pete and Pádraig go on to discuss distribution and publicity. But Pete's main point is how different a boyband type product is from a rock or indie one. How visual it is.

After Pádraig hangs up the phone, he and his two Streetwise colleagues chew over the situation. The advice points towards assembling a production team, stylists and photographers. Mary and Averyl agree. They were thinking along these lines anyway. The plan has been focused and strengthened by Pete's independent opinion. The work Averyl has already done has brought her into this area. She has contacts for some photographers and stylists. We already got some video. Melissa from the dance school has shot some footage for Mary on her own camera. That video turned out to be useful for going over problems in the show, seeing where things could be improved, and getting the boys to look at themselves. To see what a lot more work there was to be done. 'A fashion photographer? Do we know anyone doing that around here?' Averyl asks Mary.

'We need a new logo,' says Pádraig. 'Do we though?' says Averyl. 'Brenda McArdle did one for us already.' The posters she designed, with Angela Campbell's photos on them, were a big help publicising the gigs. There are still a good few left. Eamonn Cunningham is one of the best sponsors; his logo is on the poster. Essential Jeanswear, EJ's Market Cross, Sligo. Brenda did up an IOYOU logo for that. Averyl sees nothing wrong with it; it is in black and white, a nice graphic.

- Yeah, the posters were fine, but the stage the band are at now calls for something different; something that can be part of the CD cover design.
- Hm.
- It's a different ballpark. It needs to be colourful, real jazzy.

Pádraig knows of a local guy who might be good: he's an exciting talent as a graphic designer. His name is Daragh Stewart. The logo will be a vital part of creating an identity, a look for the new boyband.

Danceline are not too keen on doing a single release. But Streetwise can do it themselves. Pádraig has been through this process before. All he knows is that co-ordination is everything. To do Dublin and a national release you'd need a publicist; basically you pay them to get an inside track on radio and TV and press attention. Terry O'Neill did it at one stage for the Animals. You need to co-ordinate the advertising, appearances and radio/TV play with the release date of the single.

• If it was just local, we could plug it ourselves. And, providing you put out a good pop song, and that song is well produced, and it is daytime-radio friendly, you will get plays.

'That part we can do,' declares Pádraig. 'Of course, you won't make money with a single in Ireland nowadays. It will be a loss.' 'What's new,' says Mary, wry with her cigarette. It is a promotion exercise, designed to get you in the public eye. Designed to get a buzz going. You act like you are a pop star and then maybe you'll persuade a big—read international—record company who can help make you one.

• You can be riding high in the charts and still making nothing. But it would help . . .

• How do we get to that stage?

Distribution is one thorny issue. How do you get your single into shops all around the country? There are a few independent companies doing that job now. They will have to be talked to. But the big companies have their own networks of distribution and a relationship with the shops. The Top Ten is what everyone wants to sell. But to get in the Top Ten, you have to sell. (Well, that's what they believe. You do hear ghost stories, stories of records that have achieved prominence via phantom sales. Fellas in dark corners of music shops clicking the same CD repeatedly, bands buying up their own releases in key shops. But Streetwise have no key to this magical kingdom.)

For the small company or independent band the road beckons. The best bet is persistence and patience and . . . humility. You drive around the country to the shops yourself, ask if they will put your song on the shelf on a sale-or-return basis, and give them a good poster. You need to purchase a bar code when you manufacture or you are invisible to the charts. If you can't afford a heavyweight publicist, you have to look to being picked up by one or more of the influential DJs on the radio.

It's a task akin to moving Culleenamore beach to Rosses Point, grain by grain. But there may be a slightly easier way. Pete the Roz hinted at it. What if the record company was also the shop?

• You should try the lads. They might be into it.

The Record Room is in Castle Street, a short walk from the Café Carlton. The two owners are worldly lads who throw a sceptical eye on life and death.

Kevin is a DJ. He sported one serious mullet hairdo in the eighties. He is small when he stands beside Aidan. Aidan is jovial. His long locks emphasise his wide smile. Aidan is a committed member of Sligo Field Club and is very interested in the heritage and the archaeology of the Sligo area. The lads sell CDs and tapes. Their main competitor would be Star Records in the Quinnsworth Arcade. Aidan and Kevin run another shop on Harmony Hill, the Music Room, selling instruments and accessories. And they have their own record company, Sound Records.

They have been sporadically releasing material by local artists. They put out a record by Dervish, a local trad band, a few years ago. Dervish have their own label now and have grown hugely in status. Dervish's lush rhythmic take on traditional music has brought them respect and affection worldwide.

The Record Room lads know all the distributors.

• Aidan . . . Would ye be interested in working with us on a boyband project?

PRINCESS DI

Fintan Whelan's TASTE sandwich bar has become a popular meeting spot for IOYOU. The bandmates take the high stools by the window and watch the world go by. The Harmony Hill traffic. Michael and Graham usually get on OK, but they are always messing. Mostly in an annoying kind of way. Graham feels Michael might look down on him. Michael sees pretension in Graham, and for some reason it annoys the hell out of him. 'Ah Jesus, cut it out, lads,' says Mark.

There is always some new gossip with the boys. Such and such is shagging. Well, you know what Mary says about getting anyone pregnant. Get some young wan pregnant and you are gone. Out that door.

Bareback is the buzzword. Kian likes to boast. Just loud enough to be overheard. 'I swear to God!' Michael is always over-excited. He has some wild story. No one believes him. Others keep quiet. They have only got to the first fence. They have only *shifted.* Shifting was Sligo's term for snogging or petting for an earlier generation. And for this generation, too. Geez, it is tough being eighteen in 1997.

September is the start of a busy period. Averyl has another gig organised in the Hawk's Well. Pádraig is in the Record Room again, chatting to Aidan Mannion.

•　　You came into me before with jazz stuff, obscure stuff, but this is the business, Pádraig.

Aidan likes the idea of doing a boyband single. He has already heard on the town grapevine about Mary McDonagh's new pop group. Aidan puts on a video of a local band, Indian. Sound Records are working with them.

Pádraig knows the lads in Indian. Those guys have hung in there. Martin Harte is in it, and Joe Hunt. Christy Behan used to drum with Those Nervous Animals. Martin and some of the others have been in bands since the eighties: Reverb, Absolute Zero, The Boy The Boy. They started off as post punks, now their agenda is art-rock; they have stolen some of the clothes of David Sylvian and Bryan Ferry. Even a few Lou Reed/David Bowie touches may be detected in their songs. Their punky anger has seasoned into sarcasm. They write sharp lyrics.

Indian have just done an album independently. Eddie Lee produced. It is called *Show Me That Chihuahua Again.* There is talk that the band have signed a big record deal. There have been rumours for a long time, but they are going public with this one. It is legit. It would be good for the town. The boys are gigging in Galway and Sligo.

The song in the video is called 'So Cold'. It's a damn good pop song. Joe Hunt is on lead vocals, and there is a pretty girl in it. It is beautifully shot (the pretty girl is Michelle Feeney, one of the rotating Sandys in *Grease* in the Hawk's Well).

Aidan tells Pádraig all about the young guy from Strandhill who shot the video. He is very talented, he says. Ciaran Carty. Pádraig asks Aidan to show him the video again. It won some prize or other. Jesus, this guy is good.

Pádraig brings up Ciaran Carty at the next management and band meeting. He is strongly pushing the idea of bringing in a video guy. Mary says, 'Well . . . good, if we can afford it. See what he says. Tell him we haven't much money.' The band know Ciaran.

•　　Aw, ya, Ciaran *Carty*! He goes to school with us. Yeah, he's deadly. He'll do it no problem.

•　　Can you get me a phone number for him?

- Yeah, sound.

Mary isn't really listening first, when the news comes on. What's that about Paris? Princess Diana of Wales and her companion, Dodi al Fayed, are reported to have been involved in a car crash in a Paris tunnel in the early hours of this morning.

Further reports filter through. Diana of Wales is dead. There were paparazzi chasing the car; they have been arrested. Mary feels an eerie sense of connection to Diana; there are some curious chronological coincidences in both of their lives. She thinks how strange is fate, how shadowy. Di, just at her moment of happiness, her moment of escape from her dreary palace role and her loveless marriage, is struck down. Di's death and the big news story that surrounds it affects many people, even those with no love of the British monarchy. Elton John sings 'Goodbye, England's Rose'. Shane rings Mary's bell. They both watch the cavalcade on the telly in the sitting room. The crowds in tears.

Pádraig calls to Mary's to collect Ciaran Carty's number. He'll not delay. Yes. It's here. One of the lads—maybe Mark—has written it on the back of a purple gig flyer.

- It's wild.
- Yeah, it's wild.

The summer of '97 is over. It has been a summer of longing and frustration and laughter and dreaming. Of swimming and football . . . and IOYOU. Letters have been clattering through letter boxes. Everyone reciting their post-school plan and asking '. . . and—what are *you* doing?' Michael Garrett is staying back in Summerhill to repeat his leaving. Shane will be going to Limerick to college next week, to study business management and accountancy. He has already been down there, looking for a place to stay. Shane spends the whole day in Mary's, listening to the solemn TV commentary. Shane finds the atmosphere of drama and tragedy deeply affecting. He doesn't feel like being alone.

Michael Jackson is on the telly. Talking to Barbera Walters on '20/20'. He is very sad about Diana's death. Poor Princess Di. He felt it physically; an inner pain, in his 'stomach and chest'. After he heard the news he sat alone in his room. Wondering who would be the next (famous) person to be taken. Then it came on the radio— the news that Mother Teresa had just died.

So it wasn't him. Not this time. He had known, he says, in his oddly stylised feminine voice; he had known something was coming, real soon.

Michael Jackson knows the life that the Princess of Wales suffered. He has been a star since he was five. He has gone around the world . . . 'running and hiding'. He lists the things he can't have, the simple things, the normal things. A walk in the park. A visit to a grocery store. Privacy in a toilet cubicle. Fame, it seems, has made Michael Jackson a prisoner.

Pádraig meets Ciaran in Hargadon's Pub and asks him to come on board and shoot some footage. Ciaran, by now, has just turned eighteen. He is still in school, but now he has a digital (Mini-DV) camera. It's Panasonic. He has paid £3,000 for it. The new wonder of digital recording means that £3,000 can now buy you a camcorder with image quality that up to recently would have cost £30,000.

Pádraig is new to him, but, of course, Ciaran already knows all about IOYOU and Mary McDonagh. He has already shot footage of the last Grease, on the hi-8 camera he had at that time. Michelle Feeney asked him to do it. Mary McDonagh did not know about that video, even though she had produced the show.

Anyway, Ciaran is delighted to be part of the process. He will not charge too much. He has been doing too many gigs for nowt—people always say, 'It will be good experience for ya.' Pádraig says he can introduce Ciaran to people he knows in the video business. People who have editing gear, etc.

Carty comes to the rehearsal. He has a nice style. He likes to sling the light camera from the tripod and track close to the ground. He likes to shoot on the move. Averyl suggests that he take some close-ups from the front of the stage. The boys duly oblige with extravagant poses. The camera has been there forever. Only now it is not imaginary any more.

Mark has gotten lost in one of the dance routines. Mary wants to try that part *one more time*. Kian Egan has a theory he wants to share with everyone. 'If someone goes wrong in the dances, the person after him does the same thing, so no one notices.' Mary's voice rings from the body of the theatre. Mary says, 'Not likely. You can't get six people to go wrong together. You just stick to your part, as you have learned it.' Kian blows his top and swears. Mary takes no nonsense. 'Stop it. Now start all over again.' There's a pause. Mary's gaze doesn't waver; it is a blue blast. Kian's hair drops in his eyes, a blonde shield. No one is saying anything. Kian takes his place.

Miggles is glad to start again into his talked intro to the next song . . . Afterwards he hears Shane reassure Kian. Shane knows Kian's form. Sometimes Kian comes over all tough when completely different feelings are at work deep down. He worries if he will dance right. He worries if he will come in right. He worries about being in the right place in the song.

- It will be OK. You won't go wrong once the adrenalin of the night kicks in.

BACK IN THE HAWK'S WELL

It's not a bad evening. The south-westerly on the back of your neck makes you wonder where you left last year's wool scarf. People driving cars are turning parking lights on. Our friend the sun is away already. He is positioned down behind Knocknarea, extending his fingertips above the roof of the Presbyterian chapel in Church Street. His touch underlines the high cirrus. Herringbone in salmon-pink and crimson. A jet trail is turned to gold.

If the western sky is going for drama, the southern sky is playing it cool. The moon is out, her face nearly fully lit. Pale in the pale blue she climbs. For a lazy date with a wind-torn old rain belly. Up behind the dark bell tower of Summerhill College. Today is 14 September 1997. It is a Sunday evening, eight p.m.

Car parking is hellish to find anywhere near the Hawk's Well Theatre. They are parked on the double yellow line from the Cathedral to the theatre entrance. Pedestrians squeeze between car mirrors and the wall. The ivy-topped ten-foot wall beneath the branches of the Bishop's Garden. The oak and sycamore touching fingertips with their comrades across the road in the grounds of Summerhill.

Everywhere young girls are spilling out of cars, all denim and wool and synthetic fabrics. Mobile phones, sidebags, purses, handbags, mini-backpacks. Everyone carrying something. They come in threes and fours. A girl with long blonde shiny hair shrieks in greeting when she spots her friend. They talk and laugh on their way into the foyer.

• IOYOU are playing tonight!

Amid the backstage bedlam, Ciaran Carty appears, walking backwards and shooting mini-DV footage. There are friends, hangers on, a lot of girls milling around. People all talking at once. At the centre of the storm, the production team seems to be working smoothly. Mark and Michael sit patiently in front of the mirror. Erich is doing hair. Emily the make-up. Averyl and Mary are busy streamlining the changeovers, sorting out the clothes . . .

• Ten minutes, everybody.

The suits are ready. The gear for the second half. For the first half they will wear puff jackets from EJ's.

• If we were roasting in the rehearsal, what'll the gig be like?

Derek is cool; he has his ghetto blaster on in the dressing room, just getting in the mood with some good sounds.

• Did ya see it? It's jammed out there.

The noise level soars as the boys jog onstage to that bass drum heartbeat. Positions. The Freeze. Smoke and flashes. Out stage front, Pádraig feels a tingle of fear in his tummy. There is a trick for remembering the complex acoustic guitar rhythm pattern. A chant, a set of words that have the pattern locked inside them. You say them in your mind before you have to play. After eight kicks it comes in.

Makin'-it A-live likea-But-ter-fly-a-Beehive.
Makin'-it A-live-likea-But-ter-fly-and-ev'ry-body-
Makin'-it A-live likea-But-ter-fly-a-Beehive.

Then the power chords of 'Pinball Wizard' release IOYOU into action.

The dancing is tighter tonight. Barry McKinney has one helluva lights show going. The staff in the Hawk's Well are self-consciously manning and womaning the front-of-stage bouncer positions. They make the job look a bit more dangerous and difficult than it really is, extending their arms to each other like people lost in a

155

snowstorm. But in reality, they are kept busy enough. The crowd presses forward; young women climb over seats, jump up and down excitedly. They scream.

IOYOU power through their set. There is a carnival atmosphere. Many of the kids have never seen a band play live before. It's like being in a disco, or a club, except there are six gorgeous Sligo guys singing the songs instead of a DJ playing. In a disco the music is background. Communication over it involves shouting and lipreading. You sometimes saw bands perform on TV, usually in smartly produced videos.

Audience participation at a gig is a learnt thing. You wear your part like an accessory. Whether to wiggle? To cheer or clap? Or to stay cool and just nod to the beat. It's not exactly rocket science; you watch the cool people. You get into it. Part of being a boyband fan is learning to scream until the point of crimson-faced apoplexy on sight of your favourite singer. And follow his every move. Some just take it as fun, for others it feels like life and death. Some people end up genuinely distressed. At the end, you can help get an encore if you scream and stamp feet enough to persuade them to come back and play another song.

A good few adults are in to see what's going on. The record company guys are there, and a collection of proud band parents. Ciaran Carty's camera follows the boyband around at the interval. They are mobbed by twenty or thirty juvenile autograph hunters in the foyer. They sing happy birthday in harmony for a friend. Michael Garrett's sisters are there, saying how Michael is their brother, how great the band is. Friends together, wide-eyed teenaged IOYOU fans. They tell the lens how brilliant the boys are and which one they fancy most . . .

Shane displays some of his stagecraft and maturity when he stands under the spot for his Gary Barlow turn. Next song, Mark takes over the lead. Mark's hand dips suggestively towards his crotch as he dances. He is in full flow. Sounding strong. Everybody is doing well tonight.

The romantic bit by Kian, after the break, brings the house down.

• OK. I think we're all feelin' a little romantic up here on stage. You don't mind, do yeh? Does anyone feel like gettin' a little bit romantic? Yeah?

ACT 1

1	PINBALL WIZARD
2	BURN BABY BURN (DISCO INFERNO)
	Speech 1
3	WE'VE GOT IT GOIN ON
	Speech 2
4	I'LL NEVER BREAK YOUR HEART
5	OPEN ARMS
6	BABE
	Speech 3a
7	TOGETHER
8	GET DOWN

INTERVAL

ACT 2

1	RELIGHT MY FIRE
2	JUST TO BE CLOSE TO YOU
	Speech 3b
3	EVERYTHING CHANGES
	Speech 4
4	TOGETHER GIRL FOREVER
5	FOREVER LOVE
6	EVERLASTING LOVE
	Speech 5
7	WE GO TOGETHER
8	SANDY
9	GREASE LIGHTEN

157

- YEAH!
- OK, I think we're gonna need a little bit of help. First of all, how about a little romantic lighting—

Cue romantic lighting.

- Yeah, now how about a little *add*mosphere?

Cue smoke machine.

- And finally, let's hear a little bit of that real romantic music—does anyone . . . anyone feel like dancin'? Oww-yeeeeah. Oh baby, let's dooo it!

Truth be told, Kian is short on confidence about his singing voice. He gets by on his looks and bravado attitude, but if he *thinks* about what he is doing, while he is singing, he goes out of tune. He feels there are critics down there, waiting for him to go wrong. Lots of the audience are in bands themselves. After his song, Kian sucks in air. Mary was right. Averyl was right, her little script worked great. Shane was right. Kian has pulled it off. It worked. Just about. It is a good feeling when something works.

These days there are boybands and girlbands sprouting up all over the place in Sligo. One band, which started even before IOYOU, was Fusion, the all-girl band.

One day in the Factory rehearsal room—in October sometime—Mary invites Pádraig to step into the line and do the dance. Shane is away in Limerick, leaving a gap in the chorus. 'Try it, Pádraig.' It is just a spur of the moment thing.

- Just for the *craic*.

Pádraig declines. Nah. He is not good at remembering steps. Free dancing might be more his style, more comfortable for him. That split second makes him feel stiff, jacketed. Going out the road that evening, Pádraig says to the steering wheel, 'It's too long since I danced.'

- I used to dance at the drop of a hat.

The generation before Pádraig's, say three to five years older, were the Non Verbals. Pádraig's were the Talkers. The glam rock crowd, they learned the words of songs, thought they were some kind of intellectuals, or the tellers of secrets. They reckoned that all that was required to solve the world's problems and arrest every romantic landslide was a good heart-to-heart, one-on-one, between the players. Let's take a few days and have a chat about it. Tease out every knot till all concerned agree they feel thoroughly *understood.*

When you dance, you have no name. You confront the non-verbal on the dancefloor. The one Pádraig thought of as The Aboriginal used to dance. He turned and advanced. Don't lose eye contact, don't shrink, don't lie. The arm, fingers extended, offered. Pulled away then, the palm turned down, turned through 360 till upturned again, the shoulder pressing into his cheek from the torsion. Then the arm circling and backing away . . . Twisted by the arm's retreat, the body made to turn, forced to go, the eye still held. The upturned palm still giving to you, elbow lifted, like you were a mind-over-matter judo bouncer or school bully, twisting the arm of The Aboriginal against the joint. But this was only a dance, a swim dance, a swim through the treacle of the world, through the tinniness of the evening. Then he was gone, off in another current, nothing except a smile left to you. Turning to someone else . . . to take them by the hand . . . A man unafraid in embrace. We are music.

•   Jesus, what time is it? I have to go home, I have to get up in the morning.

'I have to, I have to,' mocked The Aboriginal.

•   The party is about four miles out. I know two of the people, and *she's* coming, and she has . . . Hey, Louise . . . *You have room for one more?* Pádraig, get some six-packs off Terry and bring the guitar. Come on. Get in.

Go with the flow. The Aboriginal had looseness, such ease with the prevailing wind you would be working hard not to feel stiff-shouldered, jacketed, old-before-your-time. A bohemian in conservative shoes? But he would never give up on you. He would invite you to take chances with him, he would listen to your songs, would be the audience always, sometimes the actor, yet never the judge.

The Aboriginal trusted his intuition, his femininity, his blood. He knew nothing was understood. He didn't bother with talking about feelings. He swam in them. This person seemed to live devoid of an invisible audience, seemed to have conquered the craving to please. He made people uncomfortable sometimes, by vibing and staring them out of it and refusing to play along with small talk or parachute jokes. He skipped the formulae. He asked for what he

159

wanted, with minimal verbals. Naturally women loved him and he loved them naturally, loved them right back.

'Don't talk so much,' Pádraig told himself.

• Keep free-dancing. Maybe something of The Aboriginal will enter my soul.

After that Pádraig danced any time the music moved him, he danced at the drop of a hat.

IOYOU have been to check out a rehearsal of Fusion. They are good friends with the girls. Most of the Fusion members are veterans of Mary McDonagh's classes, and all played some part in the '96 Grease. Avril and Gillian were even in the '93 one; they were Angels, while Shane and Olwen Morgan were doing their duet. Gillian had been in Annie, too, and Frenchie in both Greases. The Ursuline/Summerhill Grease and the Hawk's Well Grease. Now the girls in the band have sussed out St Anne's Youth Club to rehearse in. The room sounds a bit hollow and echoey, but there's lots of space. They have some good dance routines. They made them up themselves. Avril O'Hanlon has a lot of dance ideas. She is into street dance, loves the Michael Jackson style. Has done since she was seven or eight. She looks great, good body, strong attractive features and long dark hair. Avril has a friendly, open face.

Their dancing gave Fusion a great run in the All-Ireland Disco Dancing Championship in 1996. They won the heats in St Anne's in Sligo, then won the regional finals. They travelled up to Maynooth for the national final, and won there, too. They had PVC catsuits made up specially by a dressmaker. It was Avril's idea. She wanted silver rings for the belts. They looked high and low for them and eventually improvised rings from some cutlery thingy. There were a few begrudgers who said here come the Bin Liners, but the girls took no notice. The PVC looked great and was easy to move in.

The four friends were serious about the dancing. They saw themselves as a dance group. At the beginning, singing was secondary for the Fusion girls. The singing was maybe the next step. Even writing songs. Avril had already tried writing songs but had not presented them yet to the other girls.

The girls in Fusion have worked hard on their moves, and all are strong, ambitious characters. Yet Fusion have never once talked about looking for a manager or recording a demo. They don't know any managers. They are only sixteen or seventeen. But one thing is sure; they are going to enter the All-Ireland Dance Championships again next year. It was such a thrill to win last year, they saw so many other talented acts. There is a crowd of girls from Sligo called The Hill who are brilliant.

The different ends of the town, they don't mix all that much, except maybe in competitions. There are different youth clubs. They have their own football teams, bands, different youth leaders with different approaches. St Anne's serves Cranmore, giving the large young population an outlet. They are setting up a music centre in the Youth Centre. They are doing up the place and will provide recording and music training in the centre. They want to tap into all this funding that is coming on stream, Peace and Reconciliation, Leader, the Council. They are serving real needs. Cranmore is a seventies estate, an unplanned mess of houses to the west of the town, bordering the Dublin road. And facilities like these would be used by kids from all over the town and tie into some of the other youth clubs.

The Hill is a working class area of the town. A couple of young guys from up the Hill were starting a rock band around the same time Fusion started out. Jonathan in the pub, in The Weir, was giving them a few Sunday nights. The band was called Petronella. They were total independents. Trevor 'Tabby' Callaghan was lead singer and guitarist. His brother Dominic was in it, playing bass. Tabby had a great image and was hugely ambitious—a gas character. He landed over to St Anne's one day to see if they had some recording gear. Tabby had a few ideas he wanted to lay down. He was writing his own songs and playing guitar like Jimi Hendrix. Tabby and the Petronella lads were all into managers and funky hairdos and musicbiz jargon.

But for Fusion, it was just themselves. And the supportive people in St Anne's: Sr Pamela, Georgie Gorman, Frankie Langan, a lady called Anne O'Donnell with red hair. St Anne's hired the minibus for them when they had to travel, gave them a space to practise in when they could, sorted out everything.

When the IOYOU lads stroll into Fusion's rehearsal it is all very 'Good stuff, girls.'

- Good stuff, guys. How's it going for ye?

• Not bad.

The fellas out of the boyband have always supported the girls in Fusion. Going to the competitions, to the heats and all, to cheer them on. The boys mess around, posing for Ciaran Carty's camera, trying on the girls' costumes. Fusion is a four-piece. They are trying to get the attitude right—girl power attitude, like the Spice Girls. Besides Avril O'Hanlon, there is Sabrina Kiernan, Helena Heraghty and Gillian Walsh. Gillian is just great for instilling confidence in the others. They might be a bit nervous, but she would say, 'Let's get out there and *kick ass*, girls.'

The shadows are grown longer in the evenings. The light slices in at a deep raking angle, marking out the form of the land. Jaundiced autumn light, filtering through leaves. A damp smell of autumn, of rotting, fills the forest, the now-damp forest. Mushrooms flourish there. Droplets of moisture describe spider webs. The trees are still dressed up in their leaf cover, but the foliage has changed colour, fading from green to brown. Dark sickly patches have appeared on the sycamore leaves. The sky is big. It extends beyond the horizon, bearing great weather fronts in from the Atlantic on their way to England and Europe. It's dark by nine. Night is longer than day now. Morning finds Rathedmond streetlit, blinking. Needing breakfast. By seven a.m. light is filling the windows.

• At last.

His long night of tossing and turning must be coming to an end. Michael Garrett tries to calm himself down. A lot is going on for him. His heart is beating too fast. He feels the power, the awe of his life, the weight of what has been going down, *what might happen.* Michael Garrett's decision to repeat his Leaving Cert was a difficult one. Now he is back among the younger fellas from the year behind him. Trying to concentrate on English and Irish and maths. The same old problems.

Shane seems to be doing allright in college in Limerick. Management/accountancy is not too bad, so far. There are a few beauts in the class. Michael has kept his promise to keep Shane in touch with what is going on in Sligo. He has been on the phone to him regularly, telling him about rehearsals, meetings, etc. Anyway, Shane is only there four days of the week; he doesn't have classes of a Friday. Both boys are determined of one thing: nothing will get in the way of IOYOU. Our band. Shane is staying up home over Sunday night specially for the session in James Blen's studio. Everyone stayed at home yesterday. Had Sunday lunch, watched a bit of the football on the telly. Such a scrap. Kerry and Mayo in the All-Ireland Final. The two friends had a good chat after teatime. About being ready, about giving it everything, about how recording is forever, and how you can fix things in the studio if you make a mistake. Shane is not focused on mistakes. He knows it will work out fine.

- We record our song today.

THE CONTRACT

As James and Pádraig are putting down their final mixes of 'Together Girl', Mary drops in to hear the mix and see James's studio—Averyl is shuttling between word processor and phone. She has booked more gigs. Her priority now is marshalling support in the press and in the business community. And Averyl is brilliant. Averyl phones up and gets their attention right away. Everyone gets a great laugh out of it.

- We have something to sell to you that you'll be interested in, I know.
- What is that?
- Sex. We are selling sex.

Pádraig goes into James's and does a backing track mix for 'Pinball' for appearances and gigs that he won't be playing at. It has the power chords of the intro played on his trusty old Marchis Fender Strat copy. And the acoustic playing the hectic pattern of Sus Four chords.

The Marchis was one of Pádraig's great discoveries. He had spotted it in the window of Sean Allen's shop in Bridge Street. Liam 'Speedy' Farrell, who was working for Sean in 1980, sold it to him for £95. Pádraig put down £20 and his dad gave him most of the rest. The neck was one of the nicest you'd ever come across on a guitar, with beautiful action, and though the machine heads were a mix of different breeds and no breeds at all, they held tune. Pádraig played gauge ten strings, for funkiness. Later on Willie MacWhirter set the guitar up for him, replacing the original miniature controls of the Marchis and putting in Fender ones and installing EMG pickups, and active tone control. There was a hole for the battery in the back and a screw-in plate. Willie hated doing that to the guitar but Pádraig insisted.

Mary has the fashion photographer suggested by Danceline sussed. She has contacted Mike Bunn. Mike is a world-renowned fashion photographer; he has shot all the cool people, all the models. He has published a book of photographs of the Sligo landscape. Now he lives near Sligo. Mary knows someone who knows him. He has promised to help.

Shane has his back to the fireplace in Mary's sitting room. One hand up on the mantelpiece. The couch is full. Kian sits on the floor.

Mary is saying, 'We will have to get a contract organised between us and ye, a management contract.' Michael is saying, 'We trust ye, Mary'. Michael is as earnest as ever, but Shane has the conch. He stands at the fireplace.

• What do ye expect us to do? Go off with Louis Walsh?

And everyone agrees that is the one thing they would never consider doing. Shane especially. 'Jesus, guys, we would *never do that.*' 'No,' says Mary, 'but we need something.' It will be a standard contract. 'Just a piece of paper that shows we have a deal,' says Pádraig. He had felt uncomfortable about the contract thing when James asked about it in the studio. It was like a little nag in the back of his mind. His two female partners had seemed fairly nonchalant about it, when he mentioned a contract first, shortly after the band were named IOYOU. But in the last week or so Averyl has been on the phone to a top legal firm in Dublin, Matheson Ormsby Prentice.

'Hopefully we will never even need to look at it,' says Mary. 'But it protects you and it protects us.' 'When are we getting it?' ask the boys.

Averyl drives. She skilfully finds a parking space, feeds the meter. The girls spruce themselves up for the meeting. Mary and Averyl and Pádraig are in Dublin to meet the solicitor from Matheson Ormsby Prentice. 'What is her name again, Averyl?' 'Ruth. Ruth Hunter.' They sit nervously in the waiting room. It is like waiting for the dentist. Ruth is nice but a bit chilly, an impassive professional. They hear themselves telling their story. It seems so strange to explain their great adventure in these comfortable chambers.

'As two of the boys, Kian and Mark, are not yet eighteen, could their parents sign a contract on their behalf?' 'Yes, the parents could sign.' Yes, she will prepare a draft contract and send it on to Averyl. The managers stop in Mullingar for some food on the way home.

Small monsters are abroad in horrid masks. The real beginning of winter. Samhain. 'Half-nine at my place, boss.' James Blennerhasset reminds Pádraig to wind his clock back, you'll have an extra hour in the scratcher. Pádraig complains about the stolen hour of daytime.

- See ya in the mornin'.

The morning is foggy. A dusting of white on car windows, one of the first frosts of the season. The road north is narrow and winding. They cross the border at Belcoo. There is a customs post and fortified drab military towers, but no one seems to be around.

As Pádraig, James and Robyn Robins are in Enniskillen working on 'Together Girl Forever', Averyl meets photographer Mike Bunn in the Tower Hotel in Sligo. Mike is a tall fortysomething, sporting sideburns and long hair. He talks the talk. Mike has a lot of experience in the business of music and fashion. He has a sharp eye and a soothing voice.

Mike agrees to do a shoot of the boys for the CD sleeve: he is enthusiastic about the band idea; he will do a photo session for a special price. The management supply the set. Indoors or outdoors were both possible; depends what you want. Perhaps indoors would be best. A big room. Mike thinks the Model Arts Centre would be a good spot.

LOVE NOTES

After the open-air gig in Quinnsworth car park, packs of fans linger outside Mary's house for a glimpse of the boys. The gig has been a resounding success. But Mary had to have been a small bit horrified when she first set eyes on the trailer that would serve as a stage. It was a postage stamp of a stage, with four ugly pillars to the front and a canvas back. No protection at the edge.

•	Don't dance near the edge.

A second covered trailer held the public address gear. The Guards were in position. In consultation with the Chamber of Commerce, who were running the gig to promote the Sligo Shopping Spree, and Averyl Dooher of Streetwise, the Gardaí had planned the logistics at street level. All but one entrance to the park was sealed off. The stage/trailer was protected by a cordon of barriers, manned by police. From the rear of the trailer a passage of barriers led to a rear entrance of Quinnsworth supermarket. The dressing room would be the upstairs part of the supermarket, the sliding doors lifted to let in the band and management and support personnel. No fans past this point.

The boys had to start signing autographs soon after they arrived. The sky had been grey all this Sunday evening. Now it is dark. It is 2 November; someone let off a couple of Halloween bangers up the Pearse Road earlier on. But a happy and expectant atmosphere prevails in the Quinnsworth car park as the crowd begins to gather. An hour before the gig and the rain is still holding off.

Girls have been sending love notes up to the boyband members. Averyl wants to read them. '*Ohmygod!* The youth of today.' Daragh Connolly had been through a few dramas of his own. He has driven from Offaly and in his hurry forgotten the backing tracks. Now he is trying to sort out the situation: phoning, driving here and there like a lunatic; all the while the nervous band managers are pacing the car park. When he gets to the gig with the stuff, in time only by the skin of his teeth, emotions are brittle. Averyl and Daragh have a ratty exchange. Averyl is in tears. She has been under pressure organising everything—the clothes, Vinnie the soundman, meeting with the Chamber of Commerce, and the Guards, even getting in another radio spot on NWR—and now Daragh is shouting at her. Pádraig does shuttle diplomacy between Averyl and Daragh.

James Blen has come to see what IOYOU are like live. He has helped Daragh get the backing tracks into the right format for the gig. His cheery smile is infectious. The crowd is bigger now. People are selecting their viewing spots. Front row people are threading their way forward and excusing themselves. Small people are getting on big people's shoulders. The Guards between the fans and the stage are doing a great job. The autograph hunters and screamers are held back by the long arm of a good-humoured Garda. A female officer looks on, bemused. She has witnessed nothing quite like this in Sligo.

By now the boys are troupers. They soldier through slight PA difficulties, the horrible pillars on the trailer, and the tiny space to dance in. They actually manage to fit their routines on that trailer. It drizzles but doesn't rain really. The drizzle scatters a haze around the lights, orange street lights, and Vinnie's white and coloured stage lamps. The crowd keep clapping for ages after IOYOU go off. After the gig everyone runs down the tunnel and assembles in the stacked aisles of the supermarket.

It is kinda spooky to be in this place without staff or customers.

Averyl is messing. Mary gives the orders. 'Don't touch anything! That applies to you, too, Averyl,' she says, in a mock cross-teacher voice. 'What a manager!'

The boys are wired. '*Whew! Yesssss. IOYOU!*' shouts Shane. Kian Egan lurches in, shiny-faced with rain and sweat and looking for a towel. '*What do you t'ink of daat?*' demands Kian, of Ciaran Carty's camera.

This has been the biggest rush so far. How many were out there? 2,000? It looked like a helluva lot of people. The kids mobbed them at the end. Averyl sneaks most of the group back under cover to Mary's house. Pádraig lingers by the trailer, the sound guys packing up in the rain.

James Blen has a word. He really likes yer man Graham Keighron. 'He's a performer.' Yeah, he's good.

•   I think he's excellent. He really gets into the raps, doesn't he?

Speak of the devil. Graham stops briefly as he passes by Pádraig. Graham has his hands in his pockets.

•   That was deadly. These are the times. We'll probably look back on this . . .

Pádraig has a drink with some of the Chamber of Commerce people in the Adelaide. It's packed. 'They are great lads, fair play to you, fair play to Mary McDonagh. Great idea, a boyband,' says a bald man in a suit.

Back in Mary's later everyone has gathered to watch Ciaran Carty's video footage of the gig and try to wind down. Ciaran crouches by the TV and twiddles with the SCART lead, running playback from the camera. A blank screen. It's never straightforward. Derek knows what channel is for the video.

Camera with a light on, camera on the move. Wet streets, streaks, trails of fiery shop windows. View from behind, catching up with hurrying legs. Fast forward. Puppet people at ludicrous speed, then suddenly normal again, striding abreast of the group, Mary and Averyl purposeful, their camera faces on, carrying stuff. Kian walking near, in the light, smiling, some bag or something in his hand. His head bobs in and out of frame. He has turned to face the light. 'What did he say? What was that word?' asks Ciaran, aiming the remote control. Kian stops, goes into high-speed reverse, back past the frame where his head disappears, hot patches of puff jacket, something in his hand. Kian turns to the light.

- Nervous!

Make him say it again.

- Nervous!

Everyone cracks up. Fast forward again, people filling the car park like ants.

Jump cut to interior of shopping centre. Rows of cereal. Pre-gig. Everyone is looking for themselves. Pádraig going over the count-ins, Mary talking through the changes. The band members attentive. Then Kian and Graham are giving little pep talks.

- Let's give it our best, we can do it, c'mon lads.

It was Shane who started it, long ago; the little talks thing. And now he always does it. So how come it's *Graham* leading the pre-gig ritual, pulling in everyone tight, pulling everyone together, giving words of encouragement, a football coach before the match. Michael has a contribution, too. Everyone is doing it tonight. Graham squirms slightly as he watches himself.

- Shane is going to start now.

Shane's voice has the most weight . . . Shane speaks to the group, tells them to smile, tells them how to cover up if you make a mistake in your steps. When Shane says it will be OK, the other boys believe him.

The camera on the hoof again. A rush dizzily to the back of the stage, just in time to see Mark announce the band in his American Announcer voice. They are climbing up a ladder. It's very dark. 'Careful,' says Mary, and the picture lurches, goes scrambling to the front of the trailer like a fan to see the band burst onstage to a chorus of screams. Tiredness hits Shane of a sudden. He is heading off home.

- See ya, Shane.
- See ye.
- Ya can watch the whole thing on video later.

THE SHOOT

A week exactly after the Chamber of Commerce gig is the day of the photo shoot. The Model Arts Centre is an imposing and venerable stone building overlooking the Mall from atop a sloping green. Averyl has succeeded in getting permission to use it as a location. Streetwise will combine a shoot for a 'Together Girl Forever' video with the stills shoot by Mike Bunn.

Crows circle in treetops. A flight of steps up to a big red door. Everyone arrives more or less at once at half-past ten in the morning. Mike has brought along his understudy James Connolly to help out and load film. James is an up-and-coming young photographer. In the past, he has found some models for Mike. Averyl rings Mary. 'Yes, everyone is here. Ciaran is on the way. We will see you later . . . Wait till you see Mike. I told you, he is *gorgeous!*'

Mike looks at different rooms. They settle on a downstairs one. The morning is spent building a set. Ciaran Carty arrives and helps Pádraig tie up the ancient hanging UV light fittings by their dusty chains and to tidy the room. The virginal white boyband heaven is constructed from large rolls of newsprint, any gaps are filled in with sheets of Styrofoam. The whole structure is propped up at the back with a timber frame. The cameras stare in from the front; from the outside world of lamps and stands and gantries and reflective umbrellas. The long process of lighting the set begins.

The boys wait upstairs. Averyl and Emily bring tea and sandwiches. The band members roam past an exhibition of curious organic sculptures, the work of Cork artist Marie Foley. They are wearing their sharp black EJ's Menswear suits. White shirts. Averyl and Mike have agreed the colour scheme. Mary and Pádraig select an upstairs room, with delicate natural light streaming through low arched windows. Here they will do lip synch takes of 'Together Girl Forever'. This can be edited together with the CD to make a polished pop video.

The creaking floorboards. The floors are of ancient timber. The boards are cut to many different lengths, and every footfall sounds different; every fourth or fifth board yields a bit and utters a long, tortured note. Shane prowls around the large room like a Tai Chi master, listening to his echoing steps.

Averyl has brought along a ghetto blaster. The song plays in the room, the recordable CD from Robyn Robbins, and Mary puts the band through a few dance routines. Ciaran Carty moves between the dancers, shooting close-ups and tracking shots. Ciaran notices late in the shoot that the on-camera mic was not switched on. It would have been a useful guide for tying the images to the sound of the CD. He apologises to Pádraig and puts it on belatedly. Now it's working. Pádraig says, 'Not a problem. We can synch up in the editing suite, without the camera sound.' 'Yeah,' says Ciaran, 'it should be OK.'

During a break, Shane, who is growing to love the camera, continues his video diary style delivery. 'So here we are at the Model Arts Centre, doing our photo shoot for our new song,' Shane proudly announces. 'And over there is Mary, Averyl and Pádraig, our managers.'

The boys are tired and jumpy by the time they are called on to the set for the stills shoot. Their edginess is understandable. They have been five hours waiting around. It is three in the afternoon. Mary says this is the job. This is what it's like. You have to be good at hanging around, waiting endlessly and then turning on the performance like a tap. This is one of the major skills of the job. Actors have it, too. The boys are still impatient. Five hours getting ready to take a photograph does not compute. They keep peeping around the corner to see what is going on. 'Could it be . . . could the fashion shoot be *done without us*? Ha, ha.' 'No. Relax. It is just that Mike is fussy about the light. It has to be perfect.'

Jobst, the Arts Centre boss man, suddenly arrives and is not one bit happy with the number of rooms Streetwise have been shooting in. One space had been specified. Averyl goes into diplomatic mode.

Mike Bunn calls in the band. They mumble a bit. Then they walk into wonderland. *Click-bang! Click-bang!* It's hard on the eyes. Erich Conlon is kept on his toes powdering away shines and imperfections in the eager faces. Mike has a patter to keep everyone focused. He shoots a series of individual shots. Graham looks great. Mark looks moody. Shane fumbles with the chair. He switches on his smile. He seems a bit uncomfortable on his own. He is the natural band leader, but he likes the other lads to be around him. When the boys pose together, Ciaran notices stuff. Derek is never to the front. Shane always is. They seem to instinctively take up formation, like a flight of geese or fighter aircraft, everyone knowing his spot. The three to the front are usually Shane, Mark and Kian. Behind that, sometimes nudging into the front, is Graham or Miggles. No one seems to notice it but Ciaran, and he doesn't think long about it. He just registers the thought and files it away. Hmmm. Interesting.

Towards the end of the shoot, someone suggests that Mary should sit in for a picture with the boys. She has on her white Aran sweater. Erich powders her nose. 'Is this for the kitchen wall?' Averyl asks. 'The mammy shot!' jokes Mary. She looks great, in the middle of 'her' boys. But Mike is out of film. James Connolly shoots the picture on 35 mm. 'Great,' says Mike, 'let's wrap up.' It is nine in the evening. It has been a long day.

• Hargadon's for a pint?

In another room in the Model Arts Centre building, Daragh Stewart is producing a number of IOYOU logo ideas. Pádraig is delighted with having made the connection with Daragh. He is a real talent. A tall young man with long, dark, rakish hair, he works unearthly hours in his den in the Model Arts. He stares into a 14-inch Power Mac computer screen and clicks and clicks. Then he sends off a file and the results come back from the printer by post. He holds his masterwork up to the window to see the colours in the daylight. He did a great fold-out CD sleeve for Dervish's live album.

YOUR OWN PEN

Averyl comes hurrying over to Mary's at lunchtime. She will be meeting Mike Bunn later. Mary writes a cheque for Mike and gives it to Averyl. 'The management contract has come back from Ruth,' says Averyl. 'I faxed her all the info on the ages of everyone, addresses and all that stuff.'

That afternoon—it's Wednesday, 12 November—Averyl meets with Mike Bunn and pays him for the photo session. She sets up a meeting for two days time between Mike and Streetwise, plus Daragh Stewart, the graphic designer, and Aidan from Sound Records. They will be choosing the best photo for the CD sleeve. The venue for the meeting is the foyer of the Tower Hotel.

Later that evening, Mary and Averyl and Pádraig look over the management contract. It seems OK. There's a lot of legalese and gobbledygook. They make seven copies of the draft contract on the photocopier next door in Conway's Shop and leave them beside the computer in Mary's for the boys to collect next time they come in. Pádraig has collected four printouts of Daragh's suggestions for the logo at the Model Arts earlier. The pages pass between them, the three look over each in turn, and they settle on one. Yeah. That's fine.

It's a great graphic, IOYOU, clean and strong and a bit different. Daragh has retained some of the elements of Brenda's original logo.

Averyl has written and posted a letter to Jim Gray in the *Sligo Champion*. Yeah, Jim'll print it, no problem.

STREETWISE PROMOTIONS SLIGO
TO: Jim Gray
FROM: Averyl Dooher
DATE: 01/12/97
IOYOU SINGLE LAUNCH

The name on everyone's lips this festive season is IOYOU. The Sligo boys band are pleased to announce the launch of their debut single next Saturday afternoon 13 December at 3.00 p.m. in The Record Room, Sligo where you will also be able to pick up a copy of the boys' single. But be warned. Bring your own pen if you want the boys to autograph them for you.
The boy's debut single contains two tracks, both of which have been composed by the band themselves. The title track of their single is 'TOGETHER GIRL FOREVER', which is already proving extremely popular with the Sligo ladies. Also featured on the single is 'EVERLASTING LOVE', a catchy dance tune which is sure to get you off your seat and on to the floor in all the nightclubs this Christmas.
Make sure not to miss this momentous occasion, when Sligo's first boys band celebrate in style on the 13 December in Sligo town . . . Will you be there?

When the paper comes out, Averyl notices that the *Champion* edited out the 'your own pen' line.

Two meetings take place around Monday, 17 November. The photo-choosing meeting in the Tower Hotel, Quay Street, is in the afternoon. Deciding on the best photograph turns out to be easy enough. Most people agree on Mike's choice. It's useful that Daragh Stewart and Mike are now in direct contact.

That Wednesday the Streetwise partners head to an evening rendezvous with Aidan Mannion and Kevin Flannery of Sound Records, upstairs in the Journeyman Bar. Mary and Averyl and

Pádraig talk first over in Mary's. They will approach the meeting positively, but with clear ideas in mind. The Record Room guys arrive six or seven minutes late. They skip the small talk.

- Have we a deal?
- Well, we think so, but . . .

Sound Records will not be representing the band to the record companies, as they have been proposing. That was never a runner. Streetwise already have a plan for that. But the other ideas all sound good.

The light is low in the upstairs part of the Journeyman. Mary notices that they serve pizzas in here, too. The manager behind the bar is afraid of the weekend bands they have, of them being too loud, so he keeps the power amps for the wee PA beside him in there. That way the bands can't get at them. The space assigned as the bandstand is a cot, or nearly as confined, fenced off with wooden railings. It's just beside the bar, at the top of the stairs. A table has been put out there for the evening time. The five sit on high stools.

'We want to go ahead with ye,' says Kevin. 'There has to be give and take,' says Aidan. 'There's not much in it for us.' 'Well, obviously, we need to get the song released and distributed,' says Averyl Dooher, her bottom lip steering her cigarette smoke up past her nose.

- With a single out, the press, the radio play, the bit of publicity will set things up nicely for a showcase for the record companies in Dublin, or maybe even here in Sligo.

Aidan Mannion tilts his head sideways and looks at Averyl, swivels his chin on his knuckles.

- Or mebbe *both?*

The parties agree a deal. Streetwise will own the images, graphics, etc. Sound Records will own the CD masters of the Doghaus recordings. This clears the way for the record company to release the song. The plan is that—for now—it will just be a north-west Ireland release.

Before the weekend deadline, Daragh Stewart has his draft CD cover design ready for approval by Streetwise and Sound Records. His first ideas look quite appealing visually, a white/maroon thing going on. There is some white space left in, some air. It's classy. But

Aidan Mannion of the Record Room has some interesting observations. 'If they are in a rack, will the name be visible? Are the boys' faces big enough on the design?' Back to the drawing board. Daragh has done stylish work on the inside sleeve using Mike's individual shots of the boys. 'We will keep that.'

Pádraig is relieved when Daragh Stewart's redrafted design meets with everyone's approval. It's going to be a polished and professional product, one to be proud of, and no doubt about it.

On 29 November, the IOYOU boys join in singing carols around town for the charity organisation Concern. A photo of them singing with other volunteers is printed on the front page of the *Sligo Champion*.

On the day before the official launch, much to Sound Records' (and everyone's) relief, the CDs arrive, packed in cardboard boxes, with Trend Studios, Dublin, on the label. Aidan Mannion comes up to Mary's with a few copies in the afternoon.

Mary turns the finished product over in her hands. The cover design is great. Mike Bunn's photos of the boys are class. She feels a flush of pride. It looks like money was spent on it, like it was done right. Everyone is impressed. The band loves it. Pádraig looks for his name. 'There I am, producer and co-writer and guitar player, too.' *Sun CD 16.*

Mary McDonagh doesn't have to travel far for the official launch of IOYOU's new single. The Innisfree Hotel stands just across the road from her house. Gerry, the owner, was delighted to oblige. The date is Friday, 5 December. The Record Room people are in position early, with their boxes of CDs. So are a healthy crowd of fans, queued up outside the nightclub doors. There is a small core of Loyal Old Fans, who saw the first Hawk's Well gigs, and maybe even *Grease*; the rest are newbies, lower down the order, most of them only just *heard* of IOYOU last week.

Upstairs, the boys lounge in the hotel room. Emily McEvoy, Mary's assistant, interviews the band in front of Ciaran Carty's lens. Graham tells Emily how it all started . . . We were in *Grease* together . . . we were asked to do a boyband act at half-time . . . We were Six As One, and then we were approached, we got management. Look at us now. About to launch our first single! We will be lighting the Christmas lights in Sligo.

- Where do you see yourselves in a year's time?
- Well, we want to be famous. Hopefully it will happen for us. We want to meet The Backstreet Boys. And Michael Jackson.

'Michael Jackson. I want to shake that man's hand,' Miggles tells Emily. Shane makes space on the bed for Michael. Kian leans in to get in the shot.

'We want to make it big,' says Graham. He is wearing heavy black wrap Ray Bans and you can't see his eyes. 'I want to play in The Point',[†] says Shane, looking into the camera. 'In three years, I would like us to be big in England. Ahh . . . hopefully we do.'

Averyl ushers IOYOU down from the hotel room to the stage. Shielding them like a fight manager. They stream past the Sound Records lads selling their CDs in the foyer.

- Sorry, folks. They will be available to sign CDs later.

They get a mauling on their way to the stage. It is hard to climb over the monitors and front-of-stage barriers, with young ones hanging out of you. The bass drum beat starts. Is everyone here, thinks Shane. Then Mark scrambles on, having barely conquered the obstacle course. The big chords . . .

Tonight is the night Mark Feehily comes into his own.

Onstage, he is transformed. He sweats and swaggers through all the songs with a new authority. He sings his Mariah Carey song, 'Open Arms'. He has been singing it since the first Hawk's Well shows, but tonight his delivery is shiver-on-the-back-of-your neck territory. Feehily is giving of himself; he sings for everyone. Mark was born for this. Pádraig thinks of the young Elvis: was this what he was like in Sun Studios, all these years ago in Memphis? Mark has called on deep reserves, on a hidden powerhouse, on a star that has waited within him through the awkward years of adolescence.

Mary says to Averyl and Pádraig, 'You know, Mark Feehily would be a good bet just on his own.' 'Don't tempt me,' says Averyl. All the minding and putting manners on those devils. Trying to stop them drinking. 'I know how good Mark is. And he has lost a bit of weight. But wasn't Graham brilliant tonight?' Graham is growing with every performance, too. Electricity when he raps. He is actually challenging the Filan-Feehily axis for attention. 'How is Derek

---

†   The Point is a large performance space in Dublin.

doin'?' Well, Derek is OK. He knows he is probably the weakest of the band at this point. He sometimes looks uncomfortable in the dances. When he's anxious it shows in his eyes. Still, he looks good and he can sing. Derek has a melodic voice. It's not ultra-strong, but it blends well with the rest, and he is always in tune.

Michael has weaknesses, too; his are in the singing department. He is comfortable singing an octave below the lead vocal and staying out of trouble if it gets too low. But Michael can dance well and he can speak well. He exudes optimism and energy. Mary says you have to admit Michael Garrett is putting everything into it. And he looks great in photos. *'He looks like a star.'* Michael would be good on TV.

No one says much about Shane. No need.

Shane's mum brings home the IOYOU CD. She thinks Shane looks great on the front. She orders a few extra copies. She always collects things about the band. She has paid Ciaran Carty a few bob before and got copies of some video he shot of him.

KEEP YOUR SHIRT ON!

I t's the oddest thing hearing your song at a nightclub, in between the hits, Boyzone and Madonna and all. It's a mixture of pride and slight embarrassment. Still, the girls love it; and fair play to them, all the local DJs are happy to give 'Together Girl' a spin.

December is the most hectic month yet. There are a whole series of appearances arranged by Averyl. There is one in the Mercy Convent. A fair majority of the girls go stone mad. IOYOU do a special appearance at Sligo Hospital, to sing for the sick children. John McMorrow, the local stringer, comes along with his camera and RTÉ One make it an item on 'Newsround' after the evening news. It shows the boys singing *a capella*, just inside the hospital doors. And them doing Santa, giving presents to the sick kiddies.

Michael rings Shane in Limerick.

• Did you see us on the telly?

Shane tells Michael a bit about how college is going. Sometimes it can be hard being down here. You are away from home for a start. Some people get really homesick. When he is in lectures or at his digs, Sligo and the band seem sometimes to Shane like a dream, a distant dream. Bandworld and Collegeworld are so unconnected,

181

like the lives of two different Shanes, never the twain shall meet. Michael tells Shane what is going on with the band. And Mary. When he comes home on a Friday, Shane will be heading down to Mary McDonagh's.

- Christmas should be good *craic*.
- Sure, I'll see you in Mary's on Friday night.
- Yeah. Good luck.
- Good luck.

Mary is busy with the Pantomime. This year's show is *Peter Pan*. The Moment of Transformation—Mary understands that the key to panto is that moment of magic—has to be when Peter and his friends take flight. But how to create the illusion? The director, Roddy Quinn, talks over the options with Mary. Wires, ropes, black screens? They talk to the technical man in the Hawk's Well, Barry McKinney, about safety issues and approaches that would suit the theatre. The meeting to finalise the flight issue is a key meeting. It is held in Mary's house. The producer and director and technical man and Mary all describe different ways they have seen the trick done. Using people in black clothes and ladders to assist flight against a black background. Using harnesses. Using a trapeze.

Part of the effect might be achieved by projecting images of the Sligo landscape from the air on a screen behind the stage. Could you blue screen some of the characters flying over it? It was Mary's idea, or maybe Roddy's.

They set up in the room known as the Black Box in the Model Arts Centre. Everyone mucks in, painting a big canvas sky blue. Barry McKinney lights it. Ciaran Carty shoots Gemma (the girl who is playing Peter Pan) and the others doing flying poses, poised on a gymnasium horse, in front of the blue screen. Mary directs. Emily holds a fan to blow back their hair and clothes.

Next day, Pádraig drives to Gweedore with Ciaran Carty. A small company Pádraig knows called Nocht TV have an editing suite with Media 100; you can edit and add whatever effects you need. The equipment is set up in a cottage in the middle of the stark countryside. Pádraig collects the key. Once inside the house, they turn on a heater, boot up the machines and get down to work.

Ciaran has plenty of old footage of around Sligo taken from a plane; he shot it a while ago. He takes a series of little boxes of mini-DV tapes out of the top pocket of his denim jacket like a magician and stacks them up. One stack he thinks the good stuff is on. The other stack is the new 'flying' footage from the Model Arts Centre. The first job is to digitise the raw images into the computer. That takes over an hour. Then Pádraig makes tea.

The Blue Screen effect lets you turn part of a picture transparent. You can tell the computer which colour in your picture is meant to end up transparent. Say, a particular shade of sky blue. Then you can fill in the holes with a different clip, whatever you want. And of course our heroes have been filmed with a painted screen of this very shade of sky blue behind them. And they have cleverly avoided wearing anything sky blue so as not to have holes in them. So after rendering the two clips together, Peter Pan and friends can be seen on the monitor doing Superman on it, soaring over Strandhill Golf course and over Maeve's Cairn and the wooded mountain slopes of Knocknarea.

It's tricky to get it exactly right, to get it convincing. Pádraig Meehan and Ciaran Carty stay working most of the night. Pádraig's battery in the Corolla van has kicked the bucket, so he leaves the engine ticking over all night on the frozen gravel street outside the cottage.

IOYOU do a PR appearance at the Record Room on 6 December. They cause traffic chaos, with all the screaming youngsters who show up. They do an interview later that day with Robert Cullen of the *Sligo Weekender*. That evening there is a big Division One basketball match in the Sligo Sports Complex. Sligo Team Dairies are playing Burger King, Limerick. During a break in the action, St Anne's All Ireland winning disco dancing team are announced.

Avril, Sabrina, Helena and Gillian perform a couple of numbers under the name Confusion. The girls' first idea for their group name *was* Confusion, and for a while this rather unfortunate name and Fusion were used interchangeably.

Two days later IOYOU do another PR appearance in Castlerea, County Roscommon, to promote their gig in that town later in the month. They do the Strandhill golf club Christmas party, and the Eircom party in the Sligo Park Hotel. To every engagement they bring along the CD, to sell to the fans. The last two CD tracks are instrumental versions of 'Together Girl' and 'Everlasting Love'. The band uses them to sing along to at the promotional appearances. The fans can sing karaoke to those tracks at home, if they fancy themselves as singers.

Getting everyone in one place—on time—for gigs, appearances, signings, etc. is a logistical nightmare. Averyl Dooher is exhausted, trying to do her own work and co-ordinate the IOYOU machine. The weeks are slipping by. The CD is out. Streetwise are working away, but there is no sign of IOYOU signing the contract. Not just yet. They are getting advice, they say, from an accountant. Well, at least everyone will be around for the Christmas holidays.

The panto will be finishing up two days before Christmas. There is a tummy bug going around, and gaps appear in the junior chorus on a couple of nights. Daragh Connolly and Pádraig go to Beezies to see some of the girls in the show in a karaoke competition. Georgie Gorman is one of the judges. Joanne Higgins's song in *Peter Pan* is 'Perfect Day', but for the competition she does a barnstorming version of the *Titanic* theme song, 'My Heart Will Go On'.

One Saturday evening Shane Filan comes up to the Hawk's Well to try out a few song ideas with Daragh and Pádraig. He sits in one of the front auditorium seats that hedge in the music equipment, and the two lads play keyboards and guitar, and try out beats and chord changes.

There is a big storm on Christmas Eve. A deep depression sweeps in over the west coast from the Atlantic. A gale warning is in operation. Don't travel unless you have to, says the TV woman. Branches fly. Trees come down. In the forests, especially where they have sown pines in shallow, boggy soil, there is often a domino effect when a tree falls. Neighbours pull each other down. Electricity lines are damaged. Many homes in Sligo, including some of the families of the band members, have Christmas by candlelight. It's nice. Kind of old-fashioned. No TV. People stay in and talk to each other.

If the storm permitted, you could have seen that the song 'Too Much', by the Spice Girls, has nabbed the prized Christmas Number One spot in the UK charts. 'Too Much' was written by the girlband themselves and producers/writers Andy Watkins and Paul Wilson. The previous August, the same Watkins and Wilson collaboration with Eliot Kennedy (of the famous Steelworks studio in

Sheffield) and lead singer Ronan Keating, had sent Boyzone to the top of the charts with 'Picture of You'. It features in the new Mr Bean movie. The Sound Records lads report that 'Together Girl Forever' is selling pretty good in Sligo. Most of the 1,000 CDs have been shifted.

On Tuesday, 30 December, the band and a fair-sized IOYOU entourage squeeze into a minibus and head off to Castlerea, County Roscommon, to play in the River Island nightclub. Two shows are planned. Ciaran Carty is brought along with his video camera to record the occasion. The boys sing on the bus all the way up. They wave back to Mary and Averyl when they spot Averyl's car.

When the IOYOU minibus pulls up outside it, the River Island ballroom is deserted. The dance hall stands alone on its lot, a large car park with rain puddles. The front is fifties art deco. It used to be the Casino, all through the sixties and seventies and eighties. The dressing room has the souls of a thousand showband drummers burnt into the walls. The stage is about five feet off the ground, shallow and bare. Gaudy images of palm trees are painted on the wall at the back of the stage.

IOYOU are out of their element. A horrible wave of nervousness passes through the band. Shane tells them we have done this before. We can do it.

- If you lose it you know what to do, just freak out. Keep smiling, like you are really into it, and then go like this . . .

He freaks, really loose and into it.

- . . . until you get back in step with the rest. We will be fine.

Back in the dressing room, Mary says, 'Hold hands.' She and Averyl and the band embrace. 'Energy,' says Mary, 'feel the energy.'

The gigs go great. Plenty of people turn up. There are fans there that have travelled all the way from Sligo. And a great crowd of locals. In the evening gig, as Kian does his tease—his reaching out and touching the hands of fans routine while singing his big song— he is collared. A particularly determined and powerfully built girl grabs Kian's shirt. He continues to sing on, manfully, while trying to wrestle her off. But now her friends have a grip on the shirt, too. They drag him towards the edge of the stage. The shirt stretches. Kian pulls in the other direction. The shirt comes clean off, leaving a topless and vexed Kian Egan struggling to keep his balance and his place in the song. A huge cheer goes up. Averyl rushes on with a shirt to cover Kian's shapely torso while the screams go up a few decibels.

MEETING THE PARENTS

The Showgrounds is the home of Sligo Rovers Football Club. Sligo are playing the *other* reds, current league leaders Shelbourne FC. It has been a solid season for the Rovers, and they are still attracting great crowds. The rosy glow of last year's League Cup success kindles yet. Saturday 17 January 1998. Commercial Manager and goalkeeper Nicky Brujos welcomes Averyl Dooher and her boyband to his field of dreams. IOYOU's half-time performance goes out live on RTÉ TV, a first from Rovers' ground. The Rovers are losing till near the end. Then Neil Ogden hits a cracking goal in the rain. It ends a one-all draw. Sligo and their fans are relieved. And although they are soaking and cold, IOYOU and the boyband team are over the moon. They got their second bit of national TV.

• Did you see it? Why didn't you tape it?

Averyl gives Mary the £400 cheque out of the gig. Three weeks pass; the mild damp spell of the start of the month is over. Saturday dawns dry and crisp with the wind in from the north. Towards evening the biting breeze eases, and after sunset the freeze sets in, leaving the roads treacherous. Orion the Hunter and his faithful Dog

Star glitter above Sligo. Mary has been rehearsing. She is putting on a show called *Bits 'n' Pieces*, a showcase for her dance school talent. The IOYOU boys come up to Mary's house with big news. The Backstreet Boys are coming to Ireland. They will be doing a brace of gigs in Dublin in March. Everyone wants tickets. The boys queue outside Star Records for theirs. Mary orders one, too, then decides she won't need it. Kian says, 'Hold on to it, I will take it from you.'

Ciaran Carty meets up with the boyband in Strandhill to shoot more footage for lip-synch for 'Together Girl Forever'. They had gone out already in the first week of January and got some nice shots, but had to abandon because of rain. The beach thing was partly Averyl's idea. Mike Bunn was the first to speak of a beach session. Maybe a rocky coastline.

Averyl and Ciaran have been chatting. She hasn't got hold of Mike yet, but Ciaran says, 'I'll fire ahead anyway, no problem. The seaside would be perfect.'

On this morning (it's Saturday, 24 January) there are no managers around. No one giving orders. Averyl is working and can't get off. Mary is busy with her upcoming show. Pádraig Meehan is off doing something else today, too. There is something different—a change in the atmosphere—since the 7 January video shoot. The lads seem just a tad more independent. They want to direct things. There has been a lot of talking about the contract, whether it's a good thing or a bad thing. The parents of the boys have had a meeting.

The tide is on its way out, restless white breakers rolling behind the stretch of brown sand. Shane and Michael race each other, springing from boulder to boulder, boulders arranged to reinforce and protect the high water mark. Rocks so big they make a child of everyone. There are little mounds all over the mudflats, each one topped by a worm of sand. Some little animal must be making them. Further up the beach are the bigger dunes. Ciaran huddles his camera close; moisture and sand it doesn't love. The seven lads jog along the stony beach to the backdrop of towers of thundery slate-blue clouds. There are a few strollers. Half a mile away a boy kicks a ball; the sound of it bouncing comes late, comes out of synch.

Michael's hair is getting blown all over the place, a stiff wind off the sea whipping little spits of rain into his face. There was wind forecast. Hopefully it doesn't come too bad. There are old people along this coast that still remember the great hurricane of 1918; it changed the whole landscape here. There have been plenty of big storms since.

The conservation people have fenced off segments of the dunes with what look like wicker fences; it's to reduce the erosion. The fences meander up and down the hills in merry toytown patterns. As you work your way up the beach, the village houses and flags of the resort grow small and distant to the north, Ben Bulben light coloured behind them. The group of boys climb the tallest of the dunes, each set of legs labouring like on a treadmill as the sand gives way under the weight.

A primal yellow mid-morning sunlight breaks into the scene.

Maybe it's the weather, maybe the absence of 'grown-ups'. The mood of the boys turns wilder. Ciaran feels more adventurous, too. The seven, they enter a zone of play, a place of togetherness. It's a bit like the times down in the quarry, years ago. They spend a good few hours out there.

The band and Ciaran sit in a car and look down the camera after the shoot is wrapped up. As they view the footage on the tiny camera viewfinder, the boys say to Ciaran, 'Don't show Mary that bit.' This bit. 'Look!' Shane is messing, shaping to kiss Michael. 'You can't show that.' 'Look at us jumping off the big dune.' Michael jumping highest. Look at Shane and Michael on the ground, wrestling.

Actually Ciaran has shot nothing more than fairly stock horseplay and a lot of posing. He has them walking by the lapping waves. He has some lovely sweeping shots, darting around as usual. He somehow makes the camera swoop like an eagle on the heroic youths posed in their coats on high ground. The background turns dizzily behind Michael Garrett as he sings, turns from the green sea to the crumbling walls of Knocknarea. What the pictures do illustrate is the close and easy bond between the boys, particularly Michael and Shane. They frolic and mock fight, at one point getting to grips on the ground in a playful wrestling match, rolling in a grassy valley between the mountainous heaps of sand.

As the 'Together Girl Forever' CD plays distorted from a ghetto blaster, the six boys appear in long shot, western style. The sandbanks as the Nevada desert, a string of heads coming into view from behind dunes. Then the angry blue Atlantic bobs into the picture. Ciaran says the wind was awful strong.

- It was so flippin' hard to keep it steady.

And he promises to show only the good stuff. The rest will never be seen. Don't worry. The talk is about dreams again then. Ciaran is right in tune with the music business, he has always been a collector of music; now he has started work as a DJ. He knows lots of stories, all about what other bands have done to make the breakthrough; he has all the background, all the gossip. He describes his idea for the video, the style, what it should look like. Ciaran will edit something together if he gets a chance and give them a look later. No problem.

Derek calls up to Mary. He would love to see Ciaran Carty's new footage, the stuff he shot out in the sand dunes . . .

- Oh, the lip-synch, stuff, yeah.
- How did it come out?
- Great. It was very good. I have it there somewhere. Ciaran brought it in.
- Sound. When are we putting out the video? Are we putting out the song in Dublin?

Shane will probably be packing in college. Limerick is not a happy place for him. The travelling is too much. He will take some time out and maybe go back on the management and accountancy course after the summer.

Streetwise have a chance to talk among themselves after the *Bits 'n' Pieces* show on the Sunday. All three are saying the same thing.

- This contract thing is going on too long.
- We cannot continue to use our energy without something concrete on paper.
- We can't do a national release, go to record companies without these affairs sorted.
- We better lay down what we want, bring things to a head.

Averyl has gone ahead and set up an appearance for the band on RTÉ Television, a programme called 'TX Live'. They have to be in Dublin to do that on 28 March. 'Averyl,' says Mary, 'we need to get on to the boys again.' The three reach a conclusion: there has to be a meeting. Of boys, parents, everybody. Averyl makes the calls. A date in late February is agreed. A meeting of band, band parents and managers to iron out the management contract.

Pádraig has a pint in Harry's in the Point,[†] meets a bunch of good heads, and it turns into an epic night. A night of jokes and stories, the mood growing more optimistic the farther past closing time it gets. He ends the night with a walk, a walk out of range of the streetlights, down the hill to the beach car park. It is not totally deserted. Two cars are parked on the top park, one with windows fogged up. He walks on down the narrow path that leads to the first beach. The evening has been dry, windy, frosty and at the same time impossibly hazy. So it is for the night. The light is transparent; it seems to come out of surfaces, skin, metal, dogback, water, beach. The sand on the First Beach appears white, though you know it is light brown.

A dark smudge floating turns into another night beach walker. Neither party speaks. The smudge recedes. He steps out across rigid waves of packed sand, mottled and dry. Feet splish in the flats, shoes squelch on a beached jellyfish. What a sense of space. The space is enormous, it goes up and out forever. The tide is well out, its presence betrayed only by a paler line when the wave breaks with a sound that is vast and mellow and unearthly. Then he starts to sink into soft sand and wavelets surround his feet and he stops walking and looks out into the emptiness, into the coldness of the Atlantic ocean.

The lights strive bravely to keep their balance. A horizon of lights holding the line like people lost in a snowstorm. The fog blows around them, and the lights shine in different degrees of yellow. A ship at sea. The next one must be John's Point. The lighthouse at Seal Island. The Third Beach.

Walk back. Walk back from the tide. Across open sand to dunes and car park and shelter. The freezing kiss of February on bare earlobes, cheeks stinging, ears singing. Breathe. Take in the air, the space, open skyfull space. Feel the light. The scattered light of the invisible full moon coming out of everything.

---

†   The second, northern peninsula in Sligo Bay stretches long and thin but widens into a T-shape, shoulder to shoulder with Cuil Irra. The three beaches of Rosses Point lie there, Upper and Lower Rosses and the Golf Course. The village of Rosses Point is known as the Point to locals.

Two days after Valentine's Day, parents, band and band management file into a room with a long table in the Southern Hotel. The meeting is chaired informally by Michael Garrett Senior, father of Miggles. People speak in low voices. Oliver Feehily is Mark's dad. He is a nice, round-faced man with a sincere voice. He balances his head far back; he keeps a hand on the table and leans back. Mr Feehily says he wants to start by thanking Averyl and Pádraig and Mary for all they have done for the band. 'Do ye really think they can go far?'

Pádraig says there is no guarantee. But he really believes they can. 'A lot of the important elements are in place.' 'Have you looked over the contract?' The band members' parents have been to a lawyer. The Filans have concerns.

- Sure we have read it. It is very much in the management's favour.

The parents have already had a meeting, in the Sancta Maria Hotel in Strandhill, the week before. They have a sheet of paper with sixteen bullet points, changes they would like to see to the Streetwise management contract. 'Let's take them point by point,' says M. Garrett Senior. Mae Filan has a question.

- Another point first, though. Ye must have made a fair bit on them so far? The boys have not received any money from you.

Averyl takes it.

- Well, we explained early on to them that we would be working at a loss at the start. We have actually made a loss . . .

- Are you at a loss? How much?

- How can that be? The Hawk's Well was packed, how many times?

'Well,' says Averyl, 'this stage of setting up a boyband is expensive. When we started out we did not realise how expensive it would be. They haven't got any money. Neither have we. No one has been paid, except the people we brought in. You pay for photographers, preparing the music, rehearsal rooms over a long duration; we have paid Steffen for his dancing work, we have paid for ads, for printing . . .' Mary and Pádraig are nodding agreement.

- The sound system alone has cost about 1,000 pounds up to now. We pay for the use of the theatre. Yes, we got some money from the gigs, but . . .

- So how much are you out?
- A couple of thousand at least; we will show you the books. The management deal will mean that after we get a deal we can take reasonable expenses out and then distribute the money, according to the percentage agreed.

'Why didn't you come to us? We would have helped you,' says Michael Garrett Senior, sounding almost annoyed.

Mary's voice.

- Well, Michael, you know, I sold my yard, and I used that . . . I regard it as a good investment.

'We weren't aware of any of this stuff,' say the parents. Mr Feehily says, 'It's a pity this meeting did not take place months ago.'

- Well, we can make this a regular thing from now on.

All agree on this point.

Pádraig is glad that Michael Garrett Senior seems positive. He seems a man you can do business with. Pádraig has the thought; we should be explaining more to these parents. Sometimes when you know something a long time you assume everyone else knows it, too. Pádraig cuts in; he says our idea is that we will grow with the band. Learn with the band. It's good to keep things local.

He sets about explaining something of the music business as he knows it.

- You spend money to make money. In some cases managers of new bands are happy to pay out for the opportunity to support big acts on international tours to get their names up there.
- They *pay* to play? That seems an unusual arrangement.

Pádraig knows of bands/managers who have done that. It was not unusual. It might be on a British tour or whatever. It had worked for some, not for others.

- Do you intend to keep the present line-up of the band?
- Yes.
- Yes, we do.

Bernie Garrett is surprised to hear her son pose this question. The boys are saying, 'If we don't sign this, is it . . . you won't work with us any more . . . that's what you said.' 'No,' says Averyl.

- It's 'If we can't get agreement, how can we continue doing stuff—doing work—without something down in black and white.'

Pádraig can remember the question of band personnel cropping up in Streetwise chats. There had been worries, about Derek, for example. How his confidence was. Would he be OK? They were usually voiced in terms of 'How is so-and-so doing?' But as of now, there are no plans to make changes to the group. Streetwise see no need for it. But the three managers intend keeping an eye on things. People are disagreeing. Pádraig gets a speak in again.

• Well, that's why we are here. That's what we want to do. To put together that agreement. There is the possibility to make money here and have everyone do fairly well . . . And we can do a lot ourselves, from here in Sligo. There are two basic deals to be done. A *recording contract*, covering recording and merchandising, and a *publishing contract*, for the songs. They can be with different companies. You could expect to receive an advance on sales from these companies, to help you do your first album. The important thing is to make sure this money is well spent, and not blown, on limousines and clothes, as has happened to some bands in the past. £80,000 might seem a lot, but when you have a six-piece band, and studio costs . . .

• And ye can send off the CD to them, and pictures . . .

• A package . . .

• A package.

Streetwise are showing that they know a bit about the business. They acknowledge that they are not big players like people in Dublin or London. But that can be a plus as well as a minus. Once you are signed up by a company, it might be better to have it all based here.

• It can't be that easy to get signed up?

It's hard to get signed. Pádraig tells the meeting he knows this side of it all too well.

• And even when you are signed up, everything may not be sorted. You need not just *any* deal, you need a *good* deal. You need a strong relationship with the company, you need someone rooting for you. A lot of people get signed and dropped the same year. You want to be high in a record company's queue of acts and have some role, some input in decisions. Artistic control is important, even for a boyband . . . These lads—and ourselves—I think I can say—have a sense of what we want . . . You hope that what you end up doing is what you love to do. It's a tall order, and there are only a very few people who seem to have it sussed. And it's probably getting harder. So we have to be realistic . . .

- The percentage you are looking for, the managers, 24 per cent seems a lot.
- Remember there are three of us. It may not be a bottom line. There is not much room there, though.
- The duration . . . could it be two years? Five is too long.
- What about three?

Streetwise say that the duration would not be a sticking point.

Averyl explains that the contract was put together by a top showbiz law firm. 'We just asked them to put together a standard management contract. And this is what they gave us; it's standard for a boyband. This would be . . . a typical set-up in our situation. It just formalises the situation that already exists between the parties.' The biggest difficulty for the Filans and the Garretts is the fact that the management propose that they will handle and distribute monies. Pádraig speaks for Streetwise, saying, 'We will look at this.' Averyl is conciliatory, too. 'We can try to bridge these gaps.' The parties agree, in principle, that they can work around these difficulties and go ahead with the deal.

The Garretts say, 'Let the solicitors sort out the differences.' The Filans are cautions and have lots more questions. But everyone is cordial.

There is one item that parents and managers agree on. A number of the lads still have to do their Leaving Certs. This has to be a priority. This is 16 February. Paddy's day in a month. You'll never find June. Mary says, 'I have made that point all along. The schooling has to come first.' 'In fairness, you did,' says Mrs Feehily. On the way out Graham's mother says to Pádraig, 'Fair play to ye. Aren't ye great, you listen to all this stuff after all ye have done?' People are looking for allies. Pádraig says, 'In fairness they are entitled to ask questions. It is their future. It is big stuff for everyone.'

KARAOKE

Oh, hi, here! Look-a' wha's commin' now! Da-fella's a gomey adlum (a foolish person). Dark glasses onnim a' dis hour a' nigh't. Is 'e wiiide adall?

- Ah, dass caaa-t!
- C'mon, boiy, skirt! (Let's leave)
- See-ya lay-dir.

No one will lip-read us too easy in Sligo. We are wide (awake). Top lip rigid—lips close—the tongue explodes off the roof of the mouth.

- Dis is *I_O_yeaow* w'deir newyh song, day roid id demself's . . . Es called Dogeddergurl *F'rahver*.

It's funny how things can change in a few months . . . Graham goes to the karaoke bars now, but he doesn't sing. He listens to other people sing his band's song. He always says, 'Fair play to ye.' Graham speaks with that strong Sligo town accent, that crosses Noo Joisey, Noo Yoak and God knows where. It's a great accent, expressive and hearty and authentic. It is hard to imagine the Sligo accent ever becoming a cool accent, like the Liverpool one did in the wake of The Beatles. Young American kids trying to put on that accent when they sing. But no one thought the Liverpool twist on English sounded cool before the time of The Beatles.

Maybe the Sligo accent will be famous someday. There is a similar accent in Tuam, in the town, a hint of it in Ballina. In some parts of Sligo the accent is a dialect; there are words you never hear anywhere else.

Some Japanese businessmen invented the word 'karaoke'.[†] Karaoke was designed to keep the businessmen amused for the few minutes they stopped working. But it translates pretty good to the Sligo pub scene. The backing music swells through the speakers. The familiar sounds of your favourite song. The backing vocals all come lashing in in the right places. Song words trundle by on a computer screen, letters shimmering in front of a cloudless blue karaoke sky. A little highlight yoke barrells along, to the beat, telling you the word you are supposed to be singing. Karaoke-land is a democracy. A land where everyone is a star.

The DJ mouths the words, willing the singer through the key changes. Or he has a mic of his own, and he levers the performer up to the required note. There are a crowd who go up for the *craic*. The girls who go to the loo together sing 'I Will Survive' together. Beginners always smile nervously; their body language says don't look at me. A girl with a short skirt and a Tina Turner scowl blows you away in verse one. So far so good. She may not hold up. Ones like her often crumble on the third verse and have to scrutinise the lyrics screen while mumbling the words. You get some great phrasing.

A certain crew take it dead serious. Especially if there is a competition. There are the amateur Demi Rousseaus, and Joe Dolans, the sweaty crooners, and the twitchy wannabees. But there's always a Frank Sinatra or Celine Dion waiting to disgrace you after you get off.

You can always know the one who has been practising all week for his moment of glory. It's even worse if he goes on before you and the bastard sings the very same song that you are going to do. And so does the next guy. That is one thing about karaoke. You could have the same song a lot of times the one night.

---

†   Kara = empty, void. Oke = orchestra.

Graham knows you don't have that problem in a *real* band. A band that does gigs and people pay in to see. A band has a set list. A running order of songs, strategically chained, taking the audience on a roller-coaster; fast song, fast song, slow song, chatty bit. You would have decided before the gig whether to start with a bang or sneak up on them with a seductively quiet opening. You have to give the punters a structured experience.

Graham knows how fans like to rob set lists from where they are stuck by the crew to the monitors at the front of the stage, and bring them home. And how they stash them and treasure them and swap them. And that The Beatles' set lists, or maybe Michael Jackson's, sell in the likes of Sotheby's for silly money.

Your friends go mad when you get up, after you have declined first—a token show of modesty. As you are introduced, the conversations continue down the bar, the pints are lined up and topped off and handed over the counter. Spirits and ice in nice glasses. The DJ remembers most contestants from last week, it's another requirement of the job, but he sometimes mispronounces names, or mixes up sisters. Your friends correct him.

You listen to the intro and wait for the words floating in the blue to start changing colour. A few people dance, the dancers who do a jive no matter what the song is—you know the one, where the woman goes under the bridge of the arm of the man. The loyal friends at the front sing along with you. The next singer and their friends listen back a bit, smoking sceptical cigarettes. The tills rattle.

Girls Just A-Wanna Have Fun, Yeah. A good spread of age groups enjoy the karaoke. Lots of dyed blondes, lots of the DJ saying 'folks'. Study the DJ. Watch him entertain. And engineer. That lad could fly a jumbo jet. The equipment is all his own. He talks the talk and operates the machines. He keeps the levels right, avoids feedback when the mic gets too near the monitor. He dollops plenty of big echo on the singer's voice. He sings himself, too. He always takes a song on his own, in between the karaoke singers. Shows how it is done. You watch him. If you get lost in the song, the Karaoke Guy will get you back safely.

The Karaoke Guy—it seems to be mainly a male preserve—might do just straight DJ on a quieter night. He has the voice for it. Irrepressibly cheerful, folksy, the voice of someone talking to everyone. Doing requests, keeping the show rolling, making slick links between the unlinkable. He will have the confidence and sureness of touch to put the most nervous at ease, to haul ashore overlong dedications or political speeches, and keep his sense of humour in the face of the bizarre, the nutter, the drunk, the over-emotional, the messer and the just plain difficult.

The Karaoke Master has to be quick on the tongue. He may be called on at any second for a quip to take the harm or embarrassment out of A Situation. He is a local anyway and knows most of the punters' form. He will have witnessed proposals of marriage, and refusals. Religious conversions in the middle of songs. Breakdowns. People who insisted on singing some obscure song he didn't have a backing track for. Through it all the DJ will be nice to the guests, but *with* his audience. Winding them up, getting them going, roaring at them.

- Are ye stillll having a good time?

Cooling them down for a minute, turning the mood romantic. Spreading bonhomie and keeping an eagle eye on the clock.

It's a mighty atmosphere in the pub. Now and again there might be a bit of a scrap, but you will get that. Sure that would happen if there was no music at all. If the scrap starts down the back, the karaoke DJ continues on stoically and blinds his eyes to the swinging punches and the flying glasses. You might hear the challenge: *'Outside! Now!'* You might have to hit a few thumps on someone.

Graham Keighron never gets in fights. The boyband people have a way of sweeping in and sweeping out of places. They are very busy on their mobile phones. An entourage swims behind them. And people check them out.

- Hey, look, Veronica! Dass yer*maan* out of *I_O_Yeaw!* Sing us a song, willya, love?

▲ Mark Feehily in Quinnsworth, 2 November 1997, waiting to perform; Mary and Shane can be seen in the background. *Streetwise/Ciaran Carty*

▲ Kian, Shane and Mark on the couch in Mary McDonagh's sitting room during a lip-synch video shoot for *Together Girl Forever*.

▲ Pre-gig talk in Quinnsworth supermarket:
Pádraig, Graham, Michael, Kian.

▲ Shane Filan sings into an imaginary microphone.

▲ Michael, Kian, Mary, Derek with his
back to camera, and Shane.

▲ Gary Gillen of Redhouse Audio, Averyl, Shane,
Kian, Mary McDonagh.

▾ ▴ Mary leads the troops through the aisles
of Quinnsworth on the way to the stage.

PART 3:
WHEN ALL YOUR DREAMS
COME TRUE

NEVER STAND AT THE EDGE

Louis Walsh sits at his desk and turns the CD cover over in his hands. Three faces press forward. Three crane in from the background. What was that old rule in the showband days? Never stand at the edge of the band photo. You will be easily chopped out if they ever have to downsize. Nice production. He gets so many of these damn things, but this looks pretty cool. He sees the record company logo. Sound Records.

No management name on there. And what about this Mae Filan? She is not the usual type who delivers a new act to his door. She is an old fashioned west of Ireland mum. He thought he might vaguely remember her, years ago, at home in Kiltimagh.

Kiltimagh. A small, neat Mayo town, pop. 1,000, forty miles south-west of Sligo. Just north of Knock, where the Blessed Virgin appeared. Kiltimagh, market town, with its neat houses and pretty shopfronts; hilly ground to the north, narrow far roads, small farms. Suffered badly—as other places in the west—from emigration in the seventies and eighties. Lost a lot of the youth. Not many blow-ins came to replace them. Everyone knew everyone, knew their business and how they were related. In the sixties, as Louis grew up, black was big in Kiltimagh. The black Raleigh bicycle, the black Ford Prefect car, the black cassock of the priest. Black porter. Black stone-turf. Louis didn't like saving turf. He didn't like football. He read *Spotlight* magazine and listened in to Radio Luxembourg.

Kiltimagh gave Dublinese a word—'culchie', a catch-all word for a country bumpkin (anyone born in Ireland outside the Pale). Coill—pronounced a bit like quill—is the Irish word for a forest. Maghach was a chief of ancient times.

Louis Walsh has lived in Dublin most of his life. He is a wiry little guy in his forties. He grins and giggles a lot, like a kid at the counter of a village shop, asking for his third Choc Ice in succession. He blinks rapid fire. Lives in denim and casual jackets. No tie. He is forever on his mobile phone. Louis is a businessman.

Louis Walsh did not get to be Ireland's most successful pop manager overnight. It has been a long and bumpy road to where he is today. But he is having a terrific run with Boyzone. The initial band he had done almost on a whim, after a couple of enthusiastic lads rang him up. He set up auditions and threw a band together. He got Gay Byrne to give him a slot on 'The Late Late Show'. Just one day after the auditions. Boyzone mimed to a backing track they had had little time to get used to. They didn't pretend to sing. In colourful outfits that included red overalls, they gamely attempted a 'dance routine'. Each boy stretched out his arms in front of him and waved a lot. It was awful. Or was it a stroke of genius? Was Louis calculating in revealing this degree of rawness and naiveté? It seems unlikely, but in later years it all added to the legend of Louis. Anyway, it worked. People remembered it. Now Boyzone are huge in Europe and Britain and the Far East.

The US is the market that eludes them. The US of A is huge, the market Louis wants most to break. Louis understands Ireland and Europe. What works here. The slushy ballads. Blanket radio play. Television, television, television. And the tabloid newspapers. You have to keep the band in the public eye. Feed the press angles. Good stories. True or not doesn't matter, just keep feeding the monster and it won't eat you. He didn't know all this stuff when he started off, of course. Louis has paid his dues.

Louis started off booking out a rock band called Time Machine, when he was fifteen. Louis had shoulder-length long hair then, a live wire in a jacket. He was always into jackets, denim (he got into leather ones for a while later), jackets with pockets full of notebooks, stuffed with important things. He was slim of stature, but the legend says his full pockets made him as broad as he was long. He used to go into a primrose and green phone box in Kiltimagh with his pockets laden with coins and make phone calls. Fifty new pence went a long way. You rang the operator and they got you the number.

•   Press Button A, sir.

The phone would beep when your money had run out.

Time Machine were a heavy guitar/bass/drums three-piece who used to play 'Wishing Well' by Free, and 'You Spend My Money (But Honey, Don't Waste My Time)' by Status Quo. Sean O'Halloran was the singer/bass man. David Jameson played guitar, or was he the drummer? Time Machine used to do 'relief band'. A support act to the showbands of the day. They wore regulation rock denim. The money wasn't great for relief bands. Generally a tenner a night. They were happy when they got a few headline spots, in the carnivals and dance halls like the Astoria in Bundoran.

Louis went to see all the bands that came to the locality. He made friends with Doc Carroll of The Royal Blues. He got to hang around with the band, go to the gigs, travelling in Doc's car. Then Louis went to Dublin and got a gig—Doc recommended him—doing gofer with Tommy Hayden, ex The Nevada Showband. Tommy had started off playing trumpet. Two of his brothers were in the Nevada. Now he was a major showband promoter, and he managed The Royal Blues. It was the early seventies. Showbands were doing fierce business. They had been doing good business for the best part of ten years.[†] Young Louis learned fast. He got into booking out acts himself, initially under the umbrella of Hayden Enterprises of Hawkins Street. Sean O'Farrell and Chips and all those other bands. Chips were a pop/rock showband, a bit of a mould-breaker.

The showbands used to travel the length and breadth of the country (and England, too) from gig to gig in a van, with all the gear packed in the back. They played in dance halls and at carnivals, in

---

†   The Clipper Carlton from Strabane seemingly started it all in the mid-fifties, when they kicked over their big band chairs and folded up their music stands. It was pure sex for the dancing public of the time.

five-pole marquees. The showbands played what the public wanted to hear. The music was bland, conservative and sentimental. They mixed country music and songs from the charts, singing in strange copies of American accents. They sang songs by Tom T. Hall and Hank Williams and Merle Haggard.

Dim Lights, Thick Smoke and Loud, Loud Music
It's the only kind of life you'll ever understand.
Dim Lights, Thick Smoke and Loud, Loud Music
You'll never make a wife for a home-lovin' man.
(Fidler/Maphis/Maphis)

There was a strict formula: four songs to the set, fast and slow sets alternating, so the boys and girls got a chance to mix. No one clapped after a song. The National Anthem was the last song at the end of the night. Everyone stood to attention then. When the Anthem was over, the band members lingered at the front of the stage to autograph their band photos—'complimentary photos'—and chat to the fans.

The classic showbands all played more or less the same basic repertoire. The idea of writing a song, or experimenting somehow, was akin to sacrilege. There were a few subtle variations in style. There would be some fellas into exchanging cassette tapes with strange-sounding names written in biro on the cases. The Flying Burrito Brothers. Poco. These lads listened to this rarefied stuff in the band wagon while the rest of them talked about drink and women.

But the core notion, the central tenet of the showband mindset, was to copy—faithfully, and without mistake—the work of those from beyond these shores Who Knew What They Were Doing, Musically. You did the show, got paid, and went home.

Perhaps the feeling of this era of the seventies is best encapsulated in the sense of pride we all felt when The Memories got the better of Queen. The Memories—one of our biggest earning showbands—had managed to perfectly emulate, live on stage, the many-times-overdubbed-in-the-studio vocal harmonies (the song was 'Bohemian Rhapsody') of Freddie Mercury's Queen.

Queen, it was reported at many's a bar, couldn't do it live themselves. People had been to England and seen them. They always left that one out when they played live. Then, the story went,

Freddie came to Dublin and he jaw-dropped as The Memories showed him how it was done.

A few radicals like Ray Lynam and Brendan Quinn might lean towards American country. Billy Browne of The Freshmen (Louis Walsh was a fan; he ended up booking out The Freshmen) was a maverick. He wrote his own songs. The Times Showband wrote good pop songs. But the majority stuck to the stock repertoire of country and Irish, songs on the subject of guilt, and the love of the Irish son for his mother. And the songs out of the Irish top ten that were playable live.

There were loads of showband rules. The bass player could play the country stuff one way, and one way only. Even though he's just going first—fifth. Plink—plonk. A strict pattern had to be followed, two on the one, if there's only one bar, etc. Most of the tunes were in major keys, with three chords, a sixteen or thirty-two bar pattern. In fairness, there was respect for musicianship among the showband crowd. A lot of people learned their chops in that scene. You had to swing; it was harder than it sounded; the bass and drums had to nail that country shuffle.

The band leader always said, 'Your next dance, please,' at the end of the set. Then the boy could ask the girl, 'Do you want to stay on?' If she said yes, you had to buy her a Coke, and you were fairly sure of a snog and a feel out the back of the hall at the night's end. If she said no, it was back to the line on the fellas' side of the hall. The showband musicians might do a bit better in the back of the van.

Fortunes were made—and lost—in the showband era. Most people in 1970 on an industrial wage were taking home less than £20 a week. Big showbands that time were going out for £700 or £800 per night. That's about €10,000 in today's money. It was a useful gig for a young fella. Mind you, it wouldn't be an equal divvy up between the players. Managers would be secretive, you had to work your way up. Band leaders got more. Sometimes—if there was a star singer—he/she got top dollar and travelled by car.

Getting paid was not always straightforward. The band leader had to be real tough at the end of the night and put on his hardest face, while extracting the fee from a hard-boiled ballroom promoter and his cronies. Some band agents had to resort to sending a couple of hefty helpers down the country with the bands. It was the promoters and managers and dance hall owners that made the real money in the boom years of the showbands.

In England, The Beatles (who started off wearing showband uniforms) were doing 'Helter Skelter'. Over in New York City, down in the Village, The Velvet Underground were projecting movies onstage and playing 'Venus in Furs'. Whispers of the sixties and seventies emerged from a few transistor radio sets pressed to the ear late at night. The signal waxed and waned, the DJ's voice phasing. The Jocks on pirate radio stations, like Radio Caroline, sounded like the passionate priests of a new heresy. They did inspire a few impoverished rock bands in Ireland, especially in the cities, bands like Time Machine. Disregarded on the Irish airwaves, Rory Gallagher was playing blues, growing into a big name abroad. But the Irish showbands didn't care. They kept on swinging that country beat, playing crisp guitar licks, stepping in, stepping out, sounding oh-so-sincere and making buckets of money. It was the time when you knew nothing would ever change.

In Thornhill in Sligo there were five brothers of the Duggan family who loved pop music. One day their dad, a musician himself, handed out the instruments—bass, drums, guitars—to each of his five boys. Their band was called The Duggan Brothers at first. They didn't actually model themselves on American teen idols The Osmonds, but other people made the comparison. They phoned up and got a gig doing 'relief' to the big bands in the Baymount Hotel in Strandhill. The Plattermen was one of them. Red Hurley was another. He saw the lads and said, 'Ye fellas have talent to burn.' Red gave them the numbers for the big promoters in Dublin— Tommy Hayden and Louis Walsh.

Louis came to see them, liked what he saw and took them on. He was seventeen, in the same age bracket as the band. He wore his hair in a big Afro style. After that, things changed for Brotherly Love. Louis got them gigs all over the country. They bought a set of lights off Time Machine.[†] They took to the road in a twin-wheel Ford Transit wagon. There were days they made ten-hour drives. Over the

---

[†] Time Machine continued for a while; they expanded to a four piece and got a new manager. Around 1977 they broke up. Sean O'Halloran went to England and played a lot of music, solo and in different bands. David Jameson went to study in Trinity College in

years they placed six songs into the Irish charts. The blue bell-bottomed suits were made up by Tommy Hayden's sister-in-law.

Brotherly Love worked hard at getting a good sound and playing their instruments. They used to write their own songs. Drummer Joss used to figure them out on guitar. Once EMI got involved, they lost a bit of control of that process. John Drummond, who had produced the Bay City Rollers, was brought in as producer. Sometimes the backing tracks would be recorded when the boys got up from Sligo. Still, they got plenty of press and the gigs got a lot better for the band. It was hard work, especially as the band members continued with college, and some kept day jobs going as well as playing gigs at night.

Around 1979 the lads in Brotherly Love were all about to go off on a well-earned holiday. Louis Walsh said, 'Look, when ye come back ye will be giving up the day jobs. I can get ye some tours in Britain and Germany and Holland. We need to get something released abroad to take this further.' The boys weren't sure. They promised to think about it on their holidays. When the Duggans came back home, they had a meeting. They told Louis they had decided. They were going to keep their day jobs.

Nineteen eighty-one was the year of the pirates. The first pirate radio station in Sligo was Radio Sligo. But hot on its heels came Radio City. For a while before the legislation got sorted, a couple of stations seemed to have sprung up in every town in Ireland. Fellas would give you all the lowdown for nothing in conversations at the Armitage Shanks; how cheap you'd get the transmitting kit in Holland. How easy it was to install. How to actually get her on the air.

Radio Sligo was fairly professional. Slick production values there. It had a few local business heads behind it.

Radio City, on the other hand, broadcast from upstairs in an apartment in Stephen's Street. The station won a good listenership, or at least seemed to do so. Radio City had mad naiveté. It operated on the assumption that there were many forms of music in the world and Radio City should cater to them all. (Country, MOR, rock, jazz.

Dublin and got degrees in computer science. In America he worked in IBM research for thirteen years on a variety of projects, including user interfaces for the visually disabled and juggling robots. He started the IBM Computer Music Center, inventing music and multimedia software applications.

These came to mind first.) They had a big red light that went on outside the studio door for when the station was ON AIR. They had stickers and T-shirts. But the sound-proofing budget must have fallen a bit short.

The DJ—in speaking—would compete with traffic noise and, memorably, dogs barking in the alley. The late Mike Marchini did a jazz programme.[†] He was a caretaker in the Regional College, had an interest in photography and owned an impressive and eclectic jazz collection. Mike had Italian/Irish roots. No mid-Atlantic DJ accents on Radio City; everyone spoke with their natural regional accent.

Denis Murphy had his own show—which sometimes featured anarchic comic improvisations with John Siberry. Barry Brennan did a late night rock music programme on Sundays. The main daytime show for a while featured Gerry Gallagher. Gerry was the driving force behind a Sligo–based showband called Kim Newport. Kim did not actually possess the surname Newport; Gerry just saw the town as he passed a signpost in Westport, and knew it was right for them. Kim was actually his partner in life; she had a great voice, the tightest latex pants on the planet and all the classic MOR songs down pat. They wrote a few songs, too. A lot of Sligo musicians played with The Kim Newport Band. Gerry worked in Fitzgerald's Music Shop on the corner of Castle and O'Connell Street. They dreamed big. Gerry and Kim were real Americans.

Louis Walsh invested a lot of energy into a smooth young singer called Johnny Logan. The night that Johnny Logan won the Eurovision Song Contest for the first time should have been an occasion of unbridled joy. But no sooner had the flowers wilted and the tears dried than the legal flak began to fly. More than one person felt they were the manager of the talented warbler. Jim Hand, who had managed Logan before Louis came along, felt he had an interest there. The dispute was heading for the courts. Louis had put a lot of work in, but now these unresolved issues bogged him down in lengthy and expensive legal actions. Although he became a major act and sold a lot of records, it didn't happen as

---

[†]   For a time, James Blennerhasset did the jazz show. Local saxophonist, Stan Burns, presented it, too.

big as it should have for Johnny Logan.[†] He parted with his young manager.

Louis Walsh had a music collection in his apartment, mostly pop. A couple of Lou Reed and David Bowie albums, too. *The Rise and Fall of Ziggy Stardust and the Spiders from Mars.* He tried out managing rock bands again for a while in the eighties. Aslan and In Tua Nua. Didn't enjoy it much. He went on record saying he would prefer a bad showband than a good rock band. Louis was going through a fairly lean patch.

Then he hit on the boyband thing.

Bros were amongst the first Brit-pop boybands, in the eighties. Then came Take That in the early nineties. Boyz II Men and New Kids on the Block were doing something similar (but more R&B) in America.

Louis' approach to managing Boyzone in the beginning was pure showband. Mixed with some heavy nineties spin-doctoring. The performers knew who was boss. Showbands didn't generally pick their own members. That was the manager's job; he hired and fired. Anyone was replaceable.

Ronan Keating was hired after attending a series of auditions. Louis dropped two of the original members, Mark Walton and Ritchie Rock. Boyzone, like the showbands of old, had to get into a white Transit van and drive to gigs up and down the country. Ronan had the duty of asking the gig promoter for payment at the end of the night. Boyzone danced a bit, but they were not asked to play an instrument.[*] In the era of boybands, that wasn't needed. All you needed was to be real good-looking.

For song material the boybands would do covers, reruns of pop songs of the seventies or eighties. But this was a finite pool. So writers had to be brought in. These were usually teams of producers. They understood the method of putting together a jingle or a pop song. The hook, the big simple drum parts, the string arrangement, the shape, adhered to a stock formula. Acoustic guitars were in

---

[†]   Logan won the Eurovision twice as a singer—in 1980 and 1987—and his song 'Why Me?' won the competition for Linda Martin and Ireland in 1992.

[*]   Keith Duffy had been a drummer in a couple of bands.

these days. Stock, Aiken and Waterman had written a lot of the pop tunes of the eighties, and Pete Waterman et al now had lots of competitors, in Britain and Europe. Like Biff and Matt, who wrote some of the Spice Girls hits, and producer/writers Anders Bagge and Arnthor Birgisson over in Sweden. Cheiron were another Swedish-based team. They had worked with The Backstreet Boys.

Bands were money-making machines, but like any machine they could give trouble. Louis had learned a lot, including to make sure you didn't get a little bollox who was unmanageable in the band. Check them out fairly thoroughly first the next time. His favourite Boyzone is Ronan Keating. He likes Ronan, the guy's earnest innocence; maybe reminds him of himself a long time ago.

Mae Filan, it seems, had the idea of ringing Louis' brother Paul, over in her old home town of Kiltimagh, in February. Paul gave her Louis' number, but after numerous calls she had spoken only to machines. Dial tones or no tones or machines. She let Shane know about what she was doing, but he does not appear to have taken it all that seriously. It was nice having him around the house again, but Mrs Filan wondered about the future. He wanted this band thing so badly, but nothing seemed to be happening. No progress. Streetwise seemed to be hanging back a bit, waiting for the contract to be signed. Shane needed to have a go at this racket or let go his cherished dream and pursue some other goal in life. She had had lots to mull over since the contract arrived from Mary and the others. Kian wanted to sign it and let Streetwise and Sound Records get on with releasing the single nationwide. His family seemed willing to go along with that. The Feehilys did, too. Shane wasn't so sure. He had been listening; listening to his own and Miggles' parents discussing the pros and cons.

Anyway Mrs Filan was patient. She wrote a letter to Louis Walsh and enclosed the IOYOU CD. She sent off a few more CDs, to DJs and companies and people in the music business. Then she phoned Louis one more time. This time she struck lucky.

- Hello?
- Is that Louis Walsh?
- Yeah. Who's that?

Louis talked to Mae for ages. He had seen this band IOYOU on the news, doing some hospital thing. He agreed to meet her son.

Mae got off the phone in an excited state. Of course Shane, who was in Dublin visiting his sister at the time (for the twenty-first birthday party of one of her friends), could not believe what his mother was telling him when she rang him.

- Go way, Mum. Louis Walsh? Wants to meet us? I don't believe you, you're pulling my leg. Are you telling me you were actually *talking* to Louis *Walsh*?
- Do you want his mobile phone number? He says for you to ring him and go meet him.

Shane tells Kian Egan. Kian happens to be with Shane up in Dublin that day. For the moment, they are to keep it to themselves. It is still February.

Shane is a bundle of nerves getting Louis' mobile number organised. He retreats to the toilet in his sister's house for sanctuary; he wants to be alone to make the momentous call. It rings out a few times and then Louis answers. The meeting with Louis is to be in the Pod nightclub, at a gig. Louis mentions a couple of celebrity names who will be there. Shane is dizzy with excitement reporting the news to his mum and Kian.

The boys go shopping the next day. They dress up boyband for the meeting with Louis Walsh.

When Shane and Kian arrive at the venue in Harcourt Street, Dublin, the bouncers don't buy their story that they have an invite from *the man himself*. It's £10 a head into the Pod. Shane tries ringing Louis' mobile again, but he's not answering. Kian and Shane are there at the door ages, trying to convince this heavy guy, when suddenly Louis pops his head out. 'The Sligo Boys! Come on in, lads,' says Louis Walsh. They stroll smoothly by the bouncers. They have a copy of the IOYOU CD with them.

The Pod is a huge club, with a massive PA system. Upstairs is another club, the Red Box. It is literally a red box, with another serious sound and lights rig installed. John Reynolds runs both clubs. John is a partner with Louis Walsh in the management of Boyzone. The Reynolds clan, from Longford, are big in showband promotion, dogfood manufacture and politics. John is a nephew of Albert Reynolds, the ex-Taoiseach (Prime Minister) of Ireland.

Kian is taller than Louis. Kian, Shane and Louis talk in a sit-down part of the club called the Chocolate Bar. The VIP section. Louis says straight up he is not interested in managing them. He is too busy right now to do another boyband. *But do not sign a deal with anyone.* Louis will help get them a manager. He will get them some good advice, too, from some people who have been there. Who have been around the block. Louis is taking a lot of phone calls. He chats real friendly for a while, then goes off and lets the boys have a look around. Then as Louis says good luck at the end of the night he pops in a suggestion. 'How would you like to have your band do support on Boyzone's autumn tour?'

The two lads are saucer-eyed. Saucers with big black coffee cups for pupils. They have lots to tell when they arrive home.

• Then Louis was asking us, 'Could I have a look at the band performing?'

Shane told him, 'Well, we have lots of videos.' So now Shane has to get on to Ciaran Carty. Kian and Shane arrive out to Strandhill in a big panic. 'Could you put together a show reel?' Ciaran says no problem. The lads look through different bits of footage. They want it edited as soon as possible. There's a very tight deadline.

Louis and Mae talk again, a few days later. Dublin office to the Café Carlton. She has not got the video for him yet.

• Mrs Filan, do these guys have a deal with anyone?

• Oh no, Louis. No deal. Some locals helped them out and offered a contract, but it was a terrible deal. No way will we sign that.

• Who were they?

Louis has never heard of Averyl Dooher. Maybe Pádraig Meehan rings a distant bell. Billy Whelan brought someone of that name . . . Nervous Animals. Louis organised a few gigs for them ten years back. Maybe another failed rock band. Or maybe no bell rings. And Mary McDonagh. Louis remembers her OK. Choreographing stuff for RTÉ. So that's what she's up to now.

• Listen, Mae, I know you from way back, and I won't lie to you: I'm very busy, I'm up to here, I can't take these lads of yours on. But . . . Look, send up a couple of them to Ronan, Ronan Keating's twenty-first. Let them get to know some of the lads. Get to know the scene up here.

• Ronan Keating. Oh, they love Ronan.

• You say they definitely have signed nothing with these people?

Pádraig has been looking for James Blen. He wants to record another batch of songs. Shane and Graham and Kian have presented some new song ideas, one of them is called 'Angels'. It was one of the ones that Shane had worked on with Daragh and Pádraig, before Christmas in the auditorium of the Hawk's Well. The two musicians had listened to Shane's ideas and come up with some grooves and arrangements. The sequences and lyrics they invented had been stored on the hard drive of Daragh's Apple Mac.

Averyl is on the phone again to Peter, the RTÉ producer. She has faxed him the stage map and wants to know times for the arrival at the TV centre.

Kian was here, Mary hears, when she arrives home. He wanted to collect his ticket for The Backstreet Boys show. 'Oh. Kian. Haven't seen him in a while.'

Michael Garrett Senior calls the Friday meeting on 27 February in the Embassy Hotel, Sligo. Michael is a fit, young-looking dad. He feels quite sharp, quite businesslike tonight. Mae and Peter and Shane Filan sit with their backs to the window. Michael starts by putting the question—where do we go from here? Then he answers it himself.

• Seems to me, it's up to the accountants now—let's call them in and see what can be hammered out with Averyl, Mary and Pádraig. Their accountant should write to ours . . .

Michael reports to the meeting on all the work he has been doing on behalf of the parents. He has been on the phone to the solicitor representing the parents. They talked over how the meeting with the managers went, and the next move. The parents' solicitor had written a letter to Ruth, the Streetwise solicitor. Ruth had been slow getting back . . . The ball was in the management court. But Michael had persevered, believing that the goodwill was there to close the deal.

He phoned the parents' solicitor again about a week later. The response from Ruth was in. Michael and the families' solicitor looked over the letter from Streetwise's advisor. They narrowed down and bulleted the sticking points. Now Michael has a fax from the solicitor saying that neither the solicitor nor the families' accountant would agree under any circumstances to the management handling money, like the advance out of a record deal.

219

'It did not make sense to me when I heard it, and it still doesn't make sense to me,' says Michael. 'Well, what do ye think?'

Kian Egan is watching with sharp blue eyes. His elbows rest on the table, hands folded. He is saying nothing. Mae Filan has a pleasant expression on her face. Michael thinks he is doing well here. He has been spending a lot of his time trying to get closure here.

• The boys will have to handle the money themselves, and the tax side of it. I am told that no record company will sign a contract with the boys and then send a cheque to other people . . .

But Michael sees signs of progress. The management's solicitor Ruth seems to have been suggesting that the accountants might sort it out. There was goodwill there, sufficient goodwill to solve it. If the management accountant would ring the parents' accountant, it could be hammered out.

• I intend to tell them that.

Mae tells him to take it from her. 'No way are we going to sign a contract with those people.' It just comes out of the blue. Mae takes the floor.

• That's what we have been told. That's the advice now. We'll not sign.

Shane starts to say how he and Kian had met Louis Walsh and how Louis will help find us a manager, and we were afraid to tell ye and how it is not true that you always have to pay to get support on a big tour and how we have to send him a video and that Ronan's birthday party is on soon and . . . Mae hushes him. 'We have this chance now to go up and meet Ronan. Michael could go up and meet him, too.'

But what about school? What about the Leaving Cert? The Garretts don't want distractions until the exams are over. Then maybe Mary could help prepare the lads for Louis Walsh to audition them . . .

• We have to take this opportunity as it presents itself. We will not go near Mary. Mary is not their manager. We have signed nothing with anyone.

'Louis', says Mae, 'was hard to track down, but I tracked him. He is a professional.' 'Well, OK,' says Michael Senior, 'Louis Walsh is a professional.' 'He is a professional,' says everyone. Mae stands up, Shane and Kian stand up, too. Meeting over.

NUNSENSE

Ronan Keating and his girlfriend Yvonne screech to a halt outside the Red Box on a gleaming metal beast of a Harley Davidson. The bouncers scatter, but regroup quickly to clear a path for the celebrity lead singer of Boyzone. Ronan and Yvonne are in black leather; *Grease* is the theme for the night; Ronan sports a quiff. He nudges the bike through the doors and inside the building, revving up the engine savagely. The cameras chatter. It is the first time the couple have gone public as an item. Model Yvonne and heartthrob Ronan! Ronan Keating's twenty-first birthday bash is in full swing.

Michael 'Miggles' Garrett and Shane Filan arrived in Dublin earlier on the Sligo train. They have their video with them. The girl at the door leafs through six pages of names before finding theirs. They smile and move casually through the crowd, but they are not as cool as they look. Things are happening all around them. A rock and roll band blasts out classic numbers from the stage. The doors of the club suddenly swing open again and admit a 1966 green Mustang convertible, driven by Boyzone members wearing Elvis wigs. The talk is of Ronan's presents. As well as the convertible from the other Boyz, he got a microphone that belonged to Elvis Presley from Polygram, his record company.

Shane and Michael spot loads of famous people: Alan Shearer and John Barnes, the Newcastle and England footballers. Ken Doherty, snooker star. John Rocha, fashion designer. And Eamonn Dunphy, radio and TV personality. Lots of creatures in *Grease* costumes slug out of longnecks. They see Ronan on the far side of the room, a gaggle of beautiful people queueing to kiss him happy birthday. Beautiful people say 'hi' to them and float away. The two lads manage a bit of chit-chat with a pair of girls in the sexiest dresses they have ever seen. The boys' slight Sligo accents sound twice as rich as usual in their own ears. They say 'like' after each sentence, and 'cool!' a lot to compensate.

Louis Walsh introduces them to Ronan. He seems to be a real nice guy. He is a bit smaller in real life than on the telly. The lads have a great night.

The fourth of March 1998. Early, early morning. The sky is lightening, turning a paler shade of grey. Dublin's traffic is already beginning to stir. Red traffic lights, red brake lights on the dual carriageway. Trucks rumble up and hiss to a halt, salty from the ferry from England. Cars with dimmed headlights stack up behind them. Tails of white engine breath on the frosty breeze. In the living room of Shane's sister's place, where they are staying, Shane and Miggles don't slag off Boyzone any more. They drink cups of tea and go back over every moment of the night. What such-and-such a star said. What Louis Walsh said. They have met Louis Walsh: the manager and maker of Boyzone. God has spoken. He has listened to their CD. He will help them get a top manager.

• Ye could be big, lads. Ye could be one of the biggest bands to come out of Ireland.

The two best friends fall quiet. Michael feels his head spinning. 'Jesus, Michael,' says Shane, out of the blue. 'Jesus, Shane,' says Michael.

Pádraig has finished his gig with his mates Barry and Tommy and Donal in Carr's pub. It is Thursday, 12 March. Carr's was quiet. People must be saving themselves for Paddy's Day—can you believe it's only next weekend? He searches the sky, from habit. There is a halo of haze around the full moon, no stars visible. Hale-Bopp is long gone, anyway. It is still out there, of course, still speeding through space, but too faint now to see. The experts are now saying it is over 4,000 years since it was here last. On this tour, the gravity of Jupiter changed its orbit. Ah, well. Roll on the next 2,380 years. Pádraig is throwing his gear into the back of his van. A slightly slurred voice hails him from across the road. It's the lads. They are all talking at once.

- Hey, Pádraig, do you want to come to our gig?
- We are playing with The Backstreet Boys.
- We can get you a ticket, you can get backstage, the whole lot . . . Access all areas . . .
- This is a big deal, Pádraig. We are serious . . .
- I can't hear you, lads; look this is not the time or the place. Call me tomorrow.

There had been rumours flying in Martin Carr's pub all evening. The boys were in earlier and a phone call had come. Then all hell broke loose. It looked like Graham Keighron was crying. He was down on his knees anyway. And young Kian Egan had been leppin' around like a madman. The fellas were on their mobile phones bigtime. Everyone in the band had to get a mobile phone to keep in touch with the Big Stuff that is going on. And any time they were not actually on the phone they were *telling* phone calls, imaginary receiver to the ear.

- And I says, no way. Go way. Are ya coddin' me . . .?

The following day phone calls are being made all over the place. Kian Egan and Graham Keighron are looking for backing tracks. People who have been working for Streetwise, arrangers and studios, are getting calls.

- What do you want them for?
- We are doing a gig . . .
- Without Mary? An IOYOU gig?

What a night that had been, the night in Carr's when Shane's mum rang to tell the boyband they would be playing on the same bill as The Backstreet Boys. Mrs Filan told them the news just as soon as she finished talking to Louis Walsh on the phone. Yeah, he had looked at Ciaran Carty's video of the lads. He was impressed with what he saw. Then Louis says, 'I know The Backstreet Boys will be in town. Maybe I could swing that gig for ye. I could ask Jim Aiken . . .'

- Oh my God, The Backstreet Boys! I hear nothing but Backstreet Boys from my fella. They are his favourites. He would love to meet them, and to play on the same stage . . . he won't believe this, that it's even possible. They are all going up to that gig, you know. But don't you have to pay big money to do a support gig with a big name band?

It is two nights later, backstage at the Hawk's Well after the last performance of *Nunsense*. It has been a brilliant show. Tremendous fun to do. But everyone is not happy. The crowds have been disappointing. Mary hasn't enough money to pay everyone. She will have to go to the bank. And there is a rumour that the boys have gone off to play before The Backstreet Boys. They are looking for backing tracks. Averyl has been trying to contact the Dublin firm of solicitors. Bad weekend. They are not to be found. She gets a local lawyer to come in. A small group of people sit backstage as Pádraig phones Filans'.

- Hello, is Shane there?
- No, Shane is not here.
- Peter, is that you? What is happening with the boys? I am hearing talk that they are off doing stuff.
- I don't know what they are doing, but they will do what they like. They are getting good advice.
- Well, we have put a lot of effort in as their managers. There is a gig waiting for them on TV. It would only be a courtesy if you could let us know what is going on . . .
- Ah ha! Oh yes, pal of my cradle days! I bid you a good night! (Click.)

It is spring. It is the time of dreams.

The winter is over. On the long rain-filled days of winter there is never much time for dreams in Sligo. You see no mountains. The sky of leaden grey descends and blinds everyone; the rain-blind bump into each other as they trudge from pavement to street to pavement, their collars raised against the bitter wind.

But there is always a dry spell in spring, when the birds sing and people leave their coats at home and the air zings with possibility. When alcoholics wake up with hope in their hearts of new beginnings. When Sligo floats, an island amid the lush green farmland. It was on a day like today that Shane and Michael sat on a park bench in the Bishop's Garden. Now they meet on the railway platform on a crisp morning. Beams of dusty light collide in the high glass roofing of the venerable station. Blue diesel smoke rises. The early train to Dublin waiting.

• I bags the window seat.

Ciaran Carty travels with the band, his camera slung by his side. The air is electric with possibility.

Pádraig Meehan rings Michael Garrett Senior from Mary McDonagh's house. The phone in the front room. It is Monday, 16 March, just before lunch.

Mary is not there. She is on a plane to Memphis, on a flight planned long ago. She looks out the window of the plane. They are flying over a part where the dirty white cauldron of cloud is breached, exposing dark Atlantic waves five miles below. Out beyond the wingtip, the horizon is hazy. Night is in pursuit and catching up. The whisper of the plane, the hush of engines and air surrounds her, it saturates every frequency. The voices of the other passengers—so playful! So innocent!—seem distant, filtered.

Mary knew it could happen, something like this could happen. Yet somehow she did not expect it.

She tells herself the story, the story of the boyband. She knows all the players. She can see exactly what is going on. But it hasn't hit home yet. It's like a dancer's injury. Something is terribly wrong. But she just carries on. Numbly. She is waiting for the feelings to kick in.

'Howya doin'?' says Pádraig to Michael Garrett Senior.

• Howya.

• Could you give me some kind of outline as regards what is happening with the boys?

• I'll tell you now. What is happening with the boys is, they have developed a mind of their own. They are not listening to anybody. I don't agree with what they're doing, but they're doing it anyhow.

Pádraig explains that there is a TV gig called 'TX Live' booked for them. Michael acknowledges the work that Streetwise has done. He is annoyed by all this—this new disruption to Michael's study. Michael Junior and Michael Senior might have had a debate.

• I would prefer if none of this had happened at all until after June.

Pádraig is somehow surprised by Michael's frank acknowledgement of the managers' contribution.

- There has been good work done to bring them this far.

But there are other parents who are pushing. They want to try and test the water with Louis. Pádraig complains that it seems they are planning to use sequences and stuff that is not their property. Pádraig has considered looking for an injunction to stop it, but has decided against it. 'I won't queer the pitch for them.' At this stage Pádraig still feels like he is negotiating with Michael.

- I think it's a great thing that they're getting the chance to do a gig with The Backstreet Boys. I think it's fantastic. Fair play to them. Let them get out and have that experience. You know what I mean. In one way it can't be anything but good, but there is no need to do it behind our backs, with tracks we have made up.

Michael says he believes in honour.

- They'll have to include us. There's no way they can just disregard our input up to now.
- Well, this is my feeling on it as well.

Pádraig begins slowly to realise that Michael Senior has lost his position of influence at the table with the parents. 'It was all done behind my back,' Michael tells him, 'it was taken out of my hands. First thing I hear, Louis Walsh has something organised for IOYOU out at the end of March . . .'

- I'll wait—I'll give them a bit of time. Let them come back to me and talk to me.

'Well I reckon that they will,' says Michael. 'They should. They haven't signed anything with Louis.'

Mary has a bunch of CDs and photos in her bag. She had packed them already, to bring to America. She is travelling on other business but hopes to combine her visit with some exploratory promotion of her band. Mary meets with a business acquaintance in New York, and he travels with her the last leg of the journey. The well-known Irish events promoter expects her to have a CD of IOYOU for him; Mary pretends to have forgotten it. It's an uncomfortable journey, the promoter talking all about the business, about bands, about turns the market is taking, about how the time is right, about how good her ideas are.

When the plane sets down in Memphis, her companion invites

Mary to dinner. She declines and hurries away; she needs some space, time alone. When she gets to the hotel room, the hotel bar is closed, and the little fridge has wine, but only Merlot, the one grape she can't abide. Mary lies on the bed, and the tears come.

THE BACKSTREET BOYS GIG

Dame Street is bedecked in green and gold. Insistent drum rhythms, fanfares and cymbal crashes fill the air. Fantastic figures cavort and float by. A colossal dragon. Drummers, dancers, stilts-walkers, flagbearers, fireblowers. A zoo full of golden animals. And Bilbo Baggins is in town, with his friend Frodo. A uniformed majorette sends her baton spiralling high. She catches cleanly and marches on at the head of her band, making way for a 10ft tall teddy bear and a regiment of toy soldiers. Ronan Keating, with fellow band member Keith Duffy at his side, waves to the crowd. People run to him to shake his hand. He is leading the Dublin St Patrick's Day Parade, perched in the back of his new green vintage Ford Mustang convertible.

It is ten past one in the afternoon. Kian, Michael, Mark, Derek, Shane and Graham are in Dublin today, but they are not at the parade. They crowd on a couch in Mairéad Filan's apartment. IOYOU are sounding good, singing 'All I Have to Give' *a capella*. 'All I Have to Give', by The Backstreet Boys. Shane clicks his fingers and conducts, like he always does.

Michael's hair tosses about in his eyes and he does that black hand move thing. His eyes are on fire.

- We are leaving now for the RDS, we do a bit of rehearsing, a bit of a soundcheck. Then the gig. We're there, man. We're supporting The Backstreet Boys. We're there, we made it. And we're all together, living in each other's pockets—we're a *family*, maaaan, and we love it!!

Ciaran does a whip pan; Shane Filan's side look in the viewfinder.

- Ya, and there's . . . a big crowd up from Sligo.
- Thanks to all the Sligo people.
- We will be meeting The Backstreet Boys.

The Backstreet Boys are not stuck up at all. They are *soooo* sound. They are smooth and all speak with that deep southern US twang. They sound like people in a movie. The IOYOUs are introduced to four Backstreets. Howie D. isn't there. We meet him later. A.J., Nick, Brian and Kevin. Meet Graham and Kian and Mark and Derek and Michael and Shane.

- Hello.
- Hi guys.

Kevin is kind of the leader of the BSB. He looks mature. Graham has a good look at A.J. He is very striking looking. He looks relaxed, he has almost a hippyish style. He is not acting at all. He looks happy. He looks grown-up. He fits in his face and rings and clothes.

Actually the Backstreet members all look older than you'd expect; some of them are ten years older than our boys. They look Latin and moviestar and suntanned and not human. They look perfect. More like a band than a boyband. The boys later get to know the name of that look. It's called success and money.

The Backstreet Boys are mad into being fit. They have a portable basketball court they take everywhere on tour with them. IOYOU throw a few baskets with Nick and Brian. Miggles has his baseball hat on backways. Derek hangs around on the fringes. The Backstreet Boys' backing band make sounds in the background, soundchecking. The edgy power clavinets rattle through the empty hall.

- Yeah, we write our own songs, too.
- Cool, guy.

Louis comes by. Shane and Michael and Kian introduce him to Graham and Derek and Mark. They have the three backing tracks organised. 'On DAT, like you asked. Such a hassle to get them!' The studio guys were a great help. 'We got them to make up seven copies, so there's no worry about the tape getting lost. Thanks for the gig, Louis,' says Miggles. 'Best of luck, boys,' says Louis.

It has been an eventful few days. Everybody has been staying at Shane's sister Mairéad's place, on couches, on the floor. Sleeping bags, bodies everywhere. Getting up at the crack of eight o'clock. The Sunday before Paddy's Day they had been sitting in the flat fidgeting, and in a quiet moment a sound wafted into the room. It was the sound of a bass, a guitar or synth bass, booming down the road from the concert venue, the RDS, which was only a couple of blocks away. They recognised that riff.

- We've got it goin' on for years!
- That has to be The Backstreet Boys!!

Ciaran Carty and Graham Keighron went out for a prowl. They discovered a way in and around the building. They had even found a chink in a covered window by the stage. The scouts reported back. Shortly thereafter, seven lads were racing down Simmonscourt Road and skirting round the back of the buildings at the extensive Royal Dublin Society events complex. They followed that bass rumble. They went over a wall. The Backstreet Boys/IOYOU gig is not in the main arena, in the open air, like the Michael Jackson show Michael and Mark and Shane saw last year. It is in the Simmonscourt, a huge hangar-like building.

They crowded around a covered window. Through a couple of chinks they could see people moving. Familiar people. They knew those guys, like they knew people from school or from the street where they lived. Brian Littrell and his cousin Kevin Richardson. Nick Carter and Howie Dorough. And Bone McLean.

- There's A.J., Graham!

The Backstreet Boys. And their backing band. Soundchecking. And lots of roadies and other people at work. The Sligo lads watched in the cold, whispering excitedly to each other, for twenty minutes. Then they went back to the couch in Mairéad Filan's flat.

Eight thousand fans show up at the RDS for BSB. They are

230

impatient to see their band. IOYOU look down from a perch high above the scene. Derek shows his 'Access All Areas' badge. 'We are totally excited,' says Shane. 'We met four BSB guys.'

- They are pure sound.

Mark is saying everything's gone totally mad. 'Such a buzz. This is a packed RDS. We are waiting to go on. We got a big write-up in *The Herald*. We met Boyzone's manager, Louis Walsh. He was real nice. It's kinda weird. It all happened in the last two weeks.'

- We will be going to a party later, with The Backstreet Boys.

There is a pre-gig hum in the RDS, a waiting-for-the-show-to-start hum. The air is thick with excitement. The stage set looks like a futurist robotic fantasy. Lasers wander on the field of heads beyond a forest of static coloured floodlights. The mixing desk is walled off halfway down the floor, an island of intricate technology among the wheatfield of fans.

The IOYOU dressing room smells of new clothes and aftershave and toothpaste. Beyond the dressing room door there are connecting corridors, corridors full of history. They know what lies at the end of the corridor. The boys know that the futuristic robot stage awaits them at the end.

They jog along, not too fast, not too slow. Now the voice of the crowd starts getting louder. Like a train coming down a tunnel. There is a ladder to climb. On the threshold of the stage, someone stops them . . .

This heavy black dude in a jumpsuit springs onstage, from the opposite side. He has a radio mic.

- I'm the maaanager of The Backstreet Boys, and I'd like to welcome you *awwwllll*.

His spiel is like a boxing ref's intro . . .

- Annnnnnnd . . .

The pitch goes up and down again . . .

- A happy *Patrick's Day* to everyone. *Annnnnnnd* . . . First I want you to welcome to the stage . . . from yo *own* hometown, Dublin, Ireland's newest boys band. *I—O—YEWWWW!*

The bass drum pump comes first, 125 beats per minute. Then the power chords of 'Pinball Wizard' come crashing in, through the mighty BSB PA system. Pádraig Meehan's Marchis Strat power chords spurring on the manic thrash of the acoustics. The crowd waver like they're hit by a storm, then stretch out and scream. The boys jog on, moving down to the front, to the border of monitors and lamps and security men and, beyond, the paying public. IOYOU form a loose line, doing pogo jumps and holding their radio mics. The crowd scream for them. This is a different scream again, different from the Hawk's Well, an 8,000 packed scream, no adults sitting down the back smiling, just everyone lungbusting. If you put your hands over your ears, like the small ones do, it still penetrates; it enters your heart, a shrill singing, almost a whistle . . .

'*Ever since I was a young boy . . .*' Mark has learned the words of the first verse. Once the verse starts, the others are into the dance steps. The way Shane kept reminding them. The way Mary and Steffen showed them. It's loose as hell, Mary would have had a conniption, but it's high energy. Graham struts the stage, pointing the sky finger defiantly. As 'Pinball Wizard' fades out, there is a moment of vulnerability. Then the kids cheer. Derek looks out over the crowd. Derek feels feather light as he springs on the balls of his feet. He was first to reach the front after the boys burst onstage, thrusting out his arms as if to embrace everyone there.

Michael and Shane look out over the crowd. They look out over the bobbing sea of heads and hands. Kian looks, too, at all the pretty girls, the eager faces. He is loving it. After 'Pinball', the talky bit . . . . Miggles does the most chatting, he is excited. Only now it's not Averyl's script . . . this is Michael Garrett talking!

- *Helloooooooo Dublin!* Dublin, let me hear ya!

Miggles points his mic into the audience. The crowd scream on cue. Michael Garrett has never felt more alive. He exchanges a lightning glance with Shane. Shane is solid. Shane claps his hands, the chunky radio mic in the loop of thumb and palm; he winks, his trademark wink. Shane is working in wide circles, making use of the stage. It feels vast. The biggest stage they have ever played on. Shane wants to talk, too . . .

- Let me see your hands *in the air* . . . .

Four thousand pairs of hands go in the air.

'Together Girl Forever' is next. The slow song brings on the sexy screams. The arms go out. Red faces, pale faces, made-up faces, pretty faces, plain faces, all in the crush, a mass of gig happiness. The hunger of the girls. Then IOYOU are singing 'Everlasting Love'.

Shane and Mark swap vocal lines with the band. Mark has his bold face on. He is consumed in the moment. He sings.

Every now and then I get a little bit cold, then I . . .
Need somebody to hoooold MEH!
I look at you and your body of gold, and I . . .
Need somebody to hoooold MEH!

It is all over in a flash. IOYOU get a great cheer at the end. Even though they only performed three songs, they are exhausted. The manager guy is on again, announcing The Backstreet Boys.

They only saw Louis for a second. He just said good, good. Up in their perch in the hospitality box, IOYOU bop seriously to The Backstreet Boys' show. Just let the beat control your body! The BSB show is theatre. It looks great. It sounds great. It's heavy metal, it's funk. It's slinky ballads. It's got balls. They all dance great, too, so slick, lots of new moves. It's rock and roll.

ROLO MANAGEMENT

L ouis rings Ronan Keating raving about these guys from Sligo. Ronan can't make The Backstreet Boys gigs.

'I have to get you to see them! They can actually sing, not like some boybands. Not like the rest of Boyzone, ha ha. I tell you, Ro. They have energy. I am thinking of taking them on. Perhaps you might come in on the management side,' says Louis to Ronan. Maybe Louis would form a company with Ronan and manage these lads. What an idea.

• Let's combine both the names, Ronan and Louis. Rolo. *Rolo Management Limited.* It has a ring to it, hasn't it?

Ronan Keating is going through a tough patch in his life. He is grieving for his mother, Marie, who died of cancer a month ago. For a pop star, Ronan is known as a down-to-earth kinda guy. He was born into a sprawling sixties housing estate called Wilson Estate in north Dublin in March 1977. Ronan was very close to his mum.

Boyzone, with Louis as their co-manager, have sold more than twelve million albums worldwide. Ronan is the highest profile band member, a singer with a distinctive style and the looks to break teenage hearts. Still Ronan has unfulfilled dreams. He dreams of cracking the United States as a solo artist. He has been listening to country music and writing his own songs.

Louis says, you will learn from this, Ro. You will see the business from the other side. Look on it as me offering you a job. You need to get involved in something new. Something different. A challenge. If you want the gig, I will cut you in for a generous cut of the action. Maybe 10 per cent.

Louis calls in Shane and Kian from IOYOU for a talk.

• I have decided I want to manage IOYOU. What do ye think, guys?

• That would be so cool! I mean, yeah . . . I mean . . . But you said you were too busy, Louis . . .

• I changed my mind, Shane. And I might be getting a bit of help on this one. Anyway, ye did well, up there. How could I see you up there and not manage you?

Mairéad Filan tidies her flat. The lads are staying for another night. The *Evening Herald* lies open on top of a pile of sleeping bags. IOYOU cheerful in black and white all over the middle page.

THE PHONE CALL

Louis is refining this pop star thing into something of a science. He has asked himself, apart from not being troublesome, what should the characteristics of a perfect boyband unit be? He is evolving a model. Five members is the ideal number. The fans have to have something to look at. Five is easier to photograph. You only need five.

Each of the five should have a different character, a different element of the pie. Each member picked will appeal to a different type of girl. You have to accommodate different tastes. You have to give yourself every chance. The greater the difference in band members, the wider the audience they attract. There should be a macho one, a camp one, a dark one, a blonde one and a moody one. Louis would like them to be able to sing and dance. But no one guy should shine out above the team. They should be team players. And once they start wearing beads, and beards, and pronouncing solemnly on the meaning of existence, the sell-by date has been reached. They have grown past being a boyband into a manband.

Louis plays 'Together Girl Forever' for Ronan. He looks again at the CD cover, six faces staring out from Mike Bunn's boyband heaven.

The morning after the second BSB gig, the IOYOU band members wake up talking. They talk non-stop. All at the one time.

- Louis is going to manage us!
- Derek was going mental out there!
- Did you see yer wan fainting?

You don't notice how hungry you are till you stop talking. Mark and Shane are dawdling around outside when Shane's mobile tone strikes up. Private number calling. Shane saying 'yeah . . . yeah'. His eyebrows say 'Louis'. 'What? . . . OK . . . OK.' Something is wrong with Shane. His breathing is shallow. A sideways look. Mark says, 'Shane? What is it? What's wrong?' Shane looks very strange indeed.

- Tell us, for God's sake!

Shane calls the others together. All except Derek. We have to meet up in the afternoon. Forget the shopping. Cut it short.

Derek heads off happily. The rest of them meet up again shortly afterwards at an appointed landmark.

- What's the story, Shane?
- Derek has to go. Louis says he's doesn't want him.
- No way.
- Well, Louis says if he doesn't go, none of us stay, so do we have a choice?
- Jesus, Shane, how do we tell Derek?

Shane looks out at the darkening countryside flashing by the train window. Louis Walsh is going to be our manager. Now we will definitely be the biggest thing to come out of Ireland. We will probably be going over to London to record in a big studio. We will be playing support on the Boyzone tour.

Mark glances over. Shane yawns even though he doesn't need a yawn. A hush has settled over the shuffling rhythm of the train wheels. Miggles and Graham have a truce going and are chatting, all friendly, in low voices, in the seat behind. Derek is listening to music on his Walkman.

Shane is fond of Derek. Derek is easy to be around. Derek loves being in the band. Where can we break the news? Shane laughs too hard when Derek cracks a joke.

Derek has to feel that there is something up. He should guess himself. Mark drums on the table. Shane Filan sings to himself and reads his magazine.

237

The ancient hulk of Sligo station swallows the train. The platform brightly lit. The end of the line.

The tap water grows less splashy and turns warm and then steaming hot as Pádraig wets his face and hands before breakfast. The air in the cottage is chill. The sunglasses come out, dusty winter sunglasses. Always going to Dublin the sun is in your eyes, it is always morning.

Pádraig stops off at his mother's on the way to Dublin. He walks in a little abandoned lane that once led to the house but is now bypassed by a gravel road. It's muddy. There is a dank, damp smell under the trees, the smell of bour trees and twisted pines, the minty-scented ones his father used to call Gigantics.

• Pudsy is going in to Ballinvilla. Will we cut turf this year, do ya think?

• Ah yeah, let him fire ahead, the weather is supposed to be good. Yeah, I'll have time to save it.

In the end he ends up going over to Carrick-on-Shannon for a few pints. And not bothering with Dublin. He will go next week. There are a good few old contacts he should renew. He could phone up a few of the guys and maybe show them this cool new song he has.

Shane goes for a spin on his own. The turbulence in the wake of the Filan family car sets roadside daffodils nodding. Rain gear in the back seat. Wellingtons in the boot. It could be mucky. Shane needs to walk in a bit of muck. He has not seen his horses for a while. As he drives he visualises the land, the route he will take, which horse he is going to take out for a canter. We might get the *Smash Hits* tour. It will be great. There is a business meeting with Ronan Keating next week.

Someone overtakes him on a straight stretch in a four-wheel drive. Everyone is driving four-wheel drives these days.

• Derek. You are not in the band.

• We have to let you go, Derek.

• Sorry, Derek.

• Do you want to leave the band, Derek?

Nothing sounds OK. Practising his lines doesn't help the feeling in the pit of his stomach. This has to be one of the worst jobs Shane has ever had to do. The band know Shane will do it, but no one likes it. Shane arranges that they meet up in town.

- We are all heading to Graham's. Are ye coming? Derek?'

In the end, the three of them start telling Derek—Graham, Shane and Michael. They kind of blurt it out in Graham's living room. It makes no sense. So it is Shane who has to do the actual talking. Shane tells Derek the bad news. Feehily is quiet.

Derek looks stunned as he takes in the words. His jaw drops. *You won't be staying on in the band.* He sort of smiles. Tears well in his eyes. Why had they let him come all the way to Dublin?

- Why?

'It's a management decision, Derek,' says Shane, his dark eyebrows lifting, wrinkling his forehead. 'No particular reason. It's not . . . I'm so sorry . . .' Derek bursts out the door. The boys smile uneasily after he is gone. The smiles wane. They sit in silence.

Derek is all cut up. One part of his soul says, 'I knew this would happen.' The other part can't bear the loneliness of being the one left behind. His mum rings Louis Walsh. Louis rings back. Louis says, 'Sorry, Mrs Lacey. Derek was a bit mature looking. He can't dance. He is not what I am looking for. Sorry.'

Derek's girlfriend breaks it off with him, just about the same day as the band is telling him they don't need him any more.

Derek stays indoors for days. He can't bear to see anyone. Later on, he will get used to the jibes. Shelflife. The pizza deliverers . . . No life. All the smart Alecs. But just now he is in grief. He feels totally isolated. His friends have moved on and left him behind. One dry spring day he sees Mary McDonagh as he walks down Castle Street. He crosses the street and doesn't look in her direction.

THE SHOWCASE GIG

M ichael Garrett wasn't as totally blown away by meeting BSB as some of the others. OK, it was great; maybe if it was Jackson it would be different. But the feeling of the gigs had stayed with him. The buzz lasted a full week before it started to pale.

It was good. How good? Hard to measure. You could try comparing it with previous good feelings. That goal. The comfort of the solid contact between instep and football, the instant of knowing the shot will beat the keeper, and it a big match, and all the school watching and your dad there and your marker foiled at last. Or the girl? The sensation of contact, of knowledge of, that special girl. The first time, long ago, when you were real young. She teaching you with slow kisses. Firefly fingertips advancing between brastuff and skin. A nipple awakened. A date kept.

Not as good. This was the best so far. What of the place beyond the earth, in imagination, in dreams? A lap in a Formula One car? A pint with M.J. (if M.J. were to suddenly drop his teetotal ways)? Still not easy to better the week gone by.

The ceremony. The gathering. With you at its centre. An easy comfortable boyband you. Knowing what to do. You serving the audience, one of the chosen, one of the priests. Giving it loads. Better than opening Christmas presents. Or winning the lotto.

Nothing on the face of clay could come close. Except maybe if IOYOU were the main act, and the crowd had come to see IOYOU.

Pádraig has chowder and brown bread for lunch in Hargadon's. He has not bothered with Dublin. He takes a seat that places his back near the stove. A lot is going on. Some character is looking to trade millennium fifty pences. There is talk of twisters. A couple of mini tornadoes have been seen in recent months out in Ballisodare Bay. Ah, they come in all the time, you don't see them. Even on a calm day. They visit the Point, too, seemingly. Photographer Noel Kilgallen had heard a noise one morning and gone to investigate. It must have been a twister. It split the hedge in front of his house down the middle. From end to end.

• Did you take a photo, Noel?

The Hargadon's *Irish Times* is in demand. Up at Hillsboro the parties are still talking, but with no agreement in sight and an Easter deadline looming. Ken Maginnis is giving guff to Mo Mowlam. George Mitchell has the patience of Job.

• No, sorry, this is *my* paper. That guy over there has the house one.

• Sorry. OK. No problem.

Arsenal going well in the premiership. Man U. way down, eleventh. Charlie Haughey's lawyers are in the High Court, talking tough to the Moriarity Tribunal. 'I'm the king of the world,' says James Cameron at the Oscars. His blockbuster movie *Titanic* wins just about everything. 'My Heart Will Go On' sings Celine Dion, day and night, at every turn, the last couple of weeks. No escape. At least there's no TV, no singing allowed by Pat in Hargadon's.

IOYOU feel a bit like aliens on O'Connell Street, Sligo. No one really knows us. We are all alone. The five guys hang around a lot together these days. They make urgent calls on their Ready-To-Go phones. 'TX Live' is still on, on RTÉ, in a week's time. Louis sorted it out with the TV people.

On Castle Street, some of the boys nearly bump into Mary McDonagh. They dive into a doorway and scamper away. They feel dangerous and on the run, and—like, very exciting people.

241

The boys had gotten used to doing what they were told to do by Mary. She had gotten used to having the last word on everything. Well, OK, she was usually right. She was patient and firm. What a buzz to be pissing off Mary—powerful, Scary Mary.

• She must be *soooo* pissed off!

• I would love to hear what they are saying now. Averyl and Pádraig and Mary.

They don't have long to wait. Ciaran Carty goes around to Mary's. She is just back from America. He has a foot in both camps and a journalistic curiosity. Watching these acts unfold fascinates him; it's like watching a slow-mo train crash. Ciaran brings snippets of news in both directions.

• They dropped Derek Lacey.

• Yeah. I heard his mam rang Louis. I saw him yesterday in Quinnsworth.

Mary watches his video footage of The Backstreet Boys gig, in her sitting room. Ciaran crouches at the TV, ejects a video of the Oscars ceremony and put his cassette in, blue handwriting on the label. The picture emerges out of snow and noise. Dark milling packed crowds below the balcony. Small figures onstage in a storm of light. Zoom in.

Mary's first reaction is to get angry at the lads when they lose shape in the routine. They are doing her parts badly.

Then she laughs at them. She puts her hand over her mouth. More feelings are on the way. 'Don't watch it, Mary,' says Averyl. Pádraig and Averyl are at a different stage from Mary. They have been chatting to each other, they have been around, over Paddy's weekend and the week since. They have been busy blaming. They have blamed themselves. They have blamed each other. They probably even blamed Mary for a few seconds. They have blamed this boy, that boy. This parent, that parent. They blamed Louis. They cursed Louis Walsh and the horse he rode in on. Now they are in the disillusionment stage. This wine is corked. This avocado is rotten. This spud is green. I can't eat it. The stuff in my stomach makes me feel bad.

• They are terrible. They are going to get nowhere.

• No, Mary. They are going to be huge. I said it when I saw them in your rehearsal room, and I still say it. They will be mega.

'I have to go,' says Averyl.

- • Don't watch it.

Pádraig watches no more than a few seconds of Ciaran's footage, then heads home himself.

Down the road, the boys have gone all practical and pragmatic. They nod stoically to each other. Their mouths make upside down 'U's. They don't talk much about the others, and if they do it is on the lines of how it's just too bad, really, especially about Derek, but it was nothing personal. None of it was personal. Like Louis would say, it was just business. But it must be admitted that it is a good feeling all the same . . .

Anyway they have more to think about than Mary and Derek and all that stuff. They have crossed a great hurdle and landed on their feet. The field is thinner but they are galloping full tilt and wondering about the next fence on this devilish, uncharted, exhilarating pursuit. What has Louis next up his sleeve? What will The Big Meeting with Ronan Keating be like? The nearer you get to the winner's enclosure, the higher the stakes. Mrs Filan is wearing a stylish hat. She is talking to Louis. She is keeping in touch with the other parents. She is a very cool mum indeed.

Mrs Garrett has a sleepless night. She is just back from her holidays. Michael is saying what Louis Walsh said, about maybe a Showcase Gig coming up with some big record company. He has to get new stuff to wear. She rebukes Michael over the way they treated Derek. Poor Derek. And what about Mary and Averyl and Pádraig?

It has been a terrible dilemma, ever since the contact with Louis. The Garretts felt respect and gratitude towards Mary and the management team. So had all the parents.

But, at the same time, how do you stand in the way of your boy as he reaches out for his most treasured goal, when his impossible dream appears to have become just a little bit possible? Louis has been on the phone. 'Can I speak to Michael?' He seems nice. Anyway, Michael has a mind of his own. He is no longer a boy. He is eighteen years of age, nineteen this August. Bernie Garrett just hopes that whatever he chooses will work out well for him. That he will always stay the Michael that they know and love. Whether his dreams come true or not.

Did you really have to be as hard as nails to succeed? Mrs Garrett wishes that things could be some other way, where everyone would be happy, and together. She makes a wish, that everything would work out OK.

The end of March is showery. Mary and Averyl and Pádraig phone Ciaran Carty and meet him in the Innisfree Hotel. They ask him to hand over the masters of the digital footage of IOYOU. As far as they are concerned, they commissioned it; they own it. Ciaran prevaricates. He has shot footage of these fellas before and since Mary and Pádraig and Averyl were involved in their lives. There is pressure on him from all sides. It's a tense meeting. Trust has broken down.

There's a couple of Summerhill lads working in Sligo Station for Iarnród Eireann. They are used to seeing the IOYOUs on the platform for the seven fifty-five to Dublin. They always exchange hellos. Once the train stops at Connolly Station, the five boys grab their bags and bus it to Donnybrook. IOYOU have breakfast in the RTÉ canteen. They spot a few newsreaders and people from various familiar shows. Outside in the sunlight, people in suits step smartly over the concrete paths that thread through the slightly faded oasis that is the Radio Telifís Éireann centre. At the foot of the huge TV mast.

The boys are sent straight to make-up when they get to the studio. 'TX Live' is going out in the afternoon. Michael's nerves are jangling, but he is fascinated by his first encounter with the oddly clinical ritual of television. People worried you will mess up. A woman with a clipboard, shepherding a gaggle of excited young girls—the audience. Fakey-looking sets, blinding lights, bored cameramen wearing headsets. Three cameras on smooth rollers, step dancing with each other. Hunkering. The eye-lens approaching, staring large in your face. Teresa Smith, one of the presenters, talking animatedly to another camera, with one eye on the floor manager lurking behind it. When their turn comes, the band sail through 'Together Girl Forever'. They are really confident chatting to the presenter.

Once the show is done they have to hurry away. The Big Meeting with Ronan and Louis is on in the Clarence Hotel in Temple Bar. Ronan and Louis want to sit down and talk to them. Louis wants a heart to heart.

The Clarence is a fashionable place, with tastefully aged décor. Oak, velvet and leather. They sit around a low antique table. Shane has the *Evening Herald* in his hand, the week-old edition with the story and photo of IOYOU in the middle page. Mark Feehily and Graham Keighron and Kian Egan get introductions to the Boyzone frontman. Shane and Michael are able to engage in chit-chat about Ronan's birthday party.

Louis asks if they have been thinking about what all this means, and the IOYOU lads tell him they have been thinking of nothing else. He wants to get down to nuts and bolts. Inject some reality regarding what this business is all about . . .

Ronan Keating explains how it is no picnic being a pop star. He describes all the travelling. The pressures.

Louis explains how it doesn't help the fanbase if one of the boys in the band is seen in a relationship or having a baby. The competition is shit hot out there. You have to give yourself every chance. There are plenty of people out there ready to make those kind of sacrifices . . .

Ronan tells them that high profile relationships, girlfriends, won't help the image at the beginning. It won't say that in the contract . . . The 'no girlfriends' thing will just be a gentlemen's agreement.

Louis tells the band that he wants to invite Ronan Keating on board as co-manager of IOYOU. 'If you are all agreeable.' Louis looks at Ronan proudly. The boys start agreeing. They keep agreeing. Six sets of eyes follow his hand gestures. Shane checks to see if the people at the next table are listening. They're not. They are deep in discussion about some deal that seems to *them* the most important thing in the world.

The meeting lasts an hour or so. Then the band say goodbye to Louis and Ronan, shake hands with them, and leave the Clarence. Before they head home, Louis chats to Shane and Kian on their own. Kian is becoming more . . . powerful. Louis likes Kian. When Louis wants to tell the band stuff, he calls either Kian or Shane, and they pass on the news to the others. There won't be an actual contract yet, the managers have told them. Till we see how we all get on.

Louis likes talking strategy. He is always combing the future for possibilities. There is a deal he wants. A Holy Grail of a deal. A Great Boyband Deal. The time is ripe for that deal now for an Irish act. And Louis knows he is the man to get it. By sheer chance, IOYOU have come to Louis Walsh at exactly the right stage in his career.

Louis has learned some tough lessons from the past. He has learned who the key people are and the keywords to say to these people, to make them hear you. His network of contacts is now much wider. He may not be loved by all the movers and shakers in the business, but they all know who he is and respect him. He has hung in there with Boyzone, worked his way up. This time he knows how to do it right. He has a few tricks up his sleeve this time. Wait till you see.

The clocks have gone forward. The sun is up by seven o'clock. Louis rings Sligo with exciting news. *Simon Cowell* is available to look at the band on a particular day. Simon is the BMG man in London, their top talent scout. A very important guy. So the boys have a date in Dublin, in April, to sing for Simon. They organise a practice. They get five songs off pretty well. They have the harmonies down pretty good. Shane conducts. He stops them halfway when they go wrong.

• Take it from the top again, fellas.

Mary used to say, if there is a bit you are not sure of or you go off key, you can do the fish. It's kind of like miming. You just make like you are making a big effort and mouth the words. IOYOU try out a few dance moves, down in Filan's place. They feel dancing might be important. Graham has some good ideas. Good ideas are valuable. When Graham suggests moves, the others listen to him and try them out. Even Shane. All except Michael Garrett. But in the end Michael goes with the flow, too, and the dances start looking pretty tight.

Shane has just got a new short haircut. That particular session with the hairdresser didn't please him too much, but—for the moment—he is stuck with it. He finds himself thinking about Derek lately. Derek is not speaking to the band now. Shane doesn't blame him. Shane feels a real sense of loss. He used to feel kind of protective towards Derek. Derek was a really nice guy.

IOYOU go back to Dublin. To the Westbury Hotel, off Grafton Street. They go up the lift, to a nice hotel room, and meet Louis

Walsh. 'How are you doing, boys?' says Louis. 'How are the vocal chords? The BMG guy will get here in a few minutes.' The Showcase Gig turns out to be less of a gig than an audience. The boys have to sing for Simon, there on the spot.

- Right here in the hotel room?
- Yes.

They have their normal stuff on, casual gear for the journey. Their best clothes are in bags—new stuff, cool stuff, stuff packed by mothers. But there is no time to put them on. Graham tidies their plastic bags and other stuff away.

Simon is a dark, smooth kind of guy; he is nice but distant. Tall. Simon Cowell looks maybe like a guy in an advertisement for American cigarettes. Impossibly handsome in a way your mother would have liked. A sculpted jaw. Brown eyes that catch the light. He places his finger thoughtfully on a mighty chin with a dimple in the centre. Kian looks puny beside him. Louis looks small, too. His smile looks small.

Kian lifts his head to meet Simon's gaze. Simon gives a second of study to the face of each boy. Simon is delighted the band could make it. It is a bit of a trek from Sligo.

- You drove?

When he speaks you glimpse an array of even, gleaming white teeth. His clipped, educated English accent is somehow a surprise. If he had an American accent, Simon would be about to sell you something that gave you a body like his in four weeks and folded away inside a matchbox. Simon has on a short-sleeved black T-shirt, tucked inside his pants—high-waisted pants, belted at his midriff. He folds those well-toned arms and waits for IOYOU to start.

The boys are nervous. Shane clicks his fingers and brings everyone in. The harmonies sound pretty good, the deep-pile carpet means no echo, a pretty good sound. The band sing five songs they prepared. Two are originals, 'Angels'—a song Graham had a big part in writing, the one Shane had been working on with Daragh and Pádraig—and 'Together Girl Forever'. The covers they have chosen are 'Quit Playing Games', 'As Long As You Love Me', and 'Just to Be Close', by The Backstreet Boys.

Together, girl, forever, if only you could . . . (pause) See-eee-eee-ee . . .

Mark hits the high ones. Simon doesn't smile. He doesn't tap his foot or nod to the beat of the songs. He murmurs OK after each song, and Louis' expression wills them on to start the next one. Louis has his hands behind his back. After they finish, Simon thanks the boys quietly, and they go off while Louis and Simon chat.

It was never going to be 'This is my band, Simon. Take it or leave it.' Louis is there to listen to Simon. What Simon saw in the hotel room was raw talent. Raw and scruffy and naive and static. More Feis Cheoil than Michael Jackson. More community games than Backstreet Boys. But bursting with promise nonetheless.

This is the crunch, Louis knows. This is where the Flagship Act and the Great Deal must be married. It is a process. So Simon's opinion and expert advice, Simon's *belief*, is essential.

Simon has belief in Louis. Louis came to him back in '95 with another young Irish boyband, and Simon was underwhelmed. He passed. Louis never lets him forget missing out on Boyzone for BMG. But the joining of the Dream Act and the Dream Deal will require Simon's full involvement. His blessing. Simon Cowell will need—just as much as Louis does—to have a sense of ownership of the project. He has to go back to BMG with conviction in his heart that this band will make them an awful lot of money.

- What do you think?

Louis lets Simon see his genuine excitement about this latest discovery. Louis just can't stop himself thinking, hey, what could the right team plus BMG make out of these west of Ireland gents?

The lads have lunch and discuss the Westbury Showcase. They felt they sang pretty good. 'Jesus, I was *soooo* shaky,' says Mark. 'It was mad! It was just such a weird situation.' Shane thinks yer man Simon seemed to be enjoying the songs. He sees so many bands. Kian is not so sure. But everything has gone really well so far. Louis will be talking Great Deal just about now. He will be making sure that Simon and the record company give us top priority.

The long-awaited call comes to Shane from Louis. Another chat is convened.

- I'll be honest, lads. Actually the Showcase did not go all that well. Simon didn't love the band.
- We sang great.
- He didn't want to see our dances.

248

- It was the *look* of the band he was concerned about. That was what mattered to him. He liked Mark and Kian. Kian's looks, Mark's voice. But not the rest. He won't sign us. Look. We have a lot of work to do to get a deal yet, lads. Shane, you looked terrible. You were terrible. You don't come to a major audition looking like that, Shane . . .

- Jesus, Louis, you didn't give us a chance to change, I thought you were organising this.

You could hear a pin drop, if someone dropped one.

An argument ensues between Louis and Shane. Shane says it wasn't fair. Shane raises his voice. Louis looks funny when he's angry. Shane's face gets very red, then white. Louis wins. Everyone lapses into silence. Miggles forces a smile, and shrugs.

- So what do we do?

'Work,' Louis tells them. 'Work, work, work. Believe in yourselves.' Michael reminds everyone of the bright side. 'Look, fellas, we have Louis Walsh behind us. Louis has a track record.' Louis looks away, like he's impatient. Like he has other important jobs to be getting on with.

- There is going to be another Showcase, in a few months. This one will be make or break. We will record a demo for the major labels to listen to. In the meantime, those that are doing exams, better concentrate on school.

- OK, Louis.

Another long trainride west. A small group of young men in casual clothes. The mood subdued. They might be a football team that just scraped a draw after being two up at halftime. *Concentrate on school? He didn't love the band.*

- If he had seen us in front of The Backstreet Boys . . .
- If we got to use Graham's routine . . .
- The state of us!!
- The state of *YOU!*
- Why didn't we sing to the backing tracks?
- Shuddup! For feck's sake! There wasn't time—Louis told you!

It's still bright when the carriages squeak to a halt. Last stop, Sligo Station.

- Passengers at the rear of the train move forward now to reach the platform.

249

It snows in Sligo on Good Friday. Hailstones in Belfast. David Davin-Power is on telly, coming live from outside Hillsborough Castle, emotion and weariness in his voice. Bill Clinton kept in constant touch throughout the marathon talks. People have been coming out, giving hints, good news, bad news, a merry dance. But it appears that a historic peace agreement has been reached.

CHAIR RACES

Graham doesn't love flying. The seat sucks him in. He listens to the engines at full throttle and watches the outlying buildings at Dublin airport flash by. Kian and Shane and Michael are chatting excitedly. They never stop. If they are not talking shop they are messing, acting the maggot, shifting blame for farts, doing improvised impersonations. You would think they were flying out of the country in jets every day of the week.

IOYOU are off to London in the second half of April to record their new demo with Steve Mac and Wayne Hector. On the flight Graham has time to think. Things are happening fast now. Louis has organised some dance rehearsals for the band with Dublin choreographer Jane Shortall. Jane measured them with searching brown eyes. Blonde hair tied up under a baseball cap. It was shocking how unfit they all were. Jane made them sweat, she was well into street dance. She moved a few fast songs with them and demonstrated some great new moves.

Graham loved that. He enjoyed watching how Jane Shortall illustrated the moves. He took in the dance teacher's style, took in everything. He felt himself learning, making progress. Dancing is for him. He can't wait to see London. He can still see the queue for Mary McDonagh's auditions in the Hawk's Well for *Grease*. And him getting picked and he not there to audition at all. He can't wait to see the recording studio.

The businessman type in front is reading his *Sunday Times*. By the opposite window, Mark has his Walkman on, listening to the songs they are going to be doing. They all only got the recordings yesterday. When they were told about recording, all the band had piped up: 'We have some good song ideas of our own, new ones.' 'Great choruses!' 'I have a good idea for a bridge.' But no, Louis had said. We want to try something different. We have a lot of work to do. So we play it safe. You do covers for the moment. Big ballads.

• I know a couple of blokes who might supply some good songs. Steve Mac and Wayne Hector.

Louis had spoken the names gravely, like this is heavy information. Impressive stuff indeed.

• These are the guys who write the songs for *Boyzone*! And *Five*! They are the best in the business.

• Oh, yeah, Louis. Sure. Sounds good.

Fulham, south London. The White Horse Pub. Then swing off the King's Road. Parsons Green. *Rokstone Studios*. A steel door. This is it.

Quick introductions. Steve Mac and Wayne Hector have the tracks all ready. They have a little rap going between them, no point even trying to intercept and decode. Wayne is a cool black dude. He has a skinned head and some nice gold rings. His accent is mostly London with a hint of mid-Atlantic. Wayne does the vocal arrangements, sings the parts in a silky smooth soul voice.

Steve Mac wears a baseball cap, casuals. Like Wayne, Steve is in his late twenties. He's a muso/tecchie, either crouching at a keyboard or poised at Chris the engineer's shoulder at the sound desk.

There are swivel seats on rollers for the engineer and producers. A blue couch against the wall for the band. A huge control room, the ceiling painted deep blue. Gold disks mounted. The sound desk stretches forever. Boyzone used to have chair races in here, Steve tells them.

- Chair races? In a holy shrine like this?

The lads laugh politely.

OK, guys. Steve takes charge. IOYOU are to go into a vocal booth to sing each part individually. The arrangements are for five vocals. Steve doesn't believe in demos. His philosophy is: if we get the vocals right now it means we don't have to record them again.

Steve and Wayne's two songs are called 'Everybody Knows' and 'Good Thing'. Shane, as usual, helps the others, even going into the booth with Miggles, with a second set of cans, to sing the line with him in support. Steve is fussy about the harmonies and phrasing. He wants everything bang on.

- It's worth another try, I think.

He says 'thank you' after every take. Whoever is in the booth says 'thank you' back. There are a lot of 'thank you's'. It's a long day. It's work.

The band don't stay around for the mix. Louis chats to Kian later. 'Ya, ya. Ye did OK. Don't worry.' Louis will collect the CD later on.

Kian's eighteenth birthday on 29 April is celebrated in the back room of M.J. Carr's, beside the railway station in Sligo. It's set up as a surprise for him by the rest of the band. They get a local DJ in with a karaoke machine and hire out the room. It's a stroke of genius. Everyone sings; the lads really enjoy slagging each other, doing the karaoke. It's great fun, and now that they have been in a bigtime studio, IOYOU have the confidence to tread the karaoke stage once again without embarrassment. At least in private! Shane sings 'Forever Love' and the others all give him an exaggerated clap. Mark does a slightly over the top version of 'I Believe I Can Fly'. Later on Graham Keighron grabs the mic and tears the place down with 'Mustang Sally' and 'Brown Eyed Girl'.

Be-side tha stay-dee-umm with yeoooou? Van Morrison's gem of a song is a big favourite in Sligo. The pints are flowing and the performances keep getting better. Kian gets up and does a presentable version of 'Babe', the Take That song he used to do in the Hawk's Well gigs. It is a special night, a night of self-reassurance and taking stock of how far they have come, never mind the odd setback.

- She's fashionably late.

There are green monkeys in the jungle, you know. They pester the farmers. The jungle is in the background, lit sleepily by the crimson rays of an enormous setting sun. The volcanic peak at the centre of the island rises dark green into the clouds. Everywhere extravagant tropical flowers grow wild, the air sweetened by their strange perfume. Backed by a row of tall coconut palm trees, the white beach stretches for miles. Beyond the reef you can make out other rocky islands on the horizon.

Very expensive yachts ride at anchor. Irish voices, Dublin voices, rise in laughter, above the trills of a steel band combo. Here on the island of Nevis in the Caribbean, Ronan Keating, dressed all in black, is waiting for his bride. Judge Byrone—an august elder of Nevis—stands by his side, all ready to perform the marriage ceremony. Also in attendance is Ronan's older brother Gary.

Ronan has a platinum ring in his pocket. Platinum is more valuable than gold, you know. Ronan is taking a break from the treadmill at last. Today he will wed his sweetheart Yvonne.

Back in Dublin it's sunny, too. Kian Egan and Shane Filan are in T-shirts, perched in soft chairs. Seated opposite, Louis Walsh is at ease. He has his energy back. He has the mix of the new demo. It's grand. They can hear it later. 'But let's talk first.' Louis is talking again about the future. He is talking about a photo shoot. About how he plans to sell the band. About being sensible. About protecting yourself, the dangers, the pitfalls. About unsafe sex. About security. About drugs. 'Anyone doing drugs is out of the band.' 'None of us ever did drugs,' says Shane.

'Sligo Arts Festival is looking for you guys to do a gig,' Louis announces. 'I reckon the practice would be useful. Did you ever hear of a place called Merville Community Hall? Is it OK?' 'Yes,' says Shane. 'It's beside Maugheraboy, where Graham comes from.'

Louis has been wanting to talk to them about Graham. He has concerns. Graham is very skinny. His accent is too strong, Louis tells them. His look is wrong. Louis is concerned that they really blow away this record company guy next time . . . They tell Louis that Graham is the rapper of the band. Louis shrugs.

Fusion are stretching and bopping around, warming up for their set. They are looking dangerous in their shiny bodysuits. The latest version is grey. They don't work quite as well as the black ones did. Avril O'Hanlon and Sabrina Kiernan talk the girls through their dance routine *one more time*. This is the second of two gigs on the day. IOYOU have hired a huge PA for the Merville shows. The Mercy Convent and St Anne's Youth Club had earlier been considered by the band and the festival people as potential venues. But they hadn't worked out. Merville fitted the bill best.

'Great,' Louis had said. 'Good luck with it.' And then Louis turned around and asked them, 'Who is going to collect the bobs after the gig from the promoter?' Shane and Kian volunteered right away. No, they hadn't exactly done that job before, but they can handle it OK.

Not as many as expected have turned up to see the IOYOU show this evening. But those that are here are in great form. There is a load of local bands playing first. There is a Spice Girls type band, very young kids, with all the moves off to a T. A girl band is on now, by the name of Deep, all with different characters, like the Spice Girls. They don't have a Scary Spice though. How many managers have the Spice Girls fired at this stage?

Graham Keighron is getting ready for the evening gig over at home, at his mum's. He looks at himself in the mirror. Today is Saturday, 30 May. It's nearly two weeks since his birthday. He was twenty-two on the nineteenth. Everyone made a fuss. Mark Feehily's party was two days ago. Mark just turned eighteen. The end is near for you in the band, mister, Graham says to the image of himself. The mirror Graham doesn't think so. 'What would they do without me? I'm the . . .'

•   So much for the Daddy of The Band. The A.J. You are gone, son.

No one has said anything, but still Graham knows. From their eyes. You know how you just know. Nothing that is said in the pre-gig dressing room changes his mind.

THE DADDY OF THE BAND

The young lad that spread the turf with the tractor laid some of it over low patches of ground. So the serried lines of reddish brown disappear in places into black pools of water. The first day is always slow going. If the turf is on high ground it saves itself. You can assemble the dry stuff readily in little 'footings', stacks of eight or nine individual sods. But the wet turf has to be handled delicately, rescued from the flood and placed unbroken on a high spot.

Until you get used to it, the stiffness in your lower back is murder; you have to bring an old cushion in the car to ease your back on the way home. Ballinvilla Bog is deserted. The lake, swathed in reeds, glints beyond the cutaway bog. The high bog stands like an island in the foreground. The machines have left ugly marks on the faces of the fresher turf banks. Old overgrown banks, heather topped, still bear the rhythmic slanting strokes etched by the *sleán*.[†]

Bogholes should be rectangular and tidy. Everyone knew the terms for the systems of dams and drains the time the whole

---

†   A traditional hand-held turf-cutting tool.

community used to come here to save their fuel for the winter. That wasn't that long ago—only the seventies, the time of Time Machine and 'Top of the Pops' in Cahill's. The cutting was all by hand then. Once taken with the stroke of the blade, the sod of turf travelled *sleán* to hand to barrow, the barrowman packing each moist, soapy chunk into place on the wooden barrow with a resounding slap. You could end up wheeling on the low ground or on the high bank. On the high bank you kept your eyes peeled for missiles. There would be pegging—lumps of wet turf would sail over the high bog to bomb the unsuspecting workers on the far side.

When it was teatime you took a bottle of milk from a boghole fridge and wiped it. There would be tea boiling beside a fire and donkeys patient and sunburnt men that seemed old telling stories of a time before when things were different from how they are now.

They told of when the lake froze and we drove the carts across it for a shortcut home and of the time a Croghan man was lost in the bog at night. He was in a rambling house. They said stay the night but no. Poor fella went astray. His fingers had left scratch marks on the bank as he tried to pull himself out. He died standing up.

The modern bogholes made by machine are deep and dark and misshapen. The tiny island of high bog that survives is too small to turn a barrow on. Almost all the bog on Meehan's side of the pass has been cut away. The bog pass, for centuries nibbled to a narrow strip by covetous turf cutters, is almost choked by whins. The deep yellow blooms of the furze spread their sweet perfume.

Even empty, the bog is a happy place. Pádraig lifts the turf to a steady rhythm and talks to himself. He imagines everything working out just fine. He talks to Mary McDonagh and Louis Walsh and Mark Feehily and Peter Filan. He hears conversations in his head, he teases out different scenarios: he giggles to himself. Martin Mulvihill stops on the bog pass and chats for a few minutes.

• It's the best of turf. Pity he didn't spread it that bit higher.

IOYOU walk on stage wearing white T-shirts. All five sit on stools for the slow songs, Boyzone style. Most of the songs are slow. All hand movements. There is a full-on lights show, lasers, the lot. The lads all look great. Michael Garrett is a rock star; he is Michael Jackson—really, the spit of him—the hair, the countenance; ghostly pale, sinister-handsome. He doesn't overdo the energy tonight; he is more controlled, more commanding on stage. He is learning to sing *within himself*, to keep it simple, not to try to do someone else's parts. Shane is brilliant, as usual.

Graham puts every bit of his heart into the Merville gig. He sings his strongest ever. He talks to the audience, whipping them up into a frenzy. Lots of his old friends are there, cheering him on. He feels connected to them again. His mum is there, too. Graham looks out over the audience and takes in the moment.

Perhaps there is still a small flicker of hope in Graham's heart. His intuition could be totally wrong. Maybe the vibes he has been picking up from the rest of the lads might be about something else altogether. The whole birthday thing was weird. And while he is onstage, while the music plays, he still feels the sweet breeze of possibility. Maybe someone else, some manager, will see him in full flight and appreciate his movement and his rapping style. Except there are no rap songs now in the IOYOU set.

After the gig, Shane and Kian set off around the town looking for the guy with the chequebook. They finally find him in Kilgallen's pub. He is a laconic red-haired guy by the name of Danny.

He is in no hurry to part with money. He is not impressed at all by the publicity work done by the lads. That they would do publicity was their part of the deal. But he had seen no posters. 'Did you put up any posters?' He has lost money. 'Why should the festival take a loss?'

The boys are put on the defensive. 'We are very busy. Some people are doing exams.' Three of the boys are doing the Leaving. It is only a couple of weeks away. 'We gave ye photos. We did a photo session. Nearly killed ourselves climbing over the wall of Sligo Abbey to get our pictures taken in there. We put stuff in the paper. We did flyers, the lads in the Listening Post[†] helped us out. What about our money? Please, can we have it?' They have to pay for the PA. The lights. They mention Louis, their big-time manager. But even the Magic Name brings no softening in the countenance of the festival man. The way the lads remember it, they had an ace up their sleeve, so they decided to use it.

Shane goes outside and dials Louis' number. Louis laughs and

---

†   A music shop in Sligo at the time.

calls Danny. He is calling from Heathrow Airport. He is very busy. He forcefully makes the point; IOYOU have to be paid. 'They are my band.' That was the deal made with him. The organiser complains, but agrees. Louis tells Danny that these guys are going to be huge. 'Bigger than Boyzone. Trust me on that. Good luck.'

No way would Kian have talked to Graham. He has been close friends with the man since they were young fellas. Graham used to have all these Metallica and Backstreet Boys concerts on video. And Kian used to sit in Graham's and watch them with him and say, 'I want to do this. I want to get in front of that crowd of screaming girls and sing my heart out.' Graham always said 'Yeah, you will. We will.'

Graham breathes IOYOU. It's not possible to imagine the group without him. He leans his sharp elbows on your shoulders so readily getting photos taken. So it has been tense, thinking about all that. That's why the vibes have been strange. But Louis has his mind made up. 'Will you tell him or will I?'

Shortly after finishing his call to Danny, Louis calls Graham's mobile. 'Will you take a call from me on the landline?' Louis talks to Graham a long time. Louis is understanding about it. But he explains the situation fully. He explains that Graham is older than the others. He doesn't fit the look. And we have to get everything right. 'All I want is to get these guys signed.' 'That's all I want, too,' says Graham. 'It's the thing I want most in the world.'

'Then you can help us to do it, Graham,' says Louis.

GLACIATION AND CUMULUS

Shane, you are getting a new haircut. You will be off to the stylist again.

'OK, Louis. You know, it's so great that Graham is staying around tho', 'cos, like, he's our mate . . . and . . .'

'Could he be our roadie?' asks Kian. Louis talks to Kian the most. Kian is real cocky now, because Simon liked him in the Westbury Showcase. He is wearing super baggy jeans and a tight bottle-green top and tons of gold jewellery. With a deeper tan he could be a young Backstreet Boy.

- Does he *want* to be a roadie?
- Yeah, Louis, he'd do *anything* . . .
- OK, he's road manager. But about the haircut, you have to get a very different hairstyle, Shane. You have to go blonde. Let it grow long and dye it blonde.
- OK, Louis.
- Shane, do you know *why* you have to get a new haircut? So Simon Cowell won't recognise you at the next gig. Simon wants you out of the band. We might have to pull the wool over his eyes a bit . . .

- Jesus, Louis.

Shane's head has filled with noise. This was how Graham felt. And Derek. This is a new part—a part never played out in Shane's dream.

Cowell had stared him out of it for ages. 'Of course he'll recognise me. Is this just . . . how they let me down easy? Do the rest of them know?'

- Who will groom them, give them pep talks before the gig?
- Ro and Louis, of course. This band don't need me any more.
- What will life be like without IOYOU?
- It will be, like, Limerick next year, college. No management, just accountancy, like I promised mum if the band didn't work out.

Shane thinks then—*I'm still in*. Surely if Louis wants me in, I am in. Mark and Kian are in, anyway, because Simon liked them. This is a new feeling. A funny mixture of feelings. It's a feeling of worry and hurt, mixed together.

Louis tells Shane that he knows how tough it is, what they're going through now. The music business is not a nice business. Louis knew they couldn't keep Graham. Louis tells Shane he wants him in IOYOU. He tells Shane that Simon is wrong this time. Louis sees Shane as the natural leader, the Ronan Keating of IOYOU. He tells Shane to get a way-out haircut, to dye it all blond, bleach it. Simon will assume we lost the guys he didn't like. The guy sees so many boys these days.

Everybody is more zappy, more urgent, in Dublin than in Sligo. And more zappy in London than in Dublin. Questions come thicker; answers need to come quicker. Keeps you on your toes. When you come down home, you find yourself wishing your mother operated at a faster pace. Even your sisters seem too laid-back. Michael jumps when the phone rings.

- Louis here, can I speak to Michael?

A Showcase for Sony has come up all of a sudden. 'Ye have to play next Wednesday in the Red Box for a few A&R guys.' 'I'll be back Friday,' says Michael. 'Enjoy yourself,' says his mum, as he thunders upstairs.

Derek Lacey misses being in the boyband. Trying to rebuild his life is proving difficult. His mum and mates have been supportive, and he is getting strength from them. He misses being onstage, but he misses the friendship of the lads even more. And the times they spent hanging out together. He had been closest to Shane Filan. Graham must also be pining for his place in the limelight. But the band is missing its original members, too. IOYOU *sans* Derek Lacey and Graham Keighron doesn't sound like the same group at all. A third of the personnel is gone, but a far bigger slice of vocal strength. Although they are game, they are triers, neither Kian nor Michael would claim to be as accurate or as strong vocally as either Derek or Graham. The gaps in the singing became particularly evident after Graham's departure. It was kind of a threshold. Shane and Mark still sound terrific, Mark circling and Shane holding down the melody, but where has the backing gone? Louis has been talking about something called the 'cosmetic balance', but the changes have thrown the *musical* balance of IOYOU off centre.

Another Showcase Gig is upcoming, this time for Polygram. Yes, there is interest. No, no deal yet. Dad Garrett says don't rush things. Don't appear too eager. It's like selling anything. Keep your cards close. There are a series of trips up and down to Dublin. The four IOYOU members have a lot of people to meet. There's a photo shoot, three smiles and Mark's cutie macho. Ronan Keating stands in for some of the shots. Shane doesn't conduct.

Funny all you see when you are outside the circle, looking in. Michael seems real cocky lately, too, like Kian. He is talking a lot, he is in everyone's face. He is a bit over-excited. Graham makes good friends with the sound engineer in the Red Box nightclub. The guy has a sense of humour. He has seen plenty of Showcase Gigs in his time. Crew humour is different from band humour. It's cruder, more cynical. Graham better learn a few jokes. At least he looks right. He has a few keys on his belt and his mobile phone. He has checked out the Wrangler shelf in the clothes shop. He is determined to be the best road manager he possibly can. As it turns out, though, Graham Keighron gets to sing with IOYOU at both Showcase Gigs.

He sings out of sight, in the little booth where the sound engineer lives. The engineer has a special microphone set up for Graham, going straight into the desk. Graham sings his heart out. Graham would do anything to get those guys signed.

Visor down. The time traveller, suit pressurised, is working perilously far from the mother ship. But he knows the country. The Leaving Cert again. Michael Garrett sighs.

Only two lifetimes ago, last summer, he was sat here in this exam hall in familiar old Summerhill, with its familiar smells, writing about Hamlet, Shakespeare's use of simile. Glaciation and cumulus and stratocumulus. How they are different. His new, patient, deliberate boyband self eases into the seat with M. Garrett's number on it. The desk and seat is a single unit, narrow and confining. Peering narrow-eyed through his hair, he lines up his pens methodically. The supervisor is distributing the question papers. There are foolscap answer books provided.

He writes the date. Wednesday, 9 June 1998. Just a month ago Michael was standing in a booth in London recording a demo with big-name producers Steve Mac and Wayne Hector. In a studio that smelled of electricity and plastic and newness. With a desk that went on forever. Part of his soul feels about two hundred years old.

Everyone in Sligo is talking about IOYOU. There's stuff in the papers all the time and the national press have it, too, about how Louis Walsh has taken them on and they're going to be huge. Ronan Keating has been telling them about what Elton John and George Michael are really like as people. About how you can tell A-list and B-list celebrities apart. How they are different. About how the really big ones are always nice. Ronan doesn't know Michael Jackson. It's weird to be doing school stuff. Kian isn't doing the exams at all. And, of course, Shane left college in Limerick after Christmas.

Over on another island, Mark Feehily sits with his head bowed. He seems to be getting on OK this time, too. James Connolly, the photographer, an old Summerhill man himself, pulls off a coup. He gets into the exam hall and snaps a photo of Mark sitting down to do his exam.

Michael reads the questions. He starts to write. It's not so bad once you get started. He is going a bit better than last year.

The final day. The last exam paper handed up. Michael saying good luck to his friends. Michael going home. He sleeps late for a couple of days. Wimbledon on the telly. Pop, pop, pop. Fifteen—

love. Louis has been on. Next week is the audition for the new guy for the band. The days are dragging again. As they do in summer when you are nineteen, waiting for big things to happen. The World Cup is on, over in France. Lizerazu. Zidane. What a first touch. Saudi Arabia all at sea.

- Is it raining?
- Are you going out?

The west always gets the worst of the rain. But the air is warming. It might be easing off. The greenery on Strandhill Road, bowed with wet, lights up in a beam of red evening sun. A multitude of swirling suns dance beneath the leaf cover. Steam rises off the concrete, and dry patches appear. Children's voices ring across the gardens; the day is young again.

The sun starts to sit down on the horizon in the north-west corner of the sky, close to the spot where it settled yesterday. Mirages, air mirrors and phantoms dance on the Dublin road. Anyone with sense is going out with full intentions of staying up all night. There is a bonfire on the second beach in the (Rosses) Point. The girls are going. Are you heading out?

Michael has a lot of younger guys looking up to him these days. He gets a laugh out of them. He knows what it's like. To be nineteen is to be in the time of watching. Of waiting. Of wanting. Of wishing you were at centre field rather than cheering and jeering from the substitutes bench. Of finding it hard to catch a barman's eye, never mind the eye of a physically perfect, self-assured, air-and-light babe who has suddenly materialised inches from your left shoulder.

Barmen notice Michael now.

And when later, after it turns out that air-and-light babe has a friend who likes the way you laugh, you smile and try to remember her name. And when she surprises you with her hunger, and you embrace her, just out of the seafront lights, how do you know how to please her? How does she work? How do you ask? No one provides a map. Irish people, even modern Irish people, have a scarcity of names for the parts of us at the centre of our lives. We may find ourselves wishing we had a better stock of hip American slang words, like the words the writers of *Grease* and *Friends* have bestowed on us. That word is too Irish. This word too clinical. *That* word far too coarse. Would she think me naive? Would he think me a slut?

Later is debriefing, the report to the friends on how you got on. That should be good. But now, the man/boy is on his own, with the woman. What would Michael Garrett say now? What would his first move be?

She might whisper in your ear, you might remember something your friend told you, or blind and blessed instinct might kick in, and you might just magically discover you know what to say and do. You might mess up a few times before you learn that much of the map you seek is there inside you, waiting to be read. It's not a head thing. It's not an answer. It's the nature of the species that is us, that you have to somehow listen to the woman and listen to yourself. Listen to the breathing.

And it's not fair. It's never fair. Some have it instantly, it is *no problema, señorita*. Total poise and confidence, effortless smooth talk at fifteen. It is a mystery. These enviable people seem to be born with the coolness and the energy and the bone structure the prettiest girls love. Like Kian. Now Michael, too, has entered this golden domain, but in a totally different way. Not in a meatball way, in an exotic and mysterious popstar way. And Michael remembers how it feels to be on the outside. There are other lads now, who are taking the role of the drones, the workers. The fellas who push the envelope, they try everything, do everything, make fools of themselves, take a lot of crazy risks. Even if they don't succeed first off they build up an enviable repertoire of war stories. A reputation, a good name or a bad name, can be kind of sexy.

A lot of the time, the word that needs to be said, the gesture that needs getting timed, gets missed. The moment passes. Spoken after that perfect spontaneous turn, the words will always sound clichéd, always sound wrong.

> *Shyness is nice, and*
> *Shyness can stop you*
> *From doing all the things in life*
> *You'd like to*
> (Morrisey)

There are always a few Home Alones. The crowd (fellas or girls) who will return again and again to the subs bench, to watching, to inventing work-arounds and angles. But one day, they too will be called upon. In the meantime you can only rehearse familiar dreams as you walk home alone and hope that when the time comes you remember to listen. Yep, it's hard being nineteen in 1998.

Michael gets a long goodnight kiss. The dawn is breaking over Rathedmond as he pays the taxi man. It's been a great night. It seems a long time ago now since a band called IOYOU played an amazing thirteen minutes in front of The Backstreet Boys. Since Michael was at school. Since there were more than four in the band. Since Graham became a road manager.

THE DUBLIN BOYS

The nineteenth of June. Summer has landed at last, dusty and tar-spotted. It's like being at the seaside, so much bare flesh and silly headgear on Grafton Street. Down Harcourt Street, the audition for the new band guy is gas. The ad in the paper was pretty vague. *Young singers wanted for major pop act.* But the word is out that Louis Walsh will be there. He is helping veteran promoter Noel Carty to put together a new trad-type pop band. Like The Corrs, only male. A cross between Boyzone and The Dubliners. There is a poster downstairs saying Boogie An Domhain—Céilí Dancing. Beside a poster for a club called Powderbubble.

Upstairs in the Red Box three hundred Nervous Hopefuls mill around. They have all been given a number. Every one of them has their own story.

Louis and his people are seated behind a long table in the body of the venue while the Nervous Hopefuls do their thing onstage. Boyzone and B*witched[†] producer Ray 'Madman' Hedges is there,

---

[†]   B*witched are the new breaking all-girl band. They play guitars and
       fiddles in their act. Two of the girls, Edele and Keavy, are twins, sisters
       of Shane out of Boyzone.

stretching out his long legs. Noel Carty is there. He has a name for his new band—Reel. Now all he needs are some band members. Ronan Keating is there, sitting in the IOYOU corner with Michael and Kian and Shane and Mark. The Sligo guys are wondering what it will be like, having a new guy in IOYOU.

Graham Keighron watches from the sound booth.

Each singer is called up to sing over a backing track—you have a choice of singing 'Father and Son' or the traditional song 'She Moved Through the Fair'. Under the gaze of Ronan Keating. Ronan's version of 'Father and Son', produced by Ray Hedges, is a track on the album just released by Boyzone. Each person gets about thirty seconds to sing, he does the chorus, and then his shot is over. Don't bore us, get to the chorus. *Next!*

There are a few total wasters. They smile and dance and throw shapes. They sing out of tune. It's tiring just watching them. A good few are OK. Two guys—they are among the first to sing—are really good. One of them has a great voice on him. He is dressed boyband, in baggy trousers. His name is Bryan. Louis knows Bryan already. Bryan was told by Louis about the audition after he phoned trying to interest the Boyzone manager in a band he played with.

A guy called Nicky is number eighteen. He is wearing a sharp black suit. Although he comes in wrong on his song, Louis likes his style. They stop the backing track and let him finish 'Father and Son' on his own. Ray Hedges approaches this Nicky. Louis Walsh. He wants a word. Louis tells Nicky he did OK in his song.

Louis says 'I like both of these guys.' Ronan Keating likes them, too. Shane and Michael and Kian and Mark agree. They were by far the best performers.

Louis tells twenty guys to come back to the Red Box in a week's time. In the end he pares it down to Nicky and Bryan. It is a penalty shoot-out. They are asked to sing another song. To sing *a capella*. It's hard to separate them. Ray Hedges gets them to try some harmony lines with the band, to test voice and musical ear. The vocal sound of the augmented IOYOU is big. The two contenders even have to do a bit of a dance routine. Six boys turn together. Michael Garrett super-confident. Bryan does well. He asks about the steps and Shane steps them, talks them, like Jane Shortall would, or Mary

McDonagh. Nicky looks a bit uncomfortable. At the end of the day Louis talks to Kian again.

'OK, the plan is that both these boys will hang around with us for a while, and we will see who gets on best with the rest of the band. The two of them are happy with that. How do you feel?' 'Great,' says Kian. 'Great,' say Shane and Michael and Mark.

The new guys are nice guys. They say all the right things, they are still not sure of themselves. Sligo is a cool place. They have come to meet everybody. A tall lad and a shorter lad; both blondes. You introduce them to your parents. It feels weird. Your parents are people from different worlds, different universes, they would never have met these lads but for . . . IOYOU. Nicky Byrne is going out with the daughter of Bertie Ahern, the Taoiseach. Everyone is very polite, very pleased to meet each other. Bryan is staying with the Filans. Mrs Garrett will be putting up Nicky. Bryan McFadden is a good-looking blonde fellow from Artane. Some people think he has a bit of a David Beckham look to him. Bryan seems a nice lad. He doesn't have much to say. He was at The Backstreet Boys gig on Paddy's weekend, and saw IOYOU do the support slot. They were good.

Nicky leaves his bag in the hallway, and Michael shows him his bedroom. They have an evening meal in Michael's house. All the boys go out together later. First to the pub; they'll head to a club later. Warm rain is sketching circles on the Garavogue River. Shane brings a brolly. He shares it. His hair is still dark brown, but he has let it grow long enough to cover his ears.

The IOYOU's are conscious of giving equal attention to both Dublin lads, to make both feel welcome. At the auditions everyone in IOYOU had been in 'impress us' mode; Kian had asked questions, hard-faced. 'Do you have a girlfriend?' 'Are you prepared to make sacrifices?' Michael asked a few questions, too.

But it's more personal now, more there-are-guests-among-us. Everyone wants Nicky to tell his Leeds United story. Young Byrne is just back after spending a two-year spell as an apprentice with the great North of England soccer club. He was a goalkeeper. He worked very hard on his game and got to sit on the substitutes bench for Leeds' first team for one match, against Southampton.

• Oh wow, Southampton.

But that was the best it got for Nicky Byrne, footballer. The story went that newly arrived manager George Graham called him in and told him that he was too short, he would never make it as a professional footballer. But shorter guys than him had made the grade as top-flight netminders . . . He came back to Dublin. It was hard. His dad has been really supportive. He has been working since with his dad, putting on karaoke. His dad is a great singer.

Michael has stories, too. School stories, football stories. Love stories. Stories of all the famous places around Sligo where everything began. Sligo is steeped in the history of IOYOU.

You see your home place differently when you show it to a stranger. Nicholson's garage on Pearse Road has a decaying grey Fergusson Twenty tractor perched on the roof. It's invisible to the locals (sometimes you see it again after a fall of snow), but it catches the eyes of newcomers to the town. The Dublin guys slag off Sligo gently, the Sligo ones have a go at things about Dublin. They imitate each other's accents. The lads are enjoying their evening hugely. They ignore the people checking out their table in Toffs nightclub. Who are the two new boys with IOYOU? Girls come over to ask for introductions.

• Tha' fella's a beaudt!

In the morning, Mrs Garrett notices that Nicky's bed has not been slept in. He stayed somewhere else last night. He comes back in a hurry, next day, and takes away his stuff. Mrs Garrett feels something is wrong, even as she is saying goodbye to Michael. Michael is all business. Off on the 200km trip up to Dublin again. There are more Showcases to do. Tomorrow we do a Showcase for Virgin Records. But the one on everyone's mind is the big one, the second Showcase for Simon Cowell out of BMG.

THE CHAIN OF BULBS

The meeting is all a bit confusing. Michael knew a meeting was called, but not what it was supposed to be about. Everyone seems to be talking. Shane talks for a while, talks without looking at anybody in particular, like a farmer talking to a pool of water. He goes on about Louis wanting to keep *both* the Dublin boys. Everyone has been chatting behind the scenes, weighing up the pros and cons of Bryan and Nicky. No doubt about it, both the Dublin guys are sound. The talk has been that Louis likes Nicky, for his look, but Kian's favourite is Bryan, for his vocals.

Then Graham Keighron interrupts the babble of talk by raising his arms like a weary traffic cop. The rest of them look up at his hands. It's left to him. He is going to say it out loud. Graham lists the new IOYOU membership. 'Mark. Kian. Shane . . . Bryan . . . *and* Nicky. Sorry, Michael,' Graham says. 'You are out.'

Michael looks Shane in the eyes. Wide-eyed. He doesn't want to show feelings. *Please keep control,* he tells himself. The room has gone dead quiet. Miggles thinks like a pilot; the cockpit has a few red lights lit. He tries to problem solve, to correct the malfunction. He is in the process of laughing off this absurd joke, but then Miggles feels his eyes filling. He sorta checks Shane. Shane looks pale as death and close to tears himself, but he is steady. Sorry, Michael, Shane is miming, sad but serious. His wide mouth doing the fish. Michael studies those hazel-brown eyes closer than he has ever studied them before. Shane and Michael's eyes settle together. The one delivering the bad news always hopes that the person at the receiving end will *somehow* understand, *sometime* understand. Michael knows that. But just now, Michael does not understand.

Michael thinks of Michael Jackson. He thinks of the time in the Bishop's Garden. Of the two St John's fellas singing on the train, going up to Dublin for Ronan's twenty-first. He thinks of lots of times. He thinks of his sisters. He looks just once at Graham. Then Miggles gets angry. Angry words are exchanged. There had been a day, say the others, a day in Filan's, after we left Mary and Streetwise, when we stood up and shook hands and said all of us may not be here at the end of this process. But no one will stand in anyone else's way. Do you remember that, Michael?

• I remember a lot. Did ye fellas have a meeting?

Mrs Garrett answers the phone. It's Michael. He says coldly, 'I'm out.'

• Are you coming home?
• Ya. Later.

He doesn't go home straightaway. Michael stays on the scene, like an unburied corpse, a Banquo at the banquet. He sits on a stool in the Red Box, his face buried in his hands. People talk to his hands, try to get kind words through, but it's useless.

Everyone has tickets to the West End production of *Grease* at the Point Theatre in Dublin that night. Luke Goss, who used to be in Bros, is Danny. It's a great show, *Grease* on a massive canvas. They get the detail right, the fifties ads, the chain of bulbs all around the stage. An amazing car. But it's a weird night because Michael is there, Michael with a zombie look in his eyes, Michael the Helmet. Michael the Space Suit, drifting with the ship.

• You can't just walk out of a drive-in.

Shane can't stop himself glancing across the rows of seats. Michael smiles in the right places in the show. He eats sweets. He claps after the songs. He never once looks over at Shane to share his wonder.

Bernie Garrett feels numb. The world of the music business and boybands always seemed so bubbly, so out of this world, so ephemeral. A phase of growing up. Like her own dreamy days of the late seventies and early eighties. Yet it could strike a heavy blow. She had seen it with poor Derek. She had seen him mooching around town. She couldn't bear to look in his eyes when they met. But you only truly know it when it happens to yourself. It is like—a bereavement. The Garretts think about it for a while afterwards. Your head could spin trying to figure out the politics.

MORE THAN WORDS

They have to go to the gym. They have to do a lot of photo shoots. There are meetings. Mark is homesick; spending time away from home seems to be tough on him. He is moody and says little. All Mark wants to do is sing. All this other stuff, all the bullshit, just irritates him. It is a difficult time. Tempers are at breaking point. Kian Egan ends up cooling everyone down! Kian is more than pragmatic, he is being a rock of sense. He is grounded. He reminds people of what is happening to them. They see in his blue eyes their real selves, their old lives. And the Dublin guys. The Dublin guys have brought a different mood into the band, a bright, sweet, first-day-at-school optimism. Sometimes it gets a bit much. No one could be that nice. All the Sligo guys allow themselves moody patches.

The Sligo guys. Kian and Mark and Shane. They travel down home and back to Dublin together still. They are all that are left now, of the band that used to be called Six As One. The three that seemed to edge always to the front of Mike Bunn and Ciaran Carty's images.

They meet up with Ciaran any time they are in Sligo. They have stayed good friends with him. He is invited to parties. They go out together. As always, Ciaran drinks only water, the boys drink beer. Ciaran gets to know the Dublin guys. They are dead sound. Sometimes he brings his camera along, gets good footage. Ciaran talks to Shane. Shane is more grave, more reserved. He is changed subtly, but when he gets loosened up, he is still the same Shane, always ready to share a good laugh. He can give or take a slag. He is dying to pass on news updates from the front, and what is happening these days for the band is so unbelievable that you need a witness, someone from the old, normal life to help confirm that any of it is real.

The Sligo members of IOYOU enjoy going out at home. Not much problem choosing where to go. Toffs or Equinox are the only half-decent nightclubs. Most people they bump into are supportive, slapping them on the back, maybe slagging gently, asking when will ye be on 'Top of The Pops'? Sometimes though, there are weird situations—you might see three sets of former friends ignoring each other studiously in Toffs. The distance between them so yawning that they could have been isolated on islands in different seas in different centuries, rather than rubbing elbows to order drink at the one counter.

On one island would be a jolly boyband entourage, with Graham Keighron still in tow, keeping shielded whatever feelings were buried deep in his heart. Derek Lacey might be in another corner with his buddies. And if Michael Garrett came in, he would talk to mutual friends and blank out utterly anyone he didn't want to see. And at this particular stage, neither Michael nor Derek are speaking to their ex-colleagues in IOYOU.

Derek gave interviews in which he told of his anger when he saw the boys flaunting expensive jewellery and clothes, expensive cars. At times he had felt the impulse, the temptation, to 'go ballistic some night, and let it all out'. But he resisted. He ended up just letting it pass him by, shrugging and saying good luck to them, 'nice car, drive safely'. He wouldn't be looking for their phone numbers to wish any of them happy birthday. He wouldn't be ultra-friendly with Michael Garrett any more either, although he would pass him the time of day.

Michael was isolated in a different place. He had seen—and accepted, although it was questionable how much influence he might have wielded to prevent it—the shafting of his two colleagues from the original band. Right up to the end he was so sure he was home free. Now he saw grim satisfaction in the eyes of Derek and maybe Graham, too. Michael and Graham had never been that close, and now the very air between them was poisoned. The boys still inside the circle seemed to wear smug expressions. Michael never showed his hurt and talked only to a very few about his feelings. To have been replaced by the people whom you had auditioned was a particularly cruel blow. Louis and the others thought they were so smart. They didn't see the energy and charisma and heart he brought to IOYOU. Oh, how dearly he would love to prove them all wrong.

A totally different vibe is about before the second Simon Cowell Showcase. It is one of a string of Showcases for major labels. Eight labels are in the running. There is a big buzz in the business about Louis and Ronan's new act. Nearly every day there is new news. Kenny Ho—the stylist and costume designer to the Spice Girls and David Beckham—is coming to make over the IOYOUs. New backing tracks have been made up, and lots of practising has been scheduled. Louis has set up a few one-off shows for the band in Dublin. They will be doing a spot for 'Miss Ireland' in August; that one will have a big TV audience. And they will be playing support to Boyzone in England in September.

Louis has given each band member a nickname, each one is something Spice,. Homesick Spice is Mark. He's always homesick. Shane's nickname is Country Spice. Kian is Blondie Spice. Bryan is Forgetful Spice. The names are to be a secret from the press, just a gag between themselves.

A&R people—Artiste and Repertoire, the talent scouts—from the major labels have been flying into Dublin to see IOYOU. Record company people have been meeting the band and selling the charms of their particular company. Why IOYOU would be better off signing with them. The lads all asked tough questions. It was like the band was auditioning *them*.

'More Than Words', the song by Australian rock band Xtreme, is a current favourite with IOYOU. They rehearse an *a capella* version of it for the Showcase. Shane—a slightly thinner Shane, with dark eyebrows incongruous with hair that is an odd shade of dark blonde—goes around the dressing room in the Red Box, telling everyone to smile, to look like you are *really into it.*

EPILOGUE

Graham didn't turn out to be into road managing long-term. For a while, on the Beat on the Street and Smash Hits tours, he liaised with the press, helped backstage and front of house and rounded up the boys for interviews. But he tired of the gig and went back to Sligo to teach dance. He readily communicated his enthusiasm and knowledge of the subject to his students; Graham was a good teacher. He was reportedly working on a new recording project. Michael Garrett did a bit of modelling. From 1998 to 2002 he went to college, and got a degree in marketing and e-commerce. At Christmas 2002 he played Boy Hero in the pantomime *Goldilocks and the Three Bears* in the Waterfront Hall, Belfast. In the summer of 2003 Michael started training for the job of Garda Síochana.

The Garrett parents stopped thinking about IOYOU and boybands. It was painful for Mrs Garrett even to think about it. It was nice when Derek started saying hello to Michael and his mum again. It signified healing.

Mary McDonagh chatted to Derek one day, not too long after the band left him. He came up to her house. He told her what had happened to him. It was very emotional, being back in Mary's. Derek got a job doing barwork and a new girlfriend and got on with his life. He was still good-looking, he could still sing. He had his dignity.

Fusion won the All-Ireland dance championship again in 1998. After that there wasn't much else to win. The band drifted apart. Sabrina still danced; she did some teaching as well. So did Avril O'Hanlon. Avril did a degree in marketing. Avril continued to pursue her music career. She won a singing competition in 1992 and recorded a CD demo. She did a number of high profile TV spots, including *Children in Need* and the finals of *Country Cool.*

Helena and Gillian started on different life paths, paths that took them far away from the footlights. Gillian would wed Shane Filan in a glittering ceremony in December 2003. But the four girls would never forget the fun they had in the summers of '97 and '98. The years of dreams.

Ciaran Carty and Streetwise ended up in court, on opposite sides, in a dispute over ownership of the footage he had shot of IOYOU. The case was settled out of court after three years, with all parties declaring themselves satisfied. (The terms of the settlement were the subject of a confidentiality order, but the now famous tapes would eventually be put on the market.) Shane Filan gave evidence supporting Ciaran's case. In his testimony, Shane insisted that Mary and Averyl and Pádraig had never managed IOYOU. No contract had ever been signed. But he acknowledged the help they had given the boys starting out.

Prior to this there had been scant mention of Mary and the others in the official history of Westlife, or in interviews given by them. Mary had effectively been written out of history. Searches for her name in any of the Westlife websites will yield only the legend 'No pages found that include all search words'.

Averyl Dooher left the Hawk's Well. She took up a post directing the Carlow Arts Festival. Pádraig continued to play gigs with his friends and look at the sky. He got a radio play commissioned by RTÉ and wrote some new songs. Mary McDonagh got a place in Chapel Street—a new home for her dance school—organised. It was called Chapel Lane Studios. She bounced back in 1998 with *The Full Monty* in the Hawk's Well. She got new shows on the road. And continued to teach. And suddenly fire out ideas.

• Do ya know, lads, what we should do?

Louis Walsh kept having ideas, too. He upped his profile in the Irish celebrity scene by judging *Search for a Star* and other talent competitions. Simon Cowell showed up on a US variant, *American Idol*. With Simon Fuller, the ex-Spice Girls manager. The managers were becoming stars now.

IOYOU signed to BMG after the Boyzone tour. Simon Cowell never noticed that Shane, the new blond guy, was one and the same as Shane, The Reject from the Westbury Showcase. The first deal was for four million sterling over five years. IOYOU had to change their name. The record company wanted something less boybandish. Louis came up with it. He saw the name painted on the side of a skip. WESTSIDE.

After a lot of publicity was done it came to light that several bands already called themselves Westside. They had to go trawling for another band moniker. Westface. Westward. Westfive. Weststyle? They were a Sligo band (with two Dublin guys in it). Louis was determined. 'West' had to appear somewhere in the band's new name.

Thus in 1999 it became Westlife. Ronan and Louis presented them to the world press that March. Their success is well documented. The Backstreet Boys had sold forty million units. Westlife expected to equal that, maybe even beat them. Lycos Asia reported that the band members took home STG£647,000 in 2002 from touring, record sales, royalties and merchandising deals. They worked hard, in fairness. Ronan Keating says in his autobiography that Westlife had only twelve free days in 1999. Louis Walsh was reported to have earned STG£1.2 million from the band by the start of 2003.

Young female fans travelled from all over the world on pilgrimages to Sligo, to photograph the façade of the Café Carlton (and Morgan De Toi, after the change) and the Hawk's Well and Kian Egan's old house. They bought copies of 'Together Girl Forever' in the Record Room, then went over and asked Mrs Filan if maybe Shane could autograph it for them. Shane always obliged. The Sligo Westlifers spent time in Sligo any time they could. They talked to the local press regularly and were thrilled when the band was granted the Freedom of the City in June 2000. They returned, a little heavier, a little browner, to play in Markievicz Park, the Gaelic football pitch, in the summer of 2003.

Sligo smoulders still at the foot of Knocknarea. Changing and staying the same. The town skyline broken by lofty silhouettes. The cranes are here. A lot of new buildings are going up in the borough and the surrounds. Sites for houses are very pricey in any part of County Sligo. A swathe has been cut through the town, letting light in. Pools of water are gathering there. This is the route of the new road, the Mid-Block Route, long promised as the answer to the town's ugly traffic problems (and long resisted by a considerable section of the community). Seems like it might really happen.

The pre-building dig yielded a lot of stuff: mediaeval enclosures, Neolithic flint, early Christian finds. Out in Carrowkeel, in the summer of 2003, archaeologist Stephan Bergh did a preliminary excavation on a site by the passage tombs and confirmed a Neolithic date for what appeared to be a village of over 130 hut sites. There is an archaeology course now in Sligo Regional College. Except it is not a regional college any more. It has bloomed into an institute of technology; they say 'campus' down there now.

The Cooleara Pantomime celebrated its twenty-fifth season in 2003. Equinox nightclub is still going, except it is called Envy now. Toffs and the Clarence still run nightclubs, and more are springing up. The borough still has lots of problems (these are called issues now), but there is a discernible sense of optimism abroad. The arts community is perhaps stronger than ever. Sligo is home to many writers, film-makers, actors and people into the visual arts. The Sligo music scene has renewed energy. Trevor 'Tabby' Callaghan has lots of competition for twenty-something guitar hero of the town. Johnny Grennan and Caleb Gilmartin are amongst the hottest tickets. Caleb was with Legacy; of late he's cutting his teeth jamming with Séamus O'Dowd. Séamus is in Dervish now, touring regularly, but he still plays Rory Gallagher tunes in Shoot the Crows. With mouth organ and acoustic, he crouches in the corner, under Robbie Cadman's painted window, the seasonally changing window that connects all the Sligos.

Cathal McDonagh is into creating spacey guitar effects and atmospheric songs. He is one of the new names appearing at the open mic shows in Bar Eile (part of the Garavogue pub, a new

European style bar, on the banks of the river). Leon Mooney writes songs and performs them there. Many of the new batch of writers/performers are women. The new 'minimalist folk' mode is popular, influenced by Damian Rice et al. An exception to this is a red-haired rocker from Bundoran called Aine O'Doherty.

The Hooks are poised to make a breakthrough on behalf of all the original bands ever kicked up by Sligo. They have to. The two Mulligan brothers are writing mighty pop songs, funny and sharp and dissonant. The Hooks used to be Redrum, who played in the Weir. They are still only in their early twenties. Jane McCanny has changed her name to Mackenzie and penned a polished pop collection with Eddie Lee. She is looking for a deal. The Conway Sisters from Rosses Point supported Westlife in Markievicz Park. They got signed in 2003.

The oldies are still rocking on. Ex-Brotherly Love members are back gigging, enjoying themselves hugely. Joss and Ian Duggan's new group is called Take Two. Certain Nervous Animals are recording and doing an odd gig. Indian have a new album out. Kevin Conlon, too. Seamus McLoughlin is playing with a fine Scottish fiddler with big hair called Billy Stuart. Folk band Jargon are gigging again after a twenty year absence. Sligo Chamber of Commerce is hosting an event called Sligo Rocks, a free open air gig in the Stephen's Street car park. They hope it will develop into a major event of late summer and give an airing to local and out of town acts. There is still a scarcity of dedicated venues, but gigs are happening. Beezies has become the Manhattan and has a live stage. The Venue and the Strand still book bands in Strandhill. Hennigan's has been reopened under new management. There's a new place called Holborn Street. They take mainly tribute bands. Holborn Street sometimes features The Unsuspecting Public.

Ambrose Tully and his friend Mick were into self-destruction and rock and roll parody; for a while they called themselves Wastelife. They didn't really take the piss, not as much as the name might suggest. They did grungy rock covers and songs of their own. They went through a weird—but interesting—patch when Mudita Proctor joined. Mudita used to perform her enigmatic and beautiful acoustic-based songs while the lads hung around in the background and kept you on your toes with sporadic out-of-the-blue Keith

Richards licks. The lads busk an odd time in Kennedy Parade. They call themselves The Unsuspecting Public now.

Perry Blake has returned to live in his home town; his work is dark and lyric-driven. He crafts songs in the mode of Scott Walker or Bowie in the time of *Low. Pilot of Your Thighs.* Perry is working on his fifth studio album. The Sligo jazz scene is lively, and Cathal Roche has moved here. His virtuosity on the sax has been showcased by the Model Arts and Niland Centre. As well as a name change, the old Model Arts Centre has got a major renovation and has a programme of events and exhibitions.

The trad scene is rightly on fire. Jarlath McTernan went to New York, but unlike Coleman, he came back. Jarlath takes listeners to places unfamiliar in the soundscape of the uilleann pipes. He has worked with jazzers, country players, with actors. He is on the lookout for something new. Dervish have a strong new album out, recorded in their new Sligo-based studio. New players are emerging, men and women. Musicians can ask a decent wage for a gig, and sometimes get it. It took a long time to get to where we are now. There were so many false dawns.

There is an empty seat at the table of Sligo music. Finn Corrigan was a sound engineer. He was a man of diverse talents; sound engineering was just one of the things Finn was good at. He did that job with Dervish. And Those Nervous Animals and many others. Finn was one of a bunch of Offaly men brought to Sligo by bass man Ronan (Zoot) McDermott in the band The Strong Are Lonely. Daragh Connolly and Cue Egan were among them. The Strong were a bunch of middle-class lads playing long-winded instrumentals with a lot of major seventh chords (Prefab Sprout had just put out their first album). But Finn was a rock and roller at heart. He loved to play evil guitar and subversive keyboards. Finn gigged for a while with Auto da Fe, then came to Sligo.

At a time Finian Corrigan was a member of one of Barry Brennan's bands, Robinson Gruesome. (Another variation was The Milldini Brothers.) They used to play The Bearcat in the early nineties.

In the years he lived here, Finn Corrigan warmed hearts and gave those who knew him plenty of laughs and quite a few frights. He used to point his finger at the sky and show his Dracula teeth in a wide smile. He never got stuck in any musical clique. Finn was with Frannie Healy and Martin Harte in Sligo's angriest band, The Boy, The Boy. Corrigan featured bigly in The Headless Jellybabies, made up of people from different bands who would get together, dress up outrageously and do over-the-top cover versions.

Finn used to sucker guys down in Limerick and Kerry (and probably in South America and China, too, on his adventures with Dervish) into betting on pool games with him and then take them to the cleaners. One of his biggest purchases was a primitive keyboard/sampler at the dawn of sampling called an Ensoniq Mirage. The paint fell off with time and the rigours of the road; then he painted it black all over with metallic paint for a fireplace. It took on the appearance of the obelisk out of *2001: A Space Odyssey*. He didn't have a flightcase for it; he would land with it under his arm. Finn used to sample everything into it, including reports on the price of sheep by Michael Dillon and orders for Heineken, useful in the event of losing eye contact with a barman while playing Hennigan's backroom. Finn was killed in a tragic accident in his home in the Christmas of 2002. He is buried in Scardán Cemetery, by the north road to Strandhill.[†]

All the lads in Six As One, as they were, were talented young men before I met them. Those band members that went on to fame in Westlife deserve their extraordinary success. They are decent guys, and I am proud to have worked with them. They have brought a huge amount of positive attention to Sligo and made music to entertain a vast international audience.

I was deeply disappointed when the band jumped ship with Streetwise and went off to be managed by Louis Walsh, after the amount of work that Mary and Averyl and I did with them. But when I thought about it, it was obvious that Mae Filan's decision to get in touch with Louis was a wise and pragmatic business move. The music business is just that, a business, and sometimes painful decisions have to be made. On more than one occasion I have found myself making tough calls. We dropped a member of our

---

[†]   In November 2003 many musicians from different backgrounds came together to do two gigs (under the banner Simpatico, one of Corrigan's favourite expressions) in the Southern Hotel, Sligo, to celebrate Finn's life.

band Those Nervous Animals in the eighties. We thought it was best decision at the time for the band, but no one felt good about it.

What would have happened if the boys had stayed with us? Who knows? We probably would have had a good run. I knew they were going places the day I laid eyes on them. We would have done interesting things and had a lot of fun. But as the book explains, they came to Louis at just the right time in his career. That was just sheer luck, but their breakthrough was not just down to luck. So with their ability and Louis' resources, they ended up with a pretty unbeatable team.

I grant though that I did not invest as much, neither emotionally nor financially, into the band as Mary McDonagh did. She had known them and nurtured their ability since they were kids; the whole band was centred in her house. There is no doubt that she deserves acknowledgement for her vision and determination in 1996–97. As does Averyl. Averyl Dooher did a lot of the invisible work, the hard graft: assembling databases, doing mail shots, following up with phone calls. Making appointments and getting the band there.

I have done my best to achieve accuracy in telling the story of IOYOU. I am sure there are omissions. Any corrections or additions to my account are welcome. Please send suggestions or additions to me c/o Brandon/Mount Eagle Publications, Coolen, Dingle, County Kerry, Ireland. If this volume makes it to a second edition, I will endeavour to include them.

I often think of Graham and Derek and Michael. I really haven't a clue what the experience actually felt like for them. No one does. I suspect different for all three, for a start. But hard nonetheless. Perhaps they themselves can't even tell what it was like. It may take more than words to convey how it felt to have been offered so much at that age, and have it swept from under your nose. Or it would have to happen to yourself. I am proud to have worked with them, too. I wish all three the best of luck, as I do the boys whose dreams came true.